EARTH'S FINAL DAWN
(Understanding This Age in View of the Coming New Age)

Clinton E. Taber

Edited by John Roller

Xulon PRESS

Eschatology / End Times

Earth's Final Dawn
Understanding This Age in View of the Coming New Age
by Clinton E. Taber

Printed in the United States of America

ISBN 9781613792643

www.xulonpress.com

COMMENTS FROM RESPECTED LEADERS

"What could be more relevant to our times than a Biblical study of Eschatology? Who are we? What does the future hold? Is there any hope in these troublesome days? The author gives clear answers to these questions and more. This work is must reading for Advent Christians who, like the men of Issachar, need to understand the times and give a reason for the hope that we have within us. This book is filled with Biblical integrity and scholarship, yet it also is written in a way that the average laymen can understand its truths. I know that you will be blessed as you read this book!"
Looking for that Blessed Hope,
Rev. J. Brent Ross, Pastor
President ACGC

"Can any good thing come out of New Bedford, Mass.?" Yes, many, including the Tabers and Deans. To be more specific, I had expected that Clinton E. Taber's, *Earth's Final Dawn* to be a good book. Reading the first draft confirmed it. Now, having read the finished work, I would put it beside David Dean's, *Who Will Go for Us?* as the two most important Advent Christian books of the last half century.

Superintendent Taber's "goal is to give laymen an introduction to eschatology." Who is better qualified to do so than this author? He was raised in an atmosphere of intense piety and faith. His family was involved extensively in the life of the Advent Christian denomination. All four of the Taber brothers pastored AC churches. Reverend Taber graduated from the New England School of Theology, did graduate work at Wheaton College, and earned a Master of Theological Studies degree from Gordon-Conwell Theological Seminary. His more than half a century of ministry includes service at every level of the denomination.

Pastor Taber has been throughout a student of biblical prophecy. He has preached and taught it widely. His mentor, Edward K. Gedney, was a significant influence. It is a pleasure to read through this book. It is written on a popular level for laypeople, yet it demonstrates a width of reading, a thorough understanding of current views of eschatology and of the world in which we live. It is illustrated by current events and personal interest stories (could a *Yankee* batter be *raptured???*). It is filled with the Scriptures. In the near future, I will address in print any differences with Superintendent Taber about a few points, but that will not diminish my appreciation for this work. May its distribution and impact be extensive.

Dr. Freeman Barton, Author, Retired College Professor
Editor, Henceforth Theological Journal

"I considered it a privilege to receive and and review Clinton Taber's manuscript, *Earth's Final Dawn*. I have known for several years of Clint's passion for this subject and the amount of study he has spent in developing his understanding of the end times. His understanding of Christ's return has been a continuous blessing to me personally. I was pleasantly surprised at the skill with which he takes us through a study not only of where we are in that sequence of end times events, but I found myself caught up in the experience, and renewed in my hope of Christ's soon return. I was not able to put this book aside until I finished it. Each chapter challenged me to look at a new topic – leading, ultimately, to the final paragraph, where we are at last in fellowship with God in His Kingdom paradise at the return of Christ. May I challenge you to take this walk with the author as we prepare our hearts, waiting for that Blessed Hope, the return of our, Lord Jesus Christ!"

Rev. Roydon Ames
Church Planter, Pastor, Church Growth Consultant

"This is more than a primer on the subject of eschatology. It is a work that serves the layman as well as the pastor. Rev. Taber invites the reader to discover an appreciation for eschatology through an historical, theological and biblical approach. The study is rich with Scriptural support, which keeps before the reader an understanding of the urgency of our day while presenting the living hope which sustains us until Christ's second coming."
Rev. Dr. Ron Thomas, Executive Director
Advent Christian General Conference

"Clint defines eschatology in terms a layman can understand. His purpose in writing is both clear and easy to follow. The defense of conditional immortality is both logical and Biblically sound. This is must reading for anyone who is interested in prophecy."
Rev. Dr. Larry Withrow, pastor
Retired Superintendent, Southern Region ACGC

"The work of a lifetime! Courageous and stunning contribution to biblical Eschatology. Clint Tabor writes from the mind of a scholar and the heart of a pastor. Immensely practical. Infused with scripture. This will be a must read for all who are seriously interested in the signs of the times, the scenarios unraveling in our world, and the imminent return of Jesus."
Dr. David C. Alves, Author, Pastor
Founder, President, Frontline Ministries

"While I hardly considered myself worthy to be classified with the respected leaders whose recommendations you have just read, I must certainly say that it has been a great honor, and a privilege, for me to have had the opportunity to read this book in minute detail – an opportunity which came to me when the author asked me if I would serve as its editor and proofreader. I have read it, perhaps, in a different way that you will, or than these others have: I have looked at every comma, every period, every question mark, every exclamation mark, every quotation mark and every dash, until, occasionally, my eyes grew bleary with the task. Yet, I have also appreciated the broad sweep of its message. *Earth's Final Dawn* is certainly an introduction to eschatology – one of the best that I have ever read, that – but it is also a very unique book in that it gives us unique, personal insights and applications that could only have come from one source: my friend and fellow-pastor, Rev. Clint Taber. It is worth reading for many reasons, not the least of which is the simple fact that he is its author. The world (and especially the smaller "world" of the Advent Christian Church) should want to hear what this intelligent and deeply spiritual man has to say on this challenging and exciting subject."

Rev. Dr. John H. Roller, Pastor, Editor

Dedicated to those special servants of the Lord
who over the centuries have faithfully preached
and taught the full counsel of God,
with special emphasis on that Blessed Hope and the
glorious return of our Lord and Savior Jesus Christ;
and, in loving memory of my father-in-law,
Edwin K. Gedney,
and, my brothers, Vincent E. Taber and Raymond E. Taber

FOREWORD

Today's Christians display a keen interest in learning what the Bible has to say about the future. It's obvious in the books that they read (some doctrinal, others fictional) and in the motion pictures and streaming computer images that they entertain themselves with. It may be hidden in an unspoken longing to have their pastors "preach prophecy," but it is proclaimed by their flocking to conferences and seminars that promise them inside information on God's plans for what's coming. Many ordinary church members struggle to understand the days in which we live, and they don't want tomorrow to take them by surprise.

In many ways, this future orientation is good. God has revealed much about what's coming, and – in Scripture – we do have a Word from the Lord. We need godly men to wrestle with the exact meaning of that Word and to proclaim it so that equally godly people can understand and act upon it. What we do not need are superficial observations, fanciful interpretations and sensational predictions of a still obscure future. God has not given us Biblical prophecy to satisfy our curiosity, but to transform our character and to guide our conduct. He wants us to "live holy and godly lives" (2 Peter 3:11). Biblical predictions are not intended to sensationalize small details, but to magnify the Savior – Jesus Christ, the King of Kings and Lord of Lords – who remains "the same yesterday, today and forever" (Hebrews 13:6). We must never lose sight of the fact that the first and second comings of Christ are the central gems in the church's engagement ring of Biblical predictions.

In *Earth's Final Dawn,* prophetic scholar Clinton Taber addresses this widespread interest in Biblical prophecy without surrendering to the temptation to sensationalize. He declines to magnify the trivial or to find the key to understanding the future in some obscure prophetic symbol. He refuses to isolate the last things from all the other key teachings of Scripture: the first things of creation; the former things of ancient Israel and Jesus' earthly ministry; and the present things of Christian life and witness. He draws freely from the Biblical scholars who have shaped his thinking about the Bible's predictions, yet without being afraid to move beyond them in directions that they themselves might not have taken.

The book that follows is remarkably comprehensive among today's prophetic works in that the author combines the two branches of eschatology, whereas most books address only one of them. Much as did Dr. Clarence H. Hewitt in his *Classbook in Eschatology* (1941), Rev. Taber recognizes that people are interested both in their own personal destiny (individual eschatology) and what will finally happen to their world (cosmic eschatology). Not only does he treat the two, he integrates them, utilizing the biblical teaching about the kingdom of God to do so. Beginning with its relationship to the creation of the world, the author follows God's kingdom throughout history, culminating in its full embodiment in the new heavens and the new earth. This enables him to explain the pivotal role of the Second Advent of Christ as a bridge to cross over the gulf separating individual and cosmic eschatology. This unification of eschatology's two branches is a much-needed corrective to their separation in most writing about final things in our day.

In the pages that follow, Clinton Taber approaches eschatology from several distinct points of view. First of all, he writes as a perceptive and systematic theologian. He wants to bring together all that Scripture teaches about the end times into a coherent system of thought, which at the same time is consistent with the rest of the Bible. An examination of his Table of Contents reveals how comprehensive he intends this examination of eschatology to be. He wants to cover and organize the whole field. His summary of the three alternate views about death as Reincarnation, Relocation and Resurrection is equally original and helpful. Again, he writes as a careful observer and astute commentator on what is happening in today's world. In the Historicist tradition of interpreting prophecy, he looks for Biblical predictions to be fulfilled in the world in which we live. He draws on his broad range of reading and thorough research in order to correlate today's events with what the Bible has predicted. His readers may not always agree with his conclusions, but he gives them the evidence to evaluate, and they can only praise him for making the attempt. In the third place, he writes about the end times with a pastor's heart. He feels the hurts of suffering saints, and he rejoices in the final banishment of sin, disease and death from the lives of God's people. He is not afraid to embrace an unpopular argument or to oppose a widely accepted view if by doing so he can bring hope and comfort to ordinary Christians in their daily walk. He knows the heartaches and concerns of his readers, just as you would expect one of today's most widely-appreciated prophetic preachers to do.

Do not be surprised if you find in the diversity of this material and in its far-ranging argumentation some things which you have never thought about before. After all, it's hardly worth the time of either a writer or his readers if he presents only what they already believe. Like most authors, Clinton Taber aims to challenge you with fresh material and to stretch your thinking by challenging popular positions and by arguing in favor of what he proposes as better alternatives. If you are interested in doing some serious thinking about last things, you will enjoy *Earth's Final Dawn*.

Dr. David A. Dean, Live Oak, Florida
Author, Professor Emeritus,
Gordon-Conwell Theological Seminary

CONTENTS

A brief look at factors and personalities that have helped shape my interest in Biblical eschatology.

Eschatology Defined; Divisions of Eschatology: Cosmic; Individual; The Last Days; The Second Coming; The Kingdom of God; The Bible as the Source of Hope; The Meaning of the End: The End as a Cosmic Catastrophe; The End as Purpose; The End as Event.

Universal Anxiety; Globalization; Uncertainty and Despair; Man-made Deities Have Failed; Nighttime; Our View of History Has Changed; The Resurgence of Religious Hatred; False Hopes: People Are Basically Good; Scientific Advances; Medical Advances; Genuine Hope: A Divinely Provided Future.

Death; Understanding Death; Satan's Lie; Views of the Afterlife: Reincarnation; Relocation; Death as Sleep; Resurrection; The Resurrection Body.

Apocalyptic interest/frenzy; The Bible and the Future; The Second Coming of Jesus Christ; Antichrist; Understandings about the Second Coming; The Rapture; Recognition of Christ; The Glory of Deity; Purposes of Christ's Return; Judgment; Rewards and Punishment; The Reality of Hell; The Reality of Eternal Life; The Second Coming of Jesus Christ as the Transition Point between Time and Eternity.

Time and the Second Coming of Jesus Christ; Discerning the Times; The 21st Century; Distinguishing Features of the Last Days; The Nature of Prophetic Signs; The Signs of the Times; God's Last Days Kingdom Offensive; Satan's Massive Counter-Offensive of Evil; Christian Persecution; Israel and the Middle East; God's Ultimate Conquest.

Man's Quest for the Better World; The Temptation of Jesus; Satan's Counterfeit Kingdom; The Centrality of Christ; Dual Citizenship; Stages of the Kingdom; Fundamental Change; The New Heaven and the New Earth; The Glory of the Kingdom; Glimpses of Kingdom Life.

PREFACE

E ver since I was a young man starting on my spiritual journey as a minister of the Gospel, I have had a deep interest in the Biblical teaching about the Second Coming of Jesus Christ and the end of the age. That interest was spurred on by the preaching of several men of God, among who were the Reverend Raymond Beecroft, the Reverend Earl Waterman and the Reverend Dr. Edwin K. Gedney, to name a few. More recently, I have been encouraged by the counsel and writing of Dr. David A. Dean and Dr. Freeman Barton, colleagues in the work of the Gospel.

The generation in which I was born seemed to be more focused on the life to come. It was not unusual to visit a local church and hear the pastor preaching on the Second Coming of Christ. Evangelists at Camp Meetings always preached on the Second Coming and attendant developments. This was the theological climate in which I was reared.

Over the years of my ministry, I have found myself being drawn to the subject of the Second Coming and the Kingdom of God. I have preached on this theme and related subjects in churches where I served as pastor, at Camp Meetings, in Bible Conference settings, and in various special services and Prophetic Conferences. Quite often, other pastors and interested lay persons would ask if I had any of the material I spoke about in print. The answer was, "No." I don't view myself as a writer. My late father-in-law, Edwin K. Gedney, encouraged me on one occasion to do some writing. When I told him that I didn't feel gifted in that area, he advised me to simply write what I said, or record what I was preaching, and later have it transcribed. Writing and preaching are two distinct gifts. Some are blessed to have both – and others, like myself, can only pretend. I make no pretension about scholarship, but I know what I believe and why.

However, it is my conviction that some of the understandings that the Lord has given me need to be shared with others. Consequently, I have decided to put them in writing in the hope that some may better understand the clear teaching of Scripture in respect to the important teachings related to the Second Coming of Jesus Christ, the end of the age, and the resurrection to eternal life in the Kingdom of our Lord and Savior, Jesus Christ.

The focus of this writing is the wide spectrum of believers who seek for the truth of God's Word. My goal is to introduce the general public to end-time events about which they may never have thought and to give laymen an introduction to the important subject of eschatology.

INTRODUCTION

This is a book about eschatology – the study of end-time events - understanding this age in view of the New Age to come. Webster's dictionary defines eschatology as, "belief about or in the end of the world or the last things (as the second coming of Jesus Christ, resurrection, judgment, the new age)." Biblical eschatology is the study of end-time events (the working out of God's purposes for man and His world) as revealed in the Bible. The message of the Bible is all about the Kingdom of God. The story line of the Bible is God's activity in forming a people who will live in fellowship with Him in His Kingdom Paradise for His glory forever.

A study of Christian eschatology presupposes that there is a sovereign God of the universe who created all things with a purpose and who, in spite of radical opposition to that purpose advanced by the rebellion of Satan and the introduction of sin with its horrendous consequences, will ultimately triumph over evil and fulfill His eternal purpose as originally intended. In other words, we need a worldview that takes the reality of God into account. As Mullins says in his book, *Christian Religion in Doctrinal Expression*, "God's working in history and grace is purposive." Prophecy can only be understood in the context of God's creative purpose.

History is His Story faithfully recorded in the Bible. It is the story of the sovereign God of the universe who in love created the worlds and everything in them in order to form a people who would live in fellowship with Him in His Kingdom Paradise for His glory forever. This theme will reappear numerous times throughout the discussion of human history.

The Bible is not a typical story with each chapter and book following sequentially or chronologically. The Bible is a collection of 66 separate books written over a period of 1,500 years by 40 different authors. One would expect that a book written over an extended period by a variety of authors would be disjointed and disconnected. Such is not the case.

Amazingly, everything recorded in the Bible is related to the one theme: God's formation of a people who would live in fellowship with Him in His Kingdom Paradise for His glory forever. In the case of the Bible, the Spirit of God inspired the various authors as they wrote their individual parts of the story. The Bible only makes sense when understood in relation to the main theme.

It is a fascinating story in which the main characters are God, Satan and man. Man is at the center of the story as the object of God's love. The history of man is unfolded in the story of two gods (Jehovah, and Satan the pseudo-god), two trees (the tree of the knowledge of good and evil and the tree of life), two sons (Ishmael and Isaac), two Adams (the first and the last), two births (biological and spiritual), two deaths (first or natural and the second death) and two destinies (heaven and hell). Eschatology deals with the final chapters of the story.

DIVISIONS OF ESCHATOLOGY

The study of eschatology can be divided into two parts. The first is referred to as cosmic eschatology, and the second is referred to as individual eschatology.

Cosmic eschatology relates to developments of a global nature that bring the present age to a close and usher in the age to come. It has to do primarily with the future of the cosmos or universe as we understand it. It is materially oriented. Individual eschatology focuses primarily on events, actions and developments connected to the race of men such as death, resurrection, judgment, destiny and the like.

In each of these major divisions, there are numerous subdivisions. We make these divisions mainly for the sake of discussion.

You cannot really talk about one without talking about the other. Man and the environment of his existence are inseparable.

There is a subtle difference between eschatology and prophecy. All eschatology is prophetic but not all prophecy is eschatological. Eschatology focuses on the question, "What does the future hold?" Prophecy looks at the question, "What has God revealed to us about His activity in human history?" Prophecy has both a historical element and a predictive element to it, while eschatology is forward looking in the context of past history. One way to look at eschatology is to further divide it into three components.

THE LAST DAYS

The first of these components is the last days, or the season of the end. We sometimes refer to the last days by talking about the signs of the times. In other words, the last days (as used in the Bible) discusses people and events that play a part in human history in those days preceding the Second Coming of Jesus Christ.

THE SECOND COMING

Another component is the Second Coming of Jesus Christ and attendant developments. The Second Coming is viewed as the climactic event of human history. It triggers a series of events associated with it, such as the resurrection of the dead; the Great White Throne judgment; the destruction of Satan, evil and all things that offend God; and the fulfillment of God's eternal Kingdom goal. The Second Coming of Jesus Christ and related developments is the transition point between time and eternity.

THE KINGDOM OF GOD

The third component of eschatology is the establishment of the Kingdom of God with the creation of a new heaven and a new earth where righteousness reigns. In this final component, there is a restitution of all things that God had originally created before man sinned and brought upon his posterity the deadly and painful consequences of that sin.

These components of eschatology are all prominently addressed in the New Testament. New Testament Christianity was thoroughly eschatological in nature. Every generation believed that Christ could return at any time. That was largely true because it was the message of Jesus. He went everywhere preaching the good news of the Kingdom. In Luke 4:43, He said, "I must preach the good news of the Kingdom of God to the other towns also, because that is why I was sent." Many of His parables, such as the parables of the Kingdom recorded in Matthew 13, had an eschatological focus. When Jesus instituted the Lord's Supper on the evening before His crucifixion, He told His disciples that He would not eat this meal with them again until it found fulfillment in the Kingdom of God.

Following the death, burial, resurrection and ascension of our Lord, the apostles who wrote the books of the New Testament all had a strong eschatological dimension to their writing. They clung to the beliefs handed them from the teachings of Jesus about His return and kept this hope alive throughout the first century as a motivation for believers to live holy and devout lives while waiting for the Lord to come.

Some, living in great expectation (like the believers at Thessalonica), were encouraged by Paul's writing that everything that they had been taught concerning the end of the age, the Second Coming of Jesus Christ and our gathering together in Him for eternity would come true as it was previously taught to them. It was true in spite of apparent delay. It was true in spite of scoffers. It was true in spite of death taking their loved ones from their midst.

In God's own time, He will act in history to complete His eternal purpose of creating a people who will live in fellowship with Him in His Kingdom Paradise, for His glory, forever.

THE BIBLE AS THE SOURCE OF HOPE

Having given this sketch of the context of eschatology, I want to turn now to the other word associated with Christian eschatology – the word, "Biblical." Christians believe in, and are committed to, the Bible as the word of God in which He has revealed His overarching plan for the ages. The Bible is our primary resource. This is not to suggest that it is the only source of ideas about the future, but rather to state emphatically that it is the only reliable, authentic and authoritative source of truth about the future.

I remember preaching a sermon on Bible Prophecy many years ago (while I was serving as pastor of a church in Plainville, Connecticut), in which I stated certain things that I believed were going to happen in the future because the Bible said so. After the service, a man in the congregation came up to me and reflected that the sermon was very interesting. He found it to be rather fascinating. Then he asked me if I had ever read any of the prophecies of Nostradamus. He went on to suggest that I could get a lot more insight into the future if I read Nostradamus.

Nostradamus is not the only one who has ever appeared on the scene of human history and captured the imagination of curious seekers with projections about the future. Admittedly, his writing is compelling reading and convincing to any who are not familiar with Biblical truth and what the Lord has to say about such people.

In this age of the occult, with Satanic activity and Spiritism at an all-time high, we must be on our guard that we are not led astray by our compulsive desire to know what the future holds. In this type of thinking, there is a grave danger for the innocent seeker. Satan is the great deceiver, and there is nothing that he would like to do more than distract believers by some fascinating prophecy that he concocts that will only confuse and distort God's divinely revealed word of truth.

That is why I say that the Bible must be the standard of truth by which all speculations about the future are tested. In it, God has spoken clearly revealing His plan for the ages and the ultimate consummation of all things at the glorious, personal Second Coming of our Lord and Savior Jesus Christ.

Everything that the Bible has predicted has come true exactly as it was predicted with the exception of those prophecies that remain to be fulfilled. History confirms the reliability and the credibility of Biblical statements. The Bible is a revelation of divine activity. People wonder about the meaning of developments in life and question their relevance to the end of the age. The only reliable information about the meaning of the times and of world events is the Word of God. The track record of the Bible in speaking about human history is incredibly accurate. God's Word is true. He alone knows the future. He alone is the sovereign Lord. The Bible explains to us the how and why of civilization and reveals the ultimate end.

THE MEANING OF THE END
THE END AS COSMIC CATASTROPHE

One thing that we need to understand is that there will be an end to human history – an end to life as we know it – a climax to human history. We would be wasting our time discussing the end if there isn't any such thing as the end. The idea of an "end" to all things is a rather universal idea regardless of the age, the culture, the civilization and the religious orientation or lack thereof.

Scientists, cosmologists and geologists (as well as others) think that the days of the earth are numbered. In a program televised on the History Channel on March 18, 2007, titled, "The Last Days of the Earth," it was speculated that the earth will come to a violent end someday, either by a massive volcanic eruption or by being struck by a giant asteroid. In fact, seven different scenarios were discussed that could impact the survival of our planet. The earth and its environment are violent in respect to their structure.

On July 28, 2009, AOL News reported that the recent bruising Jupiter received from a cosmic impact is a violent reminder that our solar system is a shooting gallery that sometimes blasts earth. So far, 784 Near-Earth Objects (NEO's) more than half a mile wide have been found. "If an object the same size as the one that hit Jupiter were to hit Earth, it would have been fairly catastrophic," explained astronomer Donald Yeomans, manager of NASA's Near-Earth Object program office at the Jet Propulsion Laboratory in Pasadena, California.

Experts in the field rule out the probability of a major cosmic collision but suggest that one of lesser magnitude, with devastating effects, is a real possibility. The end of the world caused by a cosmic collision is not something that we need to worry about in the immediate future. God has His own plan about how the world will end.

THE END AS PURPOSE

Having said that, I would suggest that there are different ways of looking at the "end." The Greek philosopher Aristotle (384-322 BC) wrote about the "end," meaning the final purpose of things – that to which all things aim. What Aristotle had in mind was that the "end" of medical science was good health, the "end" of automobile manufacturing was a car, the "end" of architectural design was a building and the "end" of a race was the finish line. Applying the principle to humanity, he said that the end of humanity (its ultimate purpose) is "happiness" – that which we seek "always for itself and never for the sake of something else."

Happiness is a commendable goal and is thought to be the purpose of life for many. The United States' Declaration of Independence, written in 1776, states that man is endowed by his creator with certain unalienable rights, among which is the pursuit of happiness. For some, happiness is an "end" or goal of life. To understand "end" in this way is to miss the point, especially when life (for everyone) ends in death. There isn't any happiness in death. However, for some religious traditions in which man is thought to change from one form to another in dying until he reaches the perfect state of bliss, I suppose one could say that in this sense death is the "end" of life.

Some people see the end of life as a blessing, while others are frightened by the reality. An acquaintance of Mark Twain came to him one day with a look of deep consternation and said, "I'm worried that the world is coming to an end." The celebrated author replied, "Don't be worried; we can get along without it anyway." Well, we wish we could; but we know we can't, and we are left to ponder the question, "What does the future hold? Is there really an end of all things, and if so, when might that be?"

THE END AS EVENT

The idea of the end of the world has been the butt of many jokes over the years and has been trivialized by countless others. I remember seeing a cartoon in a religious periodical that showed a self-made prophet standing on a street corner with a sign which read, "THE END IS NEAR". He kept looking at his watch and counting, "10, 9, 8, 7..." Everybody standing around watching him was laughing. The same cartoon may have appeared in any periodical or newsprint given the attitude of society toward matters relating to the Biblical prediction of the end of the age. Despite the jokes made about it, and the weird behavior and projections sometimes made by self-appointed prophets of doom, the idea of the end of the world (the end of the age – the end of all things) is no joking matter. In fact, the Bible, in no uncertain terms, declares that the sovereign God of the universe, the creator of all things, the one and only true God beside whom there is none else – this God who sits on the throne of the heavens – will someday bring life as we know it to an end. The world, governments, life and everything associated with it will come to an abrupt end.

THE END AS SPOKEN TO IN THE BIBLE

"End" is an important word in the Bible. The idea of the end of human history comes from the Bible. No human being would have ever imagined such a thing. Man has a totally different idea about his abilities, powers and exploits. Man wants to believe that in time he can solve all the ills associated with life as we know it. Given enough time, money and resources, man believes that he can eventually create his own Paradise.

In spite of man's ego, the Bible says that there will be an end to human existence as we know it. It is necessary because God must bring this present world situation to an end in order to fulfill His original Kingdom goal.

Daniel 8:19 says, "For at the time appointed the end shall be." Daniel 11:35 says, "Some of the wise will stumble so that they may be refined, purified and made spotless until the time of the end. For it will still come at the appointed time." Daniel 12:4 says, "But you, Daniel, close up and seal the words of the scroll until the time of the end." Daniel was given specific instructions about what he was to do with this Biblical revelation. He was to seal it up until the time of the end.

In Matthew 24:3, Jesus addressed His disciples. In that conversation, His disciples said to him, "Lord, tell us, when shall these things be? What shall be the sign of your coming and of the end of the age?" They had been walking with Jesus and talking with Jesus for some time and even though they didn't always understand His teachings, they had come up with the understanding that there will be an end to life as we know it. Things will not go on forever as they are now.

In Matthew 24:14, Jesus talked about the spread of the gospel throughout the world. He suggested this will be an activity that will take place, "and then shall the end come." Jesus was speaking to His disciples, telling them that there will be an end.

The Bible also speaks about the end in 1 Peter 4:7, when Peter declares, as he is looking out across the landscape of his day (following the crucifixion, resurrection and ascension of Christ into heaven, and with the promise of His return fresh in his mind), "The end of all things is near." The Bible also uses other words and phrases to speak of the same thing. For instance, this phrase, "The day of the Lord," and also, "The last days" are terms used to speak of eschatological happenings.

According to the Bible, there is an end to all things, a climax of human history, an intervention by God in the affairs of men. This may be difficult for us to believe because we live in an age of continuation. All things continue as they were from the beginning of time – or, at least, so it seems. You go to bed at night and never think about the idea of whether or not there will be a tomorrow. You set the alarm clock for a specified time because you just take it for granted that there always is a tomorrow. You get up, you go through the activities of the day and you go to bed the next night.

On and on we go in life, planning for the next day, the next week, the next month, the next year. It's very difficult for us to believe that someday all these things called life will be no more; but, in spite of the difficulty that we may have in believing it, the Bible says that it will be. There will be an end to all things. Life as we know it will come to an end. The world as we know it will come to an end. When the Bible speaks of an end, it means precisely what it says.

Biblical eschatology has to do with the study of end-time events – the study of what God is doing in the world and where it will all come out. Fundamental to this whole discussion is the belief that God is, that He always has been and that He always will be. He is in control of history, and He will complete His plan when the time is right.

QUESTIONS FOR DISCUSSION
1. What is eschatology? *study of end-time events*
2. What is meant by the expression "the last days"?
3. Which definition of the term "end" makes more sense to you in this context, and why?

1. study of end times

2. last days = season of the end, Things or events that happen preceeding the second coming (Advent) of Christ.

3. last days because it's what's happening in human history now in my lifetime. The other is what is To come after the last days

Chapter 1

The Search for Hope

I once saw a large poster in full color depicting a teenage girl looking out her window of life at the world that she was about to enter. What she saw was a world aflame – a raging inferno – and, scrawled across the face of the poster in large black print, was the question, "Is there any hope?" At the bottom of the poster was this response, "Yes. I am coming again" – signed, "Jesus Christ." Unfortunately, many people in our world have never read the print at the bottom of the poster.

UNIVERSAL ANXIETY

This is a generation that is destitute of hope. Times are bad; life is foreboding; troubles abound. It's hard to believe that things can go on much longer as they are now. Something has to give, and we are rapidly reaching a point of no return.

People the world over are scanning the horizon, looking for some ray of hope. Nothing seems to have any meaning; and, without meaning, life is empty. In a decaying age, we need to hope in the right things. Nothing that we encounter in our daily living offers any real or substantial hope. Man searches in vain for wholeness, meaning and hope. Myles Monroe, in his book, *Rediscovering the Kingdom*, says, "All religions are the result of man's search for a Supreme Being – identified as God." The idea is that once this Being is found, one can find meaning.

My sense is that man's search for the Supreme Being stems from the realization that without this One, man has no hope for the future. There must be a Messiah – someone who can enter our world and our realm of being and make things right.

Every generation is engaged in the search. It is a desperate search, often misdirected.

GLOBALIZATION

One factor that contributes to this futility is the globalization that characterizes the dawning of the 21st century. We no longer live in a small community, city, state or country; we are now part of a global village, in which developments in one part of the village impact life in every other part of the village.

There is a global economic crisis, a global moral crisis, a global political crisis and a global terror crisis – all of which create a state of instability, unrest, uncertainty and distress not experienced in previous generations.

These crises – for which there are no easy solutions – breed a state of hopelessness. People everywhere are worried about the future. Amidst the confusion, distress, evil and violence of the times, people are searching for hope – anything – something that will alleviate the fear and brighten the prospect for tomorrow.

In a time like this, where can one find hope – real hope, hope with substance that you can pin your future on? We have discovered where it can't be found.

We know that it can't be found in the genius and boasts of man.
It can't be found in the military might of the nations.
It can't be found in the philosophies of men.
It can't be found in the good intentions of men.

Doug Foss says, "Real hope can be found in Christ alone, received by faith alone, provided by grace alone, revealed in the Bible alone, and all for the glory of God alone."

Unfortunately, the world has yet to discover this truth.

UNCERTAINTY AND DESPAIR

For many, these are days of uncertainty and fear. Anything on the world scene that looks ominous only heightens that fear. One thing that contributes to that fear is the rapidity with which things in life change. One day, we seem to be sailing along enjoying the ride. The next day, we find ourselves in the midst of a firestorm. The suddenness of change and the scope of change put people into a tailspin. From those who work in the behavioral sciences, we know that the emotional state of society at large is fragile. We often hear of a bizarre crime committed by someone who has suddenly fallen off the deep end. No one can explain the behavior; it is totally uncharacteristic of the person in question. Change may be the most unsettling aspect of life. Harry Emerson Fosdick, writing shortly after the turn of the last century, is quoted as saying, "The world is moving so fast these days that the man who says that it can't be done is generally interrupted by someone doing it." If that was true at the turn of the last century, what might he say about this age?

In an increasingly interdependent and interconnected world, we are rapidly discovering that events happening elsewhere can have a direct impact on our thinking and living here. A generation ago, we only heard about developments in other parts of the world – but today, we watch the revolutions, the terror attacks and the domestic violence live on our television screens.

Change – the type of change that we are experiencing and the dizzying speed at which it is taking place – is breeding a dysfunctional society, filled with distress and perplexity. I've thought about inventing a perplexity meter that would be capable of measuring the level of perplexity that we are experiencing in society. I think that I could become a wealthy man. Think of all the TV stations that would want one of these devices to report on the evening news, "The perplexity quotient today reached 78, the highest we have seen in 8 years!"

Jesus talked about this when He said, "There will be signs in the sun, moon and stars. On the earth, nations will be in anguish and perplexity at the roaring and tossing of the sea. Men will faint from terror, apprehensive of what is coming on the world, for the heavenly bodies will be shaken." (Luke 21:25-27)

As people observe the cataclysmic potential of life at the beginning of this new century, two words flow concurrently from their lips: "Apocalypse" and "Armageddon." There is restlessness and uneasiness in the human spirit – a gnawing fear which grips society – a tension of the spirit. In spite of what appears for some to be good times, many people are experiencing a crisis of hope. A mood of skepticism, anxiety and fear characterizes this generation. There is a sense of impending global disaster. It's as if someone has placed a giant time bomb in the midst of society that is waiting to explode. We can hear it ticking. We just don't know what is going to set it off or when.

A crisis of hope hangs like a dark cloud over society. Economic bailouts, bank failings, lost jobs and home foreclosures only contribute to that despair. Things are not working out the way they are supposed to, and people are growing more wary day by day. All we have lived for, all we have worked for, all we have hoped for seems to be crumbling into ashes at our feet.

There was a time when men thought that everything would go on forever as it always has, but now we are not so sure. Serious questions are being raised about the future – not only by doomsday preachers, but by scientists, historians, statesmen and philosophers as well.

Dr. Billy Graham tells of a scientist who told him that it is now possible to destroy the whole human race in about a day. Another scientist, overhearing the conversation, responded that in his understanding it was now possible to destroy the entire human race in an hour or so. Billy Graham, in his book, *Approaching Hoof Beats*, remarks in his opening statement, "Many writers are predicting that the headlines in this next decade will continue to scream war, violence, assassination, torture, World War III, and the real war, Armageddon."

Bertrand Russell reflected on this growing despair when he said, "All the labor of the ages, all the devotion, all the inspiration, all the noonday brightness of human genius are destined to extinction."

Philosopher Will Durant observed, "It seems impossible any longer to believe in the permanent greatness of man, or to give life any meaning that cannot be annulled by death."

We are beginning to hear our generation described as the terminal generation. We also hear talk of global genocide, and there is a wave of religiously inspired terrorism stalking the planet. We are told that everything will be all right; but, deep down inside, we find it difficult to believe.

I once heard a story about a new high-tech experimental cross-country aircraft that was set to take its maiden flight from the East Coast to the West Coast. When it came time to board the aircraft, passengers were guided to their seats by a set of instructions that came over a loudspeaker, explaining that the electronic gadget that they held in their hand would direct them to their assigned seat. Once in their seat, a display screen in front of them illustrated safety arrangements including what to do in the event of an emergency. There were no flight attendants or crew members on board. When all the passengers were on board the aircraft, it taxied from the gate to the runway, where it took off smoothly. Shortly after the aircraft was airborne, this announcement came over the loud speaker of the plane: "Congratulations on being the first to ride this new supersonic high-tech aircraft on its maiden flight from New York to Los Angeles. The plane has no pilot or crew. It flies with the latest technological advances in mechanics and guidance. Sit back and relax. Enjoy the flight. We want to assure you that nothing can go wrong, go wrong, go wrong, go wrong..." That's the way life is for many. Nothing that is happening seems to go the way it is supposed to. Nothing gives us a great deal of confidence for the future.

The hopelessness that we sense is the fruit of godlessness and unbelief. Leaving God out of life's equation produces hopelessness.

Bruce Lockerbie, in his book, *Dismissing God*, talks about unbelief and disbelief. He says that people today have basically dismissed God as a viable factor in the ebb and flow of life. For this generation, there is a new mindset, in which religion is essentially ignored as irrelevant and in which the Christian faith is regarded with condescension and contempt. This is the age of the obsolescence of God, the age of secularism, the age of the deification of humanism.

At a library lawn sale in Maine, I came across a catalog, *The Millennium Whole Earth Catalog*. In it the author, Stewart Brand, wrote, "We are as gods and might as well get good at it." The idea is that we don't need God. We can define our existence on our own terms. We don't need anyone telling us what we can do and what we can't do. We are perfectly capable of making our own rules.

I once saw a Toyota television commercial that showed someone in a sport utility vehicle driving through the city on a Tuesday heading for the beach. An onlooker is amazed. It is Tuesday, he reasons, and he must go to work. Then the last line appears on the screen: "Make your own rules."

Kept in context, there is nothing necessarily disturbing about that line. It only refers to the rules of which day one goes to work and which day one heads for recreation. However, taken alone, the sentence represents the thinking of a great many people in today's society. In every area of life the attitude is, "Make your own rules." It reminds us of a time described in the book of Judges when "Every man did that which was right in his own eyes" (Judges 17:6).

We know the origin of this type of thinking. It is as old as time itself. When Adam and Eve were together in the Garden of Eden, Satan came to them with the same lie, essentially telling them they didn't need God. "Make your own rules. Go ahead and eat the forbidden fruit. Your eyes will be opened, and you will be like God and not need Him anymore." Modern man sits on the throne of life as god, thinking that he is perfectly capable of finding his way, like the college student who said, "I used to believe in God, but not anymore. There are just too many things that you can't explain. Anyway, it's not cool in this generation." Secular humanism is the new religion on campus.

T.S. Eliot talks about these days as the phase of those who have never heard the Christian faith spoken of as anything but an anachronism or something really out of touch with the times. Eliot noted that as a result, "The whole of modern literature is corrupted by what I call secularism." To Eliot, secularism is the new religion.

REASONS FOR REJECTING GOD

Very few people take God seriously today. Some people reject God or dismiss Him because of spiritual indifference. They have never really concerned themselves with life's great questions. They are like surfers riding whatever wave comes along.

Others reject the idea of God because they are comfortable in their way of life. They don't want anyone or anything to mess things up. They tend to prefer license to restraint. They love the world and the world's way of life.

For others, it's a matter of joining the crowd. They feel the pressure of peers who are not Christians, and they fear they may not be liked anymore. There are others who know the Christian life is true and that they should someday make a decision, but not now.

Still others excuse themselves because some professed Christian that they know is really a hypocrite, no better than they are. If that is what Christianity is all about, why become a Christian?

One might ask, "What does any of this have to do with the mood of society and the crisis of hope?" Very directly, as I stated earlier, hopelessness is the fruit of godlessness and unbelief. As human civilization becomes more sophisticated and self-reliant, God becomes less necessary and of little consequence, being consigned to the scrap-heap of history. This is an age that denies God; and, in the words of the apostle Paul in Ephesians 2:12, to be without God is to be "without hope in the world."

OUR MAN-MADE DEITIES HAVE FAILED US

We look at those things in which we placed so much hope, and we wonder what has gone wrong. Many believed that science, technology, education, strong government or money could give us the life that we have always dreamed of having; but our man-made deities have failed us. As a result, people feel controlled, trapped, manipulated and in despair. Where can we find hope? What else is there to turn to?

NIGHT HAS COME

We are living in the nighttime of human civilization. Darkness has eclipsed our day, dimming the promise of a better tomorrow. A person without a life-changing experience with God cannot make sense of world developments and becomes totally disillusioned. Mankind is confronted by one crisis after another, each of which threatens to consume him. The greatest crisis is not what is happening outside of us, but rather what is happening to our spirit inside of us. A person who loses hope (or who simply has no hope) is destitute and miserable.

Authorities are speaking of the various crises that characterize our age as being the greatest crises ever to confront civilization, any one of which is capable of destroying us. Hope, which is a critical element in life, has escaped our grasp. We all need hope or life is reduced to a struggle for survival against forces that we believe will someday overcome us. No one wants to live like that. No one can live like that for very long.

If you look at life as a journey or passage, you see hope as a flower that blooms along the way, brightening the journey and making the hardships and trials more bearable. Hope gives us something to live for by its inspiring beauty. Hope gives us confidence about the future, but for many today, the flower of hope along life's journey often appears faded and dying. We have done everything that we know of to address the problem, but to no avail.

OUR VIEW OF HISTORY HAS CHANGED

Our view of history has changed dramatically in this generation. It was not that long ago that we were looking at the future with optimism and promise. Plans were being made to build a great global society that would be free from all the privations of war, poverty, injustice and disease. Education, energy, science and technology were the gods that would create for us a new and better world; but, somewhere along the way, they didn't produce.

Life is a contrast between plenty and poverty. For some (the haves), it is the best of times; while, for others (the have-nots), it is the worst of times. For some in our society, there is optimism. Life is pleasant. In fact, they have never had it so good. They look at their home, their family, their job, the fact that they have developed adequate safety-nets like IRAs and retirement plans – and they feel good about it all. The problem is that money and things can't buy hope. At best, they are transient – here today, gone tomorrow. When we look to the future, we seem afraid to even ponder what tomorrow might bring. Whether we are among the haves or the have-nots, life seems empty, unfulfilled and hopeless. It is a strange paradox. On the one hand, we are the most advanced civilization to have ever lived. In our generation, we have exceeded the combined achievements of the previous 40 or more generations. One would think that we should be optimistic – even euphoric – about the future, but such is not the case.

Disillusionment characterizes our outlook on life despite noble efforts to alter the course of human history for the better. We try hard; we dream big dreams; but, when the dust settles, we discover that we are not really any better off. One of the dominant characteristics of this generation at the start of the 21st century is hopelessness. It appears to be spreading like an epidemic as our mental institutions are crowded with people who are dysfunctional – who have no rudder for their lives – and, consequently, no direction and no meaning.

This is a world that in a single century has experienced two world wars as well as a number of lesser wars. This is a world that in the span of two generations has witnessed the calculated extermination of millions simply by virtue of their ethnicity. We have also seen the nuclear destruction of entire cities and live in the constant fear of some type of nuclear attack set off by a deranged despot.

Other countries threaten the world with the adaptation of modern technology into weapons of mass destruction. More than 25 countries of the world are estimated to have nuclear capabilities today. In spite of the presence of world superpowers, the international scene is extremely unstable.

THE RESURGENCE OF RELIGIOUS HATRED

Added to these problems is the fact that there has been a resurgence of religious hatred and persecution in this generation resulting in terrorist activities that have become commonplace in 21st century life. In 2001, following the terrorist attacks on the World Trade Center in New York City, the United States developed a coalition with several other countries and launched a war on terrorism – a war we are told may never end in our lifetime.

The motivation for this global distress is religious hatred. The conflicts that characterize our times and create this state of global distress are not related to weapons of mass destruction or political situations. The Islamic world has a strong hatred for the West growing out of our support for Israel. In all likelihood, we will be battling this enemy indefinitely. In June of 2003, Eddie Smith, of the U.S. Prayer Center, made the observation: "Every war that is fought in the future will be a Muslim war."

We may not recognize these conflicts as wars. The era of traditional warfare is ended. The winner will no longer be the nation who has the largest army or the most modern and lethal arsenal of weapons. Wars will be fought differently in the years ahead as we seek unconventional strategies to combat terrorism.

This is a generation that is experiencing an unprecedented spread of evil and violence. This is a world that, in the words of Robert Bork, is slouching toward Gomorrah. In his book by that title, he writes, "It is a decadent society that is angry, polarized, anti-intellectual and anti-family." I would add, anti-Christian. He goes on to describe how our culture has lost its moral underpinnings, leaving us to wander though life making up rules as we go. There are no longer any absolutes to give stability and meaning to our existence. Everything is relative. Whatever makes you feel good is all right.

IS THERE ANY HOPE?

As a result, society is in a state of flux, and people feel helpless and hopeless. There is a general feeling of distress about the nature of life, creating worry about the future. In a Gallup poll taken in the mid-1990s, a cross section of Americans were asked, "If you could ask God one question, what would it be?" The top five answers were: "Why is there suffering in the world?" "Why is there evil in the world?" "Will there ever be lasting world peace?" "Will man ever love his fellow man?" "What does the future hold for me and my family?" These pressing concerns can all be summed up in one question: "Is there any hope?"

FALSE HOPES

THE GOODNESS OF MAN

There are some who would say, "Yes, of course, there is hope. Man is essentially and inherently good. We just need a little more time and determination to work things out." Robert Bork, in his book (which I quoted earlier), says, "Those with a sentimental view of human nature believe that we are infinitely perfectible or are bent only on good if left alone." In other words, given enough time, material resources and resolve, man will extricate himself from the mess in which he now finds himself and create a beautiful world.

Such thinking is like whistling in the dark – or, at best, the height of naiveté. It is like giving a monkey a computer to play with and thinking that in time he would learn how to use it and write an exciting novel. Of course!

Martin Hengel, writing in the June 11, 2001, issue of *Christianity Today*, likens the Biblical account of the tower of Babel to much of man's self-centered optimism about the future. He says of the account in Genesis 12, "Does this not sound rather similar to the programs of self-confident scholars who, looking upon our own millennium, proclaim their prophecies of hope? Some of them predict that humanity should, with the progress of science, recreate itself by breeding a superior species and become its own creator, overcoming fear and death, and gaining for the elite a much longer and happier life, perhaps even life everlasting. All possibilities seem to be open." The thinking is that God (whoever –whatever that is) didn't do a very good job when he made man. Science is the real god and can do a better job creating human life. "Unbelievable dreams of science fiction can become reality. Babel seems to have become our Cosmo polis, the terrestrial globe. The tower is then the program of a new human creation, in which creators bring into being a better humanity and a better world more fitting for them." If all of this thinking is true, why are we no better off after all these years of working at it?

Despite man's best efforts to alter the circumstances of life, the world has been a place of sin, suffering, conflict and turmoil. The good that has permeated history is a testimony to God's grace, not a reflection of the nobility of man.

SCIENTIFIC ADVANCES

Science and technology have dramatically changed our lives. A little more than a century ago, it took about two years to sail from Europe to China – while today, you can make that same trip in a matter of hours. Tomorrow you may be able to make the trip by rocket ship in a matter of minutes. The twentieth century was a century of wonders. Up until the nineteenth century, man moved along at a snail's pace. The time that it took him to go from one place to another depended on how fast the horse could run or the ship could sail.

In 1771, a stagecoach made the trip from New York City to Philadelphia in a day and a half, and they called it "the flying machine." In a century, we have moved from horseback to stagecoach to railroad to automobile to aircraft. Today, on a commercial aircraft, you can fly from Jacksonville, Florida, to Boston, Massachusetts, (a distance of 1,160 miles) in less than three hours.

In a pamphlet from the World Future Society, dated in the winter of 2007, a series of projections are offered concerning the future. Among them was Forecast #3: "By 2015, New York, Tokyo and Frankfurt may emerge as hubs for high-speed, large-capacity supersonic planes. NASA's X-43A Scramjet has flown at 7,000 mph (nearly ten times the speed of sound). These hyper-speed planes will whisk passengers across continents in the time it takes most people to drive to the airport." The most radical of these changes have occurred in this generation.

MEDICAL ADVANCES

Advances in medical understandings have leaped ahead exponentially in this generation. Fifty years ago, a person having a gall bladder removed would have been hospitalized a minimum of seven days. I recently talked to a person who told me that he went into the hospital at 2:00 in the afternoon to have his gallbladder removed and was home by 7:00 that evening. We are living in a different world – a world in which we have made remarkable advancements in science and technology, but have regressed in the more critical areas of morals and meanings.

We are a generation that squeezes the moment for everything that we can get out of it, fearful that there may not be another moment. Nothing seems to offer much hope. We have learned that science and technology cannot answer the basic needs of the human heart. We have discovered that man-made human governments, however well intentioned and powerful they may be, cannot create the world that our heart yearns to experience. We have learned that the answers that we need are greater than what education, social reform, military might or religious tolerance can provide.

The Second Coming of Jesus Christ is the hope of the world – not education, not human government, not military might, and not science and technology! In times like these, our focus should be on Jesus and His imminent return.

GENUINE HOPE: A DIVINELY PROVIDED FUTURE

What we have failed to learn is the basic truth that the Lord revealed to Jeremiah many years ago when he said, "It is not in man to direct his steps" (Jeremiah 10:23). Modern man, like his predecessors, continues to believe that he doesn't need God. He forgets that he was made by God and for God and that he can never find any true meaning and hope apart from God. Sam Bacchiocchi, in his book, *The Advent Hope for Human Hopelessness*, writes, "Genuine hope must be grounded in something or someone who affords a reasonable ground for confidence in its fulfillment, and it cannot be divorced from the totality of one's existence."

Man's whole existence, from beginning to end, is wrapped up in the purposes of God. Many people believe that history is cyclical. While it is true that history tends to repeat itself in varying degrees in every generation, the fact of the matter is that history is a linear experience with a starting point and a terminus. Without God, it is a futile exercise of meaningless cycles of existence – possibly enlarging from one generation to the next, but always without any resolution. Life has no meaning without destiny.

Our destiny is not simply to pass through a cycle of living, but to enjoy God forever, living in fellowship with Him in His Kingdom Paradise, for His glory, forever. To understand this is to live in hope.

It is important to know that there is an ultimate resolution to all things. Life doesn't just go on forever as it is now. God has something more for man than what he has experienced or can ever experience by his own doing. Real hope comes when one believes in a future created by God and controlled by God, with all developments in the present bringing us closer and closer to that reality. In the

Bible, God has given us a glimpse of His plan for the future so that we won't give up in the present.

Our hope for the future doesn't rest on the circumstances of life that surround us, but on the sovereignty of God that transcends us. Our hope is not limited to what we can do for ourselves, but rather rests on what God has already done for us in the person of His Son, Jesus Christ. History is His Story, and it will culminate in glorious victory for the people of God. This is the good news of the gospel. Jesus lives! Jesus reigns! Jesus is coming again!

To believe in a future created and controlled by God is what we call Biblical Eschatology. It is the engine that drives hope. There is no hope that can begin to compare with the eschatological hope centered in the person of Jesus Christ and His glorious return to complete God's eternal Kingdom purpose. Until that day, the search goes on.

QUESTIONS FOR DISCUSSION
1. What worries you the most about the present situation of the world?
2. Why do people no longer believe that God is active in the world?
3. What is your view of history? Is it going anywhere? If so, where?
4. What are some of the false hopes that modern people have?
5. If a person were to ask you if there is any hope, how would you answer them?

CHAPTER 2

WHAT IN THE WORLD
IS GOD DOING?

Everything in the Bible is rooted in the first three chapters of Genesis. The end of all things is clearly stated in the beginning of all things. God's Kingdom plan is introduced in the opening chapters of the Bible, followed by the Kingdom problem and countered with the Kingdom promise. The goal of Biblical Eschatology is the Kingdom of God. It begins with the fact of God.

GOD IS

The Bible opens with the declaration, "In the beginning God." God is, was and always will be. The story of the Bible has no credibility apart from a belief in the God it depicts. The most fundamental truth known to man is the fact of God. People are actually born with this truth implanted in their heart, which explains why in every time and in every culture there is a multiplicity of gods that men worship. Idolatry has always been a part of mankind's religious experience. The fact of God is inescapable.

GOD ALONE

When God gave Moses the Ten Commandments, the first one spoke to this reality. Exodus 20:3 reads, "You shall have no other gods before me." Idol worship has always been a factor in people's lives. As early as the time of Joshua, he gathered the people of Israel together at Shechem and said to them, "This is what the Lord, the God of Israel says: 'Long ago your forefathers, including Terah (the father of Abraham and Nahor), lived beyond the river and worshipped other gods.'" There is within everyone a sense of a superior being who must be discovered and experienced to satisfy the longing of the human heart. Men fill this vacuum with a variety of objects of veneration.

The apostle Paul reflected on this during his first missionary journey when he passed through Athens and grieved over the number of gods that he found there. As he wandered around the city, he was not only impressed by the number of idols he discovered there, but also by the fact that the people were so religious as to create an "altar to an unknown god."

GOD IS AWESOME

The apostle Paul explained to the philosophers of Athens that it is not a matter of creating a god for every circumstance that man may encounter, but rather a matter of knowing the one true God who is without equal or comparison and who is greater than any circumstance that man will ever experience. Paul established a case for God as the sovereign God who rules over all. He created the heavens and the earth and everything in it. He is self-existent and self-sufficient, giving life and sustenance to all flesh.

Man's existence and ultimate destiny are intertwined with this reality. All things begin and end with God. He is "the Alpha and the Omega" – the beginning and the ending. No one existed before Him; no one will exist after Him; and no one can exist without Him. He is beyond comparison.

His creative act is spoken of as nothing to Him. The Bible speaks to the greatness and majesty of God in Isaiah 40:12-17, where it says that God's mind and thoughts are far above anything known to man. Isaiah went on to dare a comparison between this one true God and any god that man has created. All other gods are the creation of man's imagination and craftsmanship. They may be seen and venerated, but are powerless to act. By comparison, the sovereign God of the universe is not visible to the human eye, but His power is seen throughout His creation. When put to the test, there is only one God – eternal, immortal, holy, all-powerful and all-knowing. In other words, the God who is revealed to us in the Bible is distinct from all created things, above and beyond anything known to man. He is God in a unique sense.

GOD IS HOLY

God is distinct from all created beings in that God is holy. He is depicted in Scripture as holy. Isaiah had a vision of the holiness of God in the year that King Uzziah died. Isaiah 6:1-3 says, "In the year that King Uzziah died, I saw the Lord seated on a throne, high and exalted, and the train of his robe filled the temple. Above him were seraphs, each with six wings. With two wings they covered their faces, with two they covered their feet, and with two they were flying. And they were calling to one another: 'Holy, holy, holy is the Lord Almighty; the whole earth is full of his glory'" (NIV).

This is in keeping with other visions of God in Scripture. John had a vision of the holiness of God, and he recorded it in Revelation 4:1-8: "After this I looked, and there before me was a door standing open in heaven. And the voice I had first heard speaking to me like a trumpet said, 'Come up here, and I will show you what must take place after this.' At once I was in the Spirit, and there before me was a throne in heaven with someone sitting on it. And the one who sat there had the appearance of jasper and carnelian. A rainbow, resembling an emerald, encircled the throne. Surrounding the throne were twenty-four other thrones, and seated on them were twenty-four elders. They were dressed in white and had crowns of gold on their heads. From the throne came flashes of lightning, rumblings and peals of thunder. Before the throne, seven lamps were blazing. These are the seven spirits of God. Also before the throne there was what looked like a sea of glass, clear as crystal. In the center, around the throne, were four living creatures, and they were covered with eyes, in front and in back. The first living creature was like a lion, the second was like an ox, the third had a face like a man, the fourth was like a flying eagle. Each of the four living creatures had six wings and was covered with eyes all around, even under his wings.

Day and night they never stop saying: 'Holy, holy, holy is the Lord God Almighty, who was, and is, and is to come'" (NIV).

We speak of people that we know as being holy, but that is a misuse of terms. I have met some people in my lifetime I considered to be holy men and women of God. They were humble, gentle and good in a way that made them stand out from others. They seemed to be spiritual giants.

Some religious traditions identify their leaders (or leader) as, "Most Holy." As godly as some people appear to be, God alone is worthy of being called holy. Holy denotes absolute moral purity and perfection. No man has ever attained such a state. Holy is a characteristic of God alone. It is one characteristic that separates God from all other beings.

GOD IS LOVE

Besides His holiness and awesomeness of being, He is a loving God. For most people, our understanding of God tends to focus on the awesomeness of His being, but of equal importance is the understanding that God is love.

The love of God is a prominent theme in Scripture. One passage that speaks to this truth is in 1 John 4. Here the beloved disciple makes a profound reference to the love of God: "Dear friends, let us love one another, for love comes from God. Everyone who loves has been born of God and knows God. Whoever does not love does not know God, because God is love. This is how God showed his love among us: He sent his one and only Son into the world that we might live through him. This is love: not that we loved God, but that he loved us and sent his Son as an atoning sacrifice for our sins. Dear friends, since God so loved us, we also ought to love one another. No one has ever seen God; but if we love one another, God lives in us and his love is made complete in us. We know that we live in him and he in us, because he has given us of his Spirit. And we have seen and testify that the Father has sent his Son to be the Savior of the world. If anyone acknowledges that Jesus is the Son of God, God lives in him and he in God. And so we know and rely on the love God has for us. God is love. Whoever lives in love lives in God, and God lives in him. In this way, love is made complete among us so that we will have confidence on the Day of Judgment, because in this world we are like him. There is no fear in love. But perfect love drives out fear, because fear has to do with punishment. The one who fears is not made perfect in love. We love because he first loved us." (1 John 4:7-19)

God's love is demonstrated in the giving of His Son, Jesus, as our Savior from sin. The cross is an expression of the greatness of God's love. There is no other explanation for the cross.

Jesus was not a helpless victim (as it may have appeared). Consider who we are talking about! This is Jesus! No one who has ever lived can compare with Jesus. In Luke 11:29 and following, a comparison is made between Jesus, Solomon and Jonah. "As the crowds increased, Jesus said, 'This is a wicked generation. It asks for a miraculous sign, but none will be given it except the sign of Jonah. For as Jonah was a sign to the Ninevites, so also will the Son of Man be to this generation. The Queen of the South will rise at the judgment with the men of this generation and condemn them; for she came from the ends of the earth to listen to Solomon's wisdom, and now one greater than Solomon is here. The men of Nineveh will stand up at the judgment with this generation and condemn it; for they repented at the preaching of Jonah, and now one greater than Jonah is here.'" Greater than Solomon and greater than Jonah! People came from the ends of the earth to hear the wisdom of Solomon, but when Jesus spoke, everyone stood in awe at the power and profundity of His words. A greater than Solomon is here! Jonah was alive three days and three nights in the belly of a fish and survived. Jesus was dead for three days and three nights in the belly of the earth and came forth alive from this place of entombment. A greater than Jonah is here!

According to John 1:1, Jesus is the creator of all things. During His public ministry, he opened the eyes of the blind; he healed all manner of diseases; he raised the dead. He spoke peace to the raging billows of the sea, and they were calmed. Are you kidding me? This is Jesus! Jesus had the power to do anything and everything! He had the power to obliterate his enemies if he chose to exercise it. When he was arrested in the garden, and Peter wielded his sword in defense of Jesus, Jesus told him to put his sword away. He didn't need it. If he chose to fight what was ahead, he could call on His heavenly Father, who would immediately send 12 legions of angels to defend him in the face of his enemies. A legion is considered a large number – sometimes understood to be between 3,000 and 12,000 (see Luke 8:30).

When the Jews brought Jesus to Pilate, they told Pilate that he must die because he claimed to be the Son of God. "When Pilate heard this, he was even more afraid, and he went back inside the palace where he interrogated Jesus further. 'Where do you come from?' he asked Jesus, but Jesus gave him no answer. 'Do you refuse to speak to me?' Pilate said. 'Don't you realize I have power either to free you or to crucify you?' Jesus answered, 'You would have no power over me if it were not given to you from above.'"

In this contest of power, there was a greater power on display that day than the power of Rome or the nails that pinned him to the cross, and that was the power of love (John 3:16-17; Romans 5:8; 1 John 4:10; John 15:13). God's love is powerful, unconditional, inclusive, infinite, steadfast, changeless and eternal! Whenever you see a cross, it is an expression of God's love.

THE PRACTICAL BENEFITS OF GOD'S LOVE

The cross is God's answer for the problem of sin. The Bible says that if a person knows the difference between right and wrong and still chooses wrong, he has committed sin. (James 4:17) Sin is universal, and sin is personal. We are all sinners in need of a savior.

Furthermore, sin condemns and excludes us from heaven. Jesus said, "Except a man is born again, he cannot enter the Kingdom of God." If sin condemns us before God and excludes us from heaven, we all have a problem – a big problem! What is even more problematic is the fact that none of us can do anything of ourselves, to absolve us, of the guilt, power and consequence of our sin.

That's why we call Him "Savior!" He died on the cross to save us from our sin. The good news is that we can experience forgiveness in Christ. 1 John 1:9 reads, "If we confess our sin, he is faithful and just to forgive us our sin and to cleanse us from all unrighteousness." 1 John 1:7 reads, "But if we walk in the light, as he is in the light, we have fellowship with one another, and the blood of Jesus, his Son, purifies or cleanses us from all sin."

The cross is an expression of God's love. You can come to the cross, leave your burden and your past there and walk away toward the new life He has for you.

God's love has the power to forgive sin because of the cross. Knowing this gives us the freedom to come boldly into his presence, confess our sin and experience his forgiveness. We don't have to carry that burden of sin any longer.

Another practical benefit of His love is the power is has to enable us to live the Christian life and obey His commandments (John 14:15, 21, 23; 1 Corinthians 16:14). This power enables us to live in relationship with one another and to love one another (John 13:34-35).

The love of which I speak is a fruit of the Holy Spirit and is an indication of one's standing in Christ (Galatians 5:22; 1 John 3-4). The love of Christ in us has a tangible expression. It can be seen and demonstrated (John 13:35).

GOD'S PURPOSE AND PLAN

The God who is revealed in the Bible is a God of purpose. He has a plan that can be seen in the earliest revelation of His being in scripture. His purpose and plan, which is the story line of the Bible, is His activity in forming a people who would live in fellowship with Him in His Kingdom Paradise, for His glory, forever. Eric Sauer points out, "The whole plan of creation has a kingdom as its goal." The Kingdom of God and the people of God are two themes that are inseparably related in the Bible. The Bible tells the story of how God triumphantly establishes His eternal Kingdom made up of people who lovingly worship and serve Him, having been redeemed from the guilt, power and consequence of their sin by an act of this God. In other words, God had a Kingdom goal in mind when He created the world and everything in it. His Kingdom goal for man has never changed. He has given us assurance that it will become reality for man through the saving work of Jesus Christ.

THE KINGDOM ESTABLISHED AND CHALLENGED

God's plan was put into motion in the various elements of creation, each of which had a specific purpose. One stage of His earthly Kingdom is the inaugural stage. This is the prototype of a Kingdom that will exist in different stages throughout human history. All of the elements of God's Kingdom plan are present in this inaugural stage.

THE KINGDOM INAUGURATED

The first aspect of this inaugural stage is the fact of God. He is the King. His being, power and purpose are evident in the opening verses of the book of Genesis. Not only is the fact of God stated, He is also depicted as the author of creation. Everything that is has its origin in Him. Genesis 1:1 affirms that He created everything. It is important to attribute all origins to God. Things did not just happen by chance, as some would like us to think. This complex and wonderful universe came about by an act of God. The more we learn about our universe, the more impressed we are with the intricate order and balance between all aspects of it. It is obvious in the Genesis account (which remains the most plausible explanation for our universe) that there is a master designer – a prime mover – acting purposefully. What He creates is not some weird plaything or abstract disjointed cosmos, but a beautiful Paradise home for man (His special creation). This is done in order that His eternal purpose of a Kingdom Paradise populated with a people who would live in fellowship with Him, for His glory, forever, might be fulfilled.

Notice the elements of this Paradise creation. First, He created light out of darkness. Light is a characteristic of God. In Him, there is no darkness at all. This is an important understanding, which we will discover later. The first thing that God does is to create light. On the second day, He creates the sky, giving dimension to the universe and also designating the role that water will play in the operation of this Kingdom Paradise. On the third day (or in the third stage of His creation), He creates land, which has the purpose of separating the waters that cover the earth that He has created. There is a plan emerging in these steps of creation – a plan that becomes clearer with each step.

With the creation of dry land, a significantly revealing development takes place in respect to His creative purpose. He brings forth vegetation: seed-bearing plants and trees. It is important not to miss the reference to seed bearing. Everything is designed to grow and to multiply, producing food, and it is always "after its kind." There isn't any evolutionary process built into the creation. Every apple has apple seeds in it – not grapefruit seeds or orange seeds. The fruit bearing is always "after its kind." This reality is a principle of creation – a natural process in the created order.

The next stage of creation is to put the stars in place. Again, this creative act is not merely a cosmetic afterthought, but part of a design for His Kingdom Paradise. According to Genesis 1:14-15, the stars serve as signs to mark the seasons, days and years, and also to give light on the earth.

In this context, the sun and moon were created with their special purpose of giving light and providing the precise elements of temperature to sustain life on the earth. Has it ever occurred to you what would happen if the precision of the orbits of these heavenly bodies were to be altered by even the minutest degree?

God then turned his attention to the great bodies of water that had been formed, and He filled them with all the fish of the sea. Additionally, he created the birds that fly through the heavens. Again, it is important to notice that every living thing that God created had built into the creative act the ability to reproduce "after its kind."

The next stage of His creative act centered on the land, which served livestock, creatures that move along the ground, and wild animals. Again, everything is created with an "after its kind" principle.

By way of summary, the Kingdom Paradise is taking shape with light and darkness; sun, moon and stars measuring day and night; land and water with distinct functions; vegetation (plants and fruit bearing trees); fish of the sea; and birds and animals of every type and description. A bountiful Paradise has been created with order and design to fulfill the purposes of the creator, and "God saw that it was good;" but, in this place that He created, something critical to God's Kingdom plan was missing. There wasn't any creature in the likeness of God with whom he could have fellowship and in whom

He would be glorified. This is where we are told that the creation of man takes place.

According to Genesis 2:7, man was formed from the dust of the ground. He was formed of the earth – a physical body – into which "God breathed the breath of life, and man became a living being." Man was created of the earth, for the earth, and this is consistent with God's final Kingdom plan, in which there is a new heaven and new earth as man's final destiny. The linkage is still there. This tells us something important about man – that he is material substance and non-matter (the breath of life).

GOD'S INTENTION IN CREATING MAN

Before we discuss man's nature, let's look a little more closely at God's intention in creating human life. The first Biblical reference to man's creation is in Genesis 1:26 and following. In these verses, several things stand out about man. For one, man was distinct from all other aspects of God's creation in that he was created in the image and likeness of God. Man is unique in God's creation in this respect. Furthermore, man is given a position of lordship (or "dominion") over all other aspects of God's creation. He was instructed to be fruitful and multiply, to subdue the earth, and to rule over it. God's great Kingdom plan is clearly articulated here in the formation of a people who would live in fellowship with him, in His Kingdom Paradise, for His glory, forever.

God gave Adam everything that he needed for life and happiness – including a wife, along with every physical and material provision that he would ever need. The inaugural stage of the Kingdom of God has been put into place. The stage is set, with the players in position to fulfill God's Kingdom goal.

KINGDOMS IN CONFLICT

TIME

Every phase of human history is confronted by a crisis moment, the first of which occurs in the inaugural stage of God's Kingdom, in the garden Paradise. It is difficult to tell from Scripture how much time passes from the original creation to the time of Adam's sin and banishment from Eden. A case could be made that, prior to man's sin, no one was counting time, even though the measurement of time was part of the constitution of the original creation. I have always understood the act of creation to have occurred in a literal six-day period based on the definition of a day in the context of the creation narrative. In describing the various elements of creation, Genesis 1:5 says, "And there was evening, and there was morning – the first day" (NIV). Each of the days of creation is defined with the same terminology.

In the fifth chapter of Genesis, we are given time measurements in years for the first time, and generations are defined from Adam to Noah. Genesis 5:3 tells us that Adam was 130 years old when he had a son named Seth. No mention is made of Cain and Abel. Does this mean that there wasn't any need to count years until man's sin and the death penalty?

It is possible that the inaugural stage of God's Kingdom could have lasted much longer than we have normally calculated from the Biblical account, which could help to explain the discrepancies with scientific dating of fossils (which, in itself, is an inexact science) and our traditional biblical understanding. Millions of years may have passed between the original creation and man's sin. Years and dates only become important after the curse had been pronounced and death had been introduced. If man did not have an end in death, counting of years does not seem relevant. We understand from Scripture that in eternity there will be no counting of time. The dawn of God's eternal day has no time constraints. Time shall be no more!

Genesis 2 suggests that a significant period of time may have elapsed between the creation of the heavens and the earth (Genesis 1:1-2) and the actual creation of the Eden Paradise. If that is true, we can only speculate here. We do not know what existed in that pre-Eden state (if anything) and what it looked like, or what it constituted. The Bible is silent on this matter. Genesis 2:4-7 reads, "This is the account of the heavens and the earth when they were created. When the Lord God made the earth and the heavens – and no shrub of the field had yet appeared on the earth and no plant of the field had yet sprung up, for the Lord God had not sent rain on the earth and there was no man to work the ground, but streams came up from the earth and watered the whole surface of the ground – the Lord God formed the man from the dust of the ground and breathed into his nostrils the breath of life, and the man became a living being." While there are questions about the timing of certain developments, what is important in Scripture is the revelation of God's plan and man's relation to it.

THE INTRUDER

At any rate, a major development takes place at this point in time with the introduction of Satan into the Paradise scheme bringing severe consequences to man that extend to this very day. When God created man and placed him in this garden Paradise, not only did He make him ruler over all, but He also set certain boundaries for man that he must not cross. Genesis 2:8 and following describes this boundary as a commandment not to eat from the tree of the knowledge of good and evil, which was in the middle of the garden. If they did, as it says in Genesis 2:17, they would surely die.

This commandment was intended to test Adam and Eve's submission to the ultimate authority of God. They had been given dominion as an action of God's sovereign right to rule, not so that they could be independent of God, but so that in fellowship with Him His will could be done on earth as it is in heaven.

It is at this point that Satan seizes the moment to disrupt (and, in his mind, defeat) God's Kingdom plan. Scripture relates that at some point Satan was banished from heaven to earth, where he encountered Adam and Eve in the garden and deceitfully led them to an act of sin and disobedience.

Some people do not believe in a personal devil. The very existence of sorrow and evil throughout the world in every dispensation of time proves the existence of a transcendental, real, dynamic, hostile power, not willed by God. The Bible teaches the existence of a personal devil.

THE ORIGIN AND CHARACTER OF SATAN

Satan is spoken of in scripture as a master deceiver. He is a mirror manipulator. He always knows what type of mirror to use to distort reality in order to get us to believe that what we see in his mirror is real. This is his *modus operandi*. People wonder, "Where did Satan come from, and why didn't God destroy him before he could cause all this trouble?" That is a great question, which is difficult to answer. Satan is not an ordinary creature. The Bible doesn't give us a detailed account of his origin and nature, but it provides enough information for us to know that he is responsible for all the distress that we are experiencing in the world today.

According to Scripture, Satan was part of the hierarchy of God's invisible Kingdom of spirit beings. Apparently, he was in a position of leadership as an angel of light. He was created by God as a super-human spirit being. He appears to possess great power and intelligence. Scripture indicates that he became proud and ambitious, coveting the place of God for himself. At some point, there was war in heaven, and Satan (along with a third of the angelic realm, who followed him) was cast out of this invisible Kingdom into the earth – which, at the time, was probably without form and void. Genesis tells us that darkness covered the face of the deep, which is a logical place for Satan to be consigned. In fact, darkness is a major element of the universe as we know it today.

SATAN AND DARKNESS

Cosmologists have been studying the makeup of the universe for centuries, but only recently have they been able to understand how pervasive darkness really is. From recent findings by the Hubble Space Telescope, scientists now theorize that about 70% of the universe is made up of dark energy, while most of the rest is another mysterious thing called dark matter, and only a small fraction is real matter like stars, planets and living entities. The universe is largely empty, dark space.

Hubble Space Telescope images of distant exploding stars add further confirmation to the permanence of this mysterious force called dark energy that appears to dominate the universe. No one really knows what dark energy is, how strong it is, and whether or not it is growing, decaying, or remains constant.

Additionally, no one can define darkness, because it has no substance scientifically. Someone has said, "Darkness is nothing but nothing." Whether or not we can define darkness scientifically, we know that it is something because the Bible talks about darkness as a real thing. Darkness – whatever it is – references Satan, evil and hell whenever it is used in the Bible.

What we know about Satan is that he is the prince of darkness. Colossians 1:13 refers to his kingdom as a dominion of darkness. He existed in this place of darkness as his domain prior to his encounter with Adam and Eve in the garden Paradise. No one knows how long a period of time (if any) existed between Genesis 1:1 and Genesis 1:2.

SATAN THE TEMPTER

At any rate, once the creation was completed and man was placed there as God's steward (or caretaker), Satan was in a position to continue his campaign against God for dominion by attacking God's creation in this visible Kingdom. Satan recognized the moment as an opportunity to challenge God. He appeared to Adam and Eve in the garden Paradise in the form of a serpent. It is important to remember that Adam knew every creature in the garden because he had named them all. It may very well be that the serpent was a gentle and fun-loving creature that Adam and Eve enjoyed being around. The serpent in the garden at this time was not the creepy, crawly, venomous creature that we know as a snake today. It was only after Satan, in the form of a serpent, succeeded in causing Adam and Eve to disobey God that God pronounced a judgment on the serpent and changed its form to one that crawled on the ground and ate the dust of the ground according to Genesis 3:14.

At the moment of encounter with Adam and Eve, they knew the serpent and trusted the serpent. They didn't seem startled that the serpent talked to them. Apparently, there was communication between Adam and Eve and the creatures of the garden. We really don't know much about what went on in this Kingdom Paradise before man's sinful rebellion against God. What Adam and Eve didn't know is that this creature was different from the one that they named and associated with. This serpent was demonized by the prince of demons (Satan). This is in keeping with his nature as a master deceiver. His approach to Adam and Eve in the Garden of Eden shows his subtle (but effective) approach.

Think about this for a moment! God had told Adam and Eve that they could not eat of the tree of the knowledge of good and evil or they would die. Satan raised the question as to whether or not God really said that they would die. What did He mean? What is death, anyway? Adam and Eve had never seen anything die in the Eden paradise. However, they may have understood what death meant better than we sometimes acknowledge. In pronouncing the curse after the sinful act, God told Adam, "By the sweat of your brow you will eat your food until you return to the ground, since from it you were taken; for dust you are and to dust you will return" (Genesis 3:19, NIV). To become dust of the ground surely meant something different than living in the garden Paradise. Adam must have understood that to return to dust meant demise.

Whatever they understood, Satan planted a seed of doubt in their minds in respect to how God treats them. After Eve told him that she understood clearly what God had said and where He had set the boundary, Satan responded with a lie: "You will not surely die." He went on to suggest that the reason that God said not to eat of the tree was because God knew that, if they were to eat of the tree, their eyes would be opened, and they would be like God – knowing good and evil. This is a powerful deception.

To Adam and Eve, to become like God was not necessarily an appeal to be independent from God. They knew God. They were made in His likeness. They had fellowship with Him on an intimate level. In their minds, being like God in a fully realized sense would not necessarily be a bad thing.

To Satan, it meant something else. Satan is a pseudo-deity with an ego problem. His desire is not to be like God, but to be God in the sense of His dominion and rule. Isaiah 14:12-14 expresses his motivating desire. In Satan's mind, if he could get Adam and Eve to disobey God and surrender their God-given dominion to him, he could (in effect) establish his kingdom on the earth, robbing God of his Kingdom plan and bringing all creation into total and final subjection to him.

SATAN AND DEATH

The creation narrative gives every indication that Satan knew what God was up to. He knew God's plan. He knew what God said. He came to Eve and quoted God's command to her. He also knew that if he could succeed in getting Adam and Eve to disobey God, God would have to punish them with death, as He said He would. Satan knew that in the moment Adam and Eve committed sin, God's Kingdom plan was disrupted. Satan could use this moment to launch his own kingdom plan because, as long as sin and death reign, God's Kingdom plan can never be realized.

This is an important understanding, because it explains why Satan never gives up, even after the appearance of the redeemer and the cross/resurrection event. Up until Jesus Christ appears on the scene of human history, Satan is confident that he still wins because people continue to die. Resurrection is not part of the Old Testament experience. God instituted a sacrificial system whereby people made atonement for their sin, but they all still died. Death is the ultimate demise. It is the domain of Satan. It is the enemy of man, as the apostle Paul states in 1 Corinthians 15:26.

Death was never part of God's plan for mankind. Death denies man entrance into God's Kingdom Paradise. As long as death exists, Satan believes that he wins. That is why, when Jesus Christ appears on the scene of human history, Satan actively and unrelentingly dogs him in an attempt to get Jesus to fail as he did with the first Adam. If Jesus, as the last Adam, were to sin and fail, there would remain no sacrifice for sin. The cross would be robbed of its significance.

THE CONFLICT

In the great conflict of the ages between God and Satan, the first major battle was the creation Paradise battle, and (on the surface) Satan wins. The book of Genesis relates the creation story and shows the glory, majesty and power of God in what was created. There is perfection, beauty, joy and life. At some point in time, everything changed through the successful scheming of Satan, which resulted in human rebellion and the disruption of God's creative plan. Genesis, which started out as a wonderful story, moves to relate a series of human disasters: Adam and Eve's rebellion; Cain's calculated murder of his brother; global wickedness issuing in the flood destroying all human life; and man's arrogance at Babel. The conflict between God and Satan, which began in heaven, now focuses on the earth where Satan appears to have caused a set-back of God's creative plan.

The coming of Jesus Christ – the second or last Adam, the head of a new humanity – is the second and final battleground for Satan with God. Satan knows that now God has gone to the ultimate risk by sending His Son into the world – born of a woman, flesh of our flesh – to live among us in obedience to the Father. If Satan can succeed in getting Jesus to sin in an act of disobedience to God, then Jesus must die for his own sin. He cannot die for the sins of the world, because he must pay the penalty for his own sin. Satan knows that he must defeat Jesus. He must somehow deceive him into thinking that Satan is right and represents a better alternative.

For that reason, Satan is ready to devour the child when he is born (as John describes in Revelation 12). Satan works in Herod's heart to deceive the wise men so that, when they find the child, they will return to Herod with the information that he needs. Herod told the wise men that he would like to go and worship this newborn king, but God knew what Satan was up to and what Herod, as the emissary of Satan, really wanted to do, so God gave a supernatural revelation to the wise men, and they returned home another way. Subsequently, Herod was so enraged that he issued an edict that all the male children in Bethlehem and its environs who were two years old and under be killed. Satan will use every means at his disposal to stop God's plan from succeeding in Jesus.

We see him again when Christ is led by the Spirit into the wilderness at the outset of His ministry to be tempted by Satan. After Jesus spent 40 days and 40 nights fasting, hungry and in a weakened physical condition, Satan came to him with a series of three temptations. In many respects, his deception at the temptation of Jesus is styled as his original temptation to Eve. He knows why Christ is here, and he bases his appeals to Christ on what would appear on the surface to be relatively innocent, as opposed to blatantly evil inducements. He only wants Jesus to be disobedient once. That is all it will take, but – praise God! – Christ remains obedient to His Father and the purposes of His Father through him. Satan still does not give up. Throughout the life and ministry of Jesus, Satan encounters him in demonic representations, and Jesus always overcomes him.

The real test comes when Satan works in Jesus' disciple, Judas. Satan succeeds in getting him to betray Jesus, which leads to his subsequent arrest, trial and sentence of death on the cross. When Jesus is subsequently taken from the cross as a dead man and placed in the tomb of Joseph of Arimathea, the decisive moment has arrived in the saga of the conflict between God and Satan.

Jesus is the one in whom God has planned to recover His lost creation. Jesus is the last Adam – the last hope for a new race of men. Now, He is dead. The fact that He is dead proves beyond a shadow of a doubt that He took our sins upon Himself on the cross. 1 Peter 2:24 says, "He himself bore our sins in his body on the tree, so that we might die to sins and live for righteousness; by his wounds you have been healed."

If He hadn't taken our sins upon Himself, He couldn't have died. Death is a penalty for sin. Christ was sinless; consequently, death could not have overcome Him. The reality, however, is that Christ died on the cross and was buried in the grave – the turf of Satan. A stone was rolled against the door, affixed with a seal that – if tampered with – would result in the death of the perpetrator or perpetrators. Moreover, an elite Roman guard was stationed there to make sure that no one came to steal His body and spread a false rumor that He was alive. That is what is known and can be seen with the naked eye.

THE CONQUEST

What cannot be seen in this moment are forces much stronger than the legions of Rome. Satan has marshaled all his demonic powers, and he stands with them against that tomb all the while that Christ is there. He knows that he cannot allow Christ to escape from this place of death. He must keep a lid on the grave; and, if he can keep Christ there, he wins. But – praise God! – on the third day morning, as prophesied, Christ arose, victorious over sin and the grave, dealing a crushing blow to this enemy of God and man.

Jesus actually prophesied about His death and resurrection when He was speaking with His disciples about His identity. After Peter accurately reveals His identity as the Son of the living God, Jesus goes on to say, in Matthew 16:18, "I will build my church, and the gates of hell shall not prevail against it". It is interesting to note here that the word translated "hell" in the Authorized Version is the Greek word for the grave, *Hades*. David Burge, writing on the History of Hell, says, "Hades was the Greek god of death and king of the underworld." In the minds of those to whom Jesus was speaking, "Hades" was understood as the place of the dead. Jesus was telling His followers that He would experience death. He would enter Satan's domain and be locked in by Hades' gate. The cemetery is a gated community. Once you get in there, the gate is closed and locked. You can't get out. Jesus prophesied that He would go into the grave and burst the gate of the grave open, coming forth victoriously. This is precisely what happened. Christ went into the grave – into this place of captivity, into this domain of Satan – and He planted the Christian flag there, claiming the grave for God. Death has no more dominion over Him; and, because He lives, we too shall live. Satan was dealt a decisive defeat. The grave is where the battle of the ages was fought. No resurrection – no future. Resurrection – Paradise.

In Colossians 2:13-15, the Apostle Paul wrote, "When you were dead in your sins and in the uncircumcision of your sinful nature, God made you alive with Christ. He forgave us all our sins, having canceled the written code, with its regulations, that was against us and that stood opposed to us; He took it away, nailing it to the cross, and having disarmed the powers and authorities, He made a public spectacle of them, triumphing over them by the cross." Also, Hebrews 2:14-15 says, "Since the children have flesh and blood, He too shared in their humanity so that by His death He might destroy him who holds the power of death – that is, the devil – and free those who all their lives were held in slavery by their fear of death. "

Satan still has not given up.. He must believe that he still can win, because death continues to reign. Perhaps he thinks that Christ was an exception. After all, he was the Son of God. God may have won that battle, but it is not over in Satan's mind. People still die.

Good people still die. Believers still die; and, as long as there is death, Satan still thinks he has a chance.

The reason why death is so important to Satan is that it represents his dominion over man and all things earthly. Man is of the earth. A believer is a new creation in Jesus Christ, but he can never be what God created him to be without resurrection. Death is the antithesis of life. Contrary to popular opinion, it is not the same as life. Death prevents man (even a believer) from experiencing the glories of God's Kingdom Paradise. Without resurrection, there isn't any future for man.

QUESTIONS FOR DISCUSSION
1. What does the Bible say about the "existence" of God?
2. What are some differences between pagan gods and the God of the Bible?
3. What are some practical benefits of the fact that God loves us?
4. What was God's ultimate purpose in creating the universe?
5. How do we know what we know about Satan, the Devil?
6. What does it mean to describe Jesus Christ as "the last Adam"?

CHAPTER 3

THE VIEW FROM A HELICOPTER: AN OVERVIEW OF THE BOOK OF DANIEL

To stand in the middle of something limits ones understanding of what is observable, but to stand above it gives one a different perspective. Hovering over something allows us to see the big picture – like viewing it from a helicopter.

When studying Bible prophecy, it is easy to get bogged down on the details of the prophecy, which may or may not have any significance, and end up missing the main point. We need to see the big picture. The question we must ask ourselves is this: "What is the message that God is intending for us to understand from what He has revealed?" Too often, we want to fit some of the incidental aspects of the prophecy into historical developments, which may change from generation to generation, but the fundamental truth of the prophecy never changes. It makes for interesting reading to see what Bible students in each generation have made of the 10 toes of Nebuchadnezzar's image, or the little horn of Daniel 7, or the 10 horns, or the 2,300 days. However, the main theme of the Book of Daniel remains constant and is generally agreed upon by Bible scholars.

The primary message of the Book of Daniel is the sovereignty of God over the affairs of men and of nations, culminating at last in the establishment of God's eternal Kingdom of righteousness and peace on the earth made new. Everything else is incidental to this reality. This is the big picture of the Book of Daniel, which (if properly understood) will give us confidence and hope in the God who rules the nations as seen in Psalm 22:28, Psalm 45:6 and Daniel 2:44.

In Daniel's time, the people of Israel were in captivity in a foreign land. Anytime we find ourselves in a troublesome circumstance, the tendency is to wonder if God is able to help us and if He cares. What is conveyed to us in this Book is a demonstration of God's power and care in the midst of distressing circumstances. By it, the people of Israel were reminded that kingdoms come and go, but the sovereign God of the universe is always there, and He is always triumphant.

THE TRANSITORY NATURE OF HUMAN GOVERNMENT

Earlier, we came to the conclusion that the world as we know it – life as we know it, in the various nations of the world as we know them – will someday come to an end. They will be no more. Any student of history has learned that governments often rise and fall, being established with great promise, but subsequently falling in disarray and failure. Eric Sauer makes the observation, "Peoples and kingdoms emerge and vanish. Thrones and dominions rise and fall."

World governments are subject to change by an uprising, a military coup or a foreign invasion. Some governments transition peacefully by a democratic election or other natural process. Change of power is a staple of the times. In this generation alone, we have seen the reunification of the two Germanys and the dismantling of the Russian political empire. We have seen heads of government change in many countries of the world – sometimes peacefully, and sometimes by violent means. Mass protests in Middle Eastern countries at the outset of 2011 have demonstrated the instability of human government.

We look at some of these changes and wonder, "How did these changes come about? What issues or forces helped bring about these changes?" We look at other situations and wonder when the next uprising will take place – or when the next military coup will occur – and what will happen to the leadership of this nation or that. Nations of the world have historically gone to war with other nations to destroy a threat to their security. Since the war on terrorism was launched in the fall of 2001, several nations have come into the crosshairs of the United States, including Iran and North Korea. Nations who harbor terrorist groups, or who are thought to develop weapons of mass destruction, are nervous – wondering if they might be next on our hit list. In a political sense, the world is in a troubled state.

If history teaches us anything, it teaches us that the governments of the world are unstable, short-lived and doomed to failure. It teaches us one thing more: that God is the sovereign God of the universe and He is in control of the affairs of men and of nations. That's the testimony of the nations historically, and that's the message of the Bible. That understanding raises a good question. How can one look at the nations of the world today and say that God is in control – that God is sovereign over the affairs of nations? After all, some governments are oligarchies or dictatorships – oppressing their people, robbing them of their freedoms, depriving them of life's bare essentials, subjugating them to live in poverty, suffering injustices and experiencing terror and fear. Some nations are religious governments that have been established on the fundamentals of a dominant religion – a religion that is intolerant of other religions and is defiant and hostile toward Christianity and the God of the Bible. Some governments are morally and spiritually corrupt, sometimes professing a belief in the God of the Bible, but alienating Him from all arenas of public and governmental life. Some governments are atheistic, believing only in the fundamental genius and power of man to shape his own destiny. No nation demonstrates by its life and action an adherence to the teachings of Scripture and to the will of God. No nation of the world can ever hope to fulfill the Biblical qualifications for becoming the Kingdom of God.

THE KINGDOM OF GOD IS DIFFERENT

The Kingdom of God is not political in nature, but spiritual. It is not about a world government or worldly kingdom, but about God's reign over His people.

The whole Bible is the story of God's activity in creating a people that would be known as the people of God. When God created Adam and Eve, His purpose was to begin a race of beings who will live in fellowship with Him in His Kingdom Paradise, for His glory, forever. The Bible is all about God's Kingdom plan. His plan was clearly evident in creation. He was the owner who gave authority and dominion to those that He created to rule in the garden Paradise as his caretakers. However, Satan entered the scene as the adversary of God and man, and by his temptation succeeded in wresting the dominion from Adam to become ruler of the world. It is important to remember that God never gave ownership of anything to Adam. He made him ruler of the created order, and that is what Satan stole from our first parents. God was not defeated in this transgression. His plan of forming a people who would live in fellowship with Him in His Kingdom Paradise, for His glory, forever, moved now to the preparations for a second (or last) Adam who would become the head of a new humanity to complete God's plan as originally intended.

The promise of a Messiah goes back to the Genesis narrative and is worked out through the calling of Abraham, through whom all the nations of the world would be blessed. The birth of the Messiah – 2,000 years after the promise to Abraham – came about precisely as God said it would. Jesus is the "seed of the woman" and fulfills the Messianic promise.

God's purposes then centered on the formation of a people through the saving activity of His Son, the Redeemer, who gave His life on the cross, paying the penalty for our sins. Following His death, resurrection and ascension to the right hand of God the Father, Jesus will return in power and great glory at the end of the age to do away with sin and Satan and to establish His eternal Kingdom on the earth made new. The cross/resurrection event assures us that God will indeed dwell with His people forever in His Kingdom Paradise.

The outline of the future as revealed in the Book of Daniel, is generally agreed upon by evangelical scholars and Bible-believing Christians. The question is not so much, "What does the future hold?" Rather, in the words of the disciples of Jesus, the question is, "When shall these things be?" This is what everyone wants to know.

THE COURSE OF TIME TRACED THROUGH HUMAN GOVERNMENT

That is where the Book of Daniel helps us understand the course of human history. The Book of Daniel is one of four Major Prophets in the Old Testament. In fact, it is the shortest of these prophetic books, but it is distinguished from the others by the style and content of the book. In respect to style, it is an apocalyptic book. According to the *Encyclopedia of Bible Prophecy*, it exhibits the highest proportion of apocalyptic or symbolic prophecy to be found in the entire Bible, engaging slightly more than two-thirds of its prophetic content. As far as its content is concerned, it contains a significant amount of historical data – especially chapters 1, 3 and 6 – but the importance of the book is not so much in the historical content as in its prophetic content. The Book of Daniel gives us a glimpse of world history as traced through the governments of men from the time of Nebuchadnezzar, king of Babylon, to the very end of the age. It is a complete chronology of worldly governments. This is what distinguishes Daniel from all other books of the Bible.

THE BABYLONIAN EMPIRE

The Book of Daniel is set in the context of the kingdom of Babylon. Babylon was one of the most famous cities of ancient time. It was the capital city of an empire that dominated the ancient world as a center of trade, military power, culture and religion. It was situated in the land of Mesopotamia, between the Tigris and Euphrates rivers – an area thought to be the cradle of civilization. It is the same geographical area as is currently occupied by the nation of Iraq.

The area that we refer to as "Babylon" has a long and colorful history. After the great flood, the area was populated by the sons of Noah. According to the first-century historian Josephus, the area became famous by the exploits of a great-grandson of Noah by the name of Nimrod. The history of Babylon is like that of a cat with nine lives. It survived brutal and savage invasions by the Assyrians. Barbaric hordes of Assyrians ravaged the remains of Hammurabi's empire that had lasted some 1,000 years after his death. They so completely destroyed Babylon in 689 BC, under King Sennacherib, that it was said to resemble a washed-over meadow after a great flood.

However, Babylon was not finished. It re-emerged as a world power in 605 BC, when the Babylonians – under the leadership of the young Nebuchadnezzar – conquered Egypt and began a reign of power that would be unequalled in the history of world empires.

"Babylon the Great" was the largest city on earth at that time, with up to 200,000 people. It was the capital of the most dominant empire that the world had ever seen, characterized by power, wealth, opulence and decadence. Babylon was a powerful city. It was sur-rounded by a wall that was 12 miles long, 25 feet thick and 35 feet high. On top of the wall were 360 battle towers that rose 288 feet into the air. Babylon was a powerful, well-fortified city.

From its earliest days, Babylon symbolized a way of thinking that was opposed to God and his ways.

In 605 BC, probably in Nebuchadnezzar's first year as king of the Babylonian empire, he brought his armies to Jerusalem and cap-tured the city, taking important captives and artifacts from the temple back to Babylon. This was in the third year of the reign of Jehoiakim, King of Judah. Among the hostages that Nebuchadnezzar brought to Babylon was the young man Daniel about whom the Book that bears his name revolves.

Dating of these events is a little difficult, but most Bible scholars accept the 605 BC date for this first attack on Jerusalem. It would not have been a difficult thing for Nebuchadnezzar to lead his army against Jerusalem in his first year as king, since he had been the commanding officer of the Babylonian army for several years under his father, King Nabopolassar.

The Jewish people became exiles in a foreign land. That's where we are at the opening of the Book of Daniel.

What does any of this have to do with understanding where we are on the timeline of human history? The answer to that question is revealed in the overarching theme of the Book of Daniel, which is the sovereignty of God over the affairs of men and nations. Daniel 5:21 says, "The Most High God is sovereign over the kingdoms of men and sets over them anyone he wishes."

GOD'S SELECTION AND PREPRARATION OF DANIEL

Daniel, who is the author and chief character of the Book, is remembered by most people as the man who was thrown into a den of ferocious lions. This was done by an indolent king who had been tricked by his subordinates into issuing a decree, which (if enforced) would lead to Daniel's end (chapter 6). Everyone remembers the miraculous presence of God with His servant, keeping him safe in the midst of imminent danger. However, there is a great deal more to Daniel than this intriguing experience.

Daniel was not in Babylon by accident or because Nebuchadnezzar knew what he was doing when he brought him to Babylon. Daniel was in Babylon as part of God's divine plan, revealing His purposes for the kingdoms of men prior to His intervention in human history at the end of the age. God had His man in His place for His time to fulfill His purposes. The incidents of chapter 1 are necessary to Daniel's role in chapter 2. Daniel must become known to the king, and gain the respect and favor of the king, or he would never be allowed to come into the presence of the king in the hour of his crisis.

A series of unusual circumstances unfold that fulfill this objective. When Nebuchadnezzar arrived back in Babylon after his conquest of Jerusalem, he brought with him the spoils of war. Among these spoils were choice articles from the Temple, which Nebuchadnezzar put in the temple of his god. In addition to these artifacts were some of the finest young men of Jerusalem, who had been chosen because of their superior social and intellectual standing. They were young men "without any physical defect, handsome, showing aptitude for every kind of learning, well informed, quick to understand, and qualified to serve in the king's palace" (Daniel 1:4). The chief official was charged by the king to give these young men a crash course in the ways and culture of the Babylonians. In addition to the pre-scribed academic program, they were ordered to eat a special diet of food and wine from the king's table. The training regimen was to last for three years, after which they were to enter the king's service.

Daniel was among these choice young men, and he had a problem with the king's decree. He would not defile himself with the royal food and wine, and he asked the king's official to allow him to have a different menu. This caused the official a great deal of difficulty, because he reasoned that if he allowed Daniel and his friends this special diet and after a time they were found to be malnourished, the king would kill the official for not following orders.

Here, again, we have an illustration of God's sovereignty over the affairs of men and nations. The Bible says that God caused the official to show special favor to Daniel. The official accepted Daniel's proposed 10-day test even though he knew that it could result in his death. At the end of the 10 days, Daniel and his friends looked healthier and better nourished than the others, who ate the king's food. God is faithful, and He will always honor His servants who are obedient to His will and way.

At this point in the Book, we are told that God also gave Daniel and his friends certain gifts that would prove advantageous to His purposes in the days that would follow. According to Daniel 1:17 these four young men were given the gifts of "knowledge and understanding of all kinds of literature and learning. And Daniel could understand visions and dreams of all kinds." This may be the first reference to spiritual gifts in the Bible. God was preparing these young men for what would follow, when the use of these gifts would bring great glory to His name.

During this period, Daniel was prepared to be God's man. At the end of the training period set by the king, he brought everyone in for a personal examination, and he found Daniel and his friends to be superior in knowledge and understanding, setting them apart from all the others. "In every matter of wisdom and understanding about which the king questioned them, he found them ten times better than all the magicians and enchanters in his whole kingdom" (Daniel 1:20).

The developments recorded in Daniel 1 confirm God's sovereignty over the affairs of men and nations. God has a purpose in history, and everything that happens serves that purpose. God is in control of history, and He is always triumphant. One of the basic principles of Bible prophecy is the understanding that God is sovereign. The incidents recorded in this opening chapter of the Book of Daniel demonstrate how God is active in our lives, even when life appears to turn against us. His purposes are always served. Daniel was now prepared to serve God's purpose interpreting the dream of Nebuchadnezzar. The Book of Daniel revolves around a frightening dream of king Nebuchadnezzar.

DATING THE DREAM

There is some difficulty putting this dream and its interpretation in a correct chronological order. Daniel 2:1 says that the dream occurred in the second year of Nebuchadnezzar's reign, which would make it about 603 BC. If Daniel was brought to Babylon in the first year of Nebuchadnezzar's reign and was put into a training course for at least three years (Daniel 1), he would have still been in training when Nebuchadnezzar had his dream. According to the setting in Daniel 2, it appears that the king called his wise men in to interpret the dream shortly after it happened, maybe even in the middle of the night. At least three explanations are possible.

One explanation is offered by Barnes in his commentary on Daniel. "The dream was in the second year of Nebuchadnezzar's reign (Daniel 2:1). Previously to this, Daniel and his fellows had been subjected to a three years' discipline, as preparatory to waiting upon the king (Daniel 1:5). That period had passed before Daniel was presented to the king (Daniel 1:18). How, it is asked, could Nebuchadnezzar, as king, appoint to Daniel three years of discipline, and yet bring in the same Daniel, in the second year of his actual reign, to interpret his dream, when it is evident, from the author's own showing, that this Daniel had already completed his three years' course of discipline, and taken his place among the Magi before he was called to interpret the dream? (Daniel 1:20, Daniel 2:2 and Daniel 2:13)

"If the result of the preceding investigation be admitted, then is the solution of this seemingly difficult problem rendered quite easy. Nebuchadnezzar is called king in Daniel 1:1, after the usual manner of the Hebrews (compare 2 Kings 24:1 and 2 Chronicles 36:6), and in the way of anticipation. In fact, he became sole king before that expedition had ended. But when a Jewish writer in Babylon (Daniel) comes to the transactions of his actual reign as reckoned of course in Babylon (for of course the date of his reign there would be from the period when he became sole king), the writer dates the events that happened under that reign, in accordance with the Babylonian reckoning. So it seems to be in Daniel 2:1. According to the result of the preceding examination, Daniel was sent to Babylon in the latter part of 607 BC or the beginning of 606 BC. Nebuchadnezzar became actual king, by the death of his father, near the end of 605 BC or at the beginning of 604 BC. Nebuchadnezzar's second year of actual and sole reign would then be in 603 BC. If we suppose the latter part of this year to be the time when the dream occurred, then we have a period of nearly four years between Daniel's exile and his call to interpret the king's dream.

"Any part of 603 BC saves the accuracy of the Book of Daniel with respect to this matter. In fact it lies on the very face of this statement in the Book of Daniel that it is scrupulously conformed to historical truth, for how could the writer, after having announced Daniel's deportation as belonging to the third year of Jehoiakim, and his discipline as having been completed in three years, then declare that Daniel was called upon as one of the Magi, to interpret dreams, in the second year of Nebuchadnezzar? If Nebuchadnezzar was actual king in the third year of Jehoiakim, he was so when Daniel was carried away to Babylon; and plain enough is it, that Daniel's course of discipline was not complete until the fourth, or at least the end of the third year of Nebuchadnezzar. The error would, in such a case, be so palpable, that no writer of any intelligence or consistency could fail to notice and correct it.

"We are constrained to believe, then, that Nebuchadnezzar is named king merely in the way of anticipation, in Daniel 1:1 (and so in 2 Kings 24, 2 Chronicles 36:1 and Jeremiah 25:1); and that the date of his sole and actual reign is referred to in Daniel 2:1, as the Babylonians reckoned it. Thus understood, all is consistent and probable. We do not need to resort, as Rosenmuller and others have done, to a 'long series' of dreams on the part of Nebuchadnezzar, in which the same thing was repeated; nor to the improbable subterfuge, that, although he dreamed in the second year of his reign, he did not concern himself to find out an interpreter of his nocturnal visions until some considerable time afterward. Both of these representations seem to me to be contrary to the plain and evident tenor of the whole narration. The agitation was immediate, and the stronger because it was immediate. Procrastination of the matter might, and probably would, have liberated him from his fears, and blunted the edge of his curiosity.

"That Jeremiah reckons in the Palestine Jewish way, that is, anticipatively, is certain from Jeremiah 25:1 and Jeremiah 46:2. That he did not do this by mistake, but only in compliance with the usage of the Jews in Palestine, seems altogether probable. On the other hand, the state of facts as to Nebuchadnezzar's conquests, as exhibited above, shows that his invasion of Judea must have begun as early as Daniel 1:1 asserts. In truth, facts and events vouch for the writer's minute historical accuracy in this matter, in case it be conceded that Nebuchadnezzar is called king in Daniel 1:1, in the way of anticipation, and in accordance with the common Hebrew usage." (From Barnes' Notes, Electronic Database Copyright © 1997, 2003, 2005, 2006 by Biblesoft, Inc. All rights reserved.)

A second possible explanation is that some time may have passed between the time Nebuchadnezzar had his terrifying dream and his decision to call his wise men to interpret it. If that is the case, then he must have lived with these horrifying thoughts (and been troubled by them) for a long time – or, perhaps, had multiple dreams over an extended period. No time line is given in Daniel 2, but the inference is that a dream like this would call for immediate attention. While this scenario is possible, it is highly unlikely.

A third possible explanation is that the chronology as stated is accurate, but our understanding of how the details played out may not be. There is nothing in chapter 2 to suggest that Daniel and his friends were already approved and serving in the king's court of wise men. They may have still been in training. Remember, we are dealing with apocalyptic literature, in which the information conveyed isn't necessarily chronological. It is important to underscore the fact that the three-year training regimen that Daniel was subjected to was not what qualified him to serve among the wise men of Babylon and interpret dreams. His ability to interpret dreams was a gift from God.

It is interesting to note that when the king held court with his wise men, Daniel and his friends were not present (Daniel 2:13). This seems like the most plausible explanation, since when Arioch came to find Daniel and told him about the king's edict, Daniel asked for an audience with the king. If he had completed his training and was approved for service, why wasn't he there when the king called for his wise men? We already know, according to the first chapter of Daniel, that he had special gifts of understanding and wisdom along with the ability to interpret dreams (Daniel 1:17). If he was present when the king first called in his wise men, I can't imagine Daniel would have remained silent when all the others spoke about the impossibility of interpreting the dream.

THE DREAM

Daniel 2 is the focal point of the entire Book of Daniel. King Nebuchadnezzar had a dream that troubled him greatly. Daniel is later given his own vision in chapter 7 in the form of four beasts, which correspond to the sections of the image in chapter 2 and confirm the interpretation that was given. Nebuchadnezzar employed a group of astrologers, magicians, sorcerers and enchanters, who were summoned to tell him the dream and interpret it. They had been given comfortable lives in the king's palace so as to provide the king with understanding and meaning on such occasions as this. However, when they stood before the king, they needed the king to tell them his dream in order for them to concoct a meaning. They repeatedly asked the king to tell them the dream and promised to give him an interpretation. They insisted that it was only the fair thing to do. When he refused to reveal the dream to them (there is some question as to whether or not he even could recall it), and they were unable to tell him his dream, he became enraged and ordered that they all be executed. The problem was that Daniel and his friends were among the king's chosen wise men and the edict to execute everyone included Daniel and his friends even though they were not present when the king questioned his wise men and issued his decree. As the execution was under way, Daniel heard of what was going on and asked for an audience with the king. The audience was granted, and Daniel told the king essentially the same thing that he had heard from his astrologers and their friends, except that Daniel said that there was a God in heaven who could reveal the understanding. Daniel asked the king for time to beseech this God for the meaning of the dream. The king granted him his request, and Daniel and his friends went to prayer, asking the Sovereign God of the universe to reveal the answer to the king's riddle. Daniel 2:19 says, "During the night, the mystery was revealed to Daniel in a vision." This is one of the first concerts of prayer recorded in the Bible, and it was very successful. Daniel was given the understanding necessary to preserve his life and that of his friends.

The dream that troubled Nebuchadnezzar and that was so frightening was a vision of a huge shining metallic image in the form of a man. The image had a head of gold; the breast and arms were silver; the belly and thighs were brass; and the legs were of iron. The feet of the image were part iron and part clay. As the king watched this brilliant shining image, he saw a stone cut out of a mountain without hands, which struck the image on the feet, crushing the sections of the image and grinding them into dust, which the wind blew away. The falling stone that struck and destroyed the image became a mountain that filled the whole earth. Daniel described this vision to the king and proceeded to interpret it.

The first thing that Daniel did was to tell the king where he got this understanding. It didn't come from his own wisdom or from some magic that he concocted. He said to the king, "No wise man, enchanter, magician or diviner can explain to the king the mystery that he has asked about, but there is a God in heaven who reveals mysteries. He has shown King Nebuchadnezzar what will happen in days to come" (Daniel 2:27-28).

This was basically the same thing that the king's wise men had told him, except that they didn't know where to get the information. They said that he was asking the impossible of them. Daniel said that that was true, except that the God of heaven knows all things and is able to reveal them to whomsoever He chooses.

Having given credit to the sovereign God of the universe, Daniel proceeded to explain what the Lord had revealed to him. He boldly and bluntly told the king, "You are the head of gold." He reminded Nebuchadnezzar that everything he had had been given to him by the Lord, whether he acknowledged it or not. The Lord gave him dominion, power, might and glory. God made him ruler over the entire Babylonian empire. Daniel didn't ask the king if he had any questions; he merely told him what the situation was. I suppose that, at this time, Nebuchadnezzar might have puffed out his chest just a little as he contemplated the greatness of his empire. As far as Nebuchadnezzar was concerned, it was all about him and his greatness (Daniel 4:30). If that was the case, he was in for an attitude check very quickly when Daniel followed with this statement: "After you, another kingdom will arise, inferior to yours. Next, a third kingdom will rule over the whole earth; and, finally, a fourth kingdom."

After explaining about the stone cut out of the mountain without hands, he added, "The great God has shown the king what will take place in the future. The dream is true and the interpretation is trustworthy."

It is difficult for us to imagine the emotions that must have surged through Nebuchadnezzar's head. "I am a great king, and I rule over a great empire," he thought. "I am the greatest! But what about this God whom Daniel serves? He must be great also." "Surely your God is the God of gods, and the Lord of kings, and a revealer of mysteries for you were able to reveal this mystery" (Daniel 2:47). People are interesting. Here is Nebuchadnezzar, clearly impressed with Daniel, so much so that he elevates Daniel to a position of authority in his kingdom. At the same time, he is even more impressed with himself – to the degree that he erects a huge statue of himself on the plains of Dura! It is not just a statue, but it stands 90 feet high and is nine feet wide and is covered from head to toe with gold. It's as if he has forgotten the God who revealed the mystery to him and has flaunted his own sense of worth in the face of the Almighty. Daniel said that the image that he saw with the various metallic elements represented four kingdoms, and Nebuchadnezzar was the head of gold. This was terribly disturbing to the king, and his response was to create his own image in order show everyone that he wasn't just a head of gold, but he was the whole image. He thought of himself as being invincible. His kingdom would last forever. The image in the dream meant nothing to him. It didn't change a thing. For Nebuchadnezzar, it was all about him. He quickly forgot that the God who revealed the mystery was also in control of the kingdoms of men.

The image that King Nebuchadnezzar created, as recorded in Daniel 3, proved to be another opportunity for God to show His power. Nebuchadnezzar summoned all the officials of his kingdom to come to the dedication ceremony, which was staged like a Hollywood extravaganza. He assembled the "Babylonian Symphony Orchestra" to perform for him. He came before his people arrayed in his royal robes, while his herald issued the following command: "This is what you are commanded to do, O peoples, nations and men of every language: As soon as you hear the sound of the horn, flute, zither, lyre, harp, pipes and all kinds of music, you must fall down and worship the image of gold that King Nebuchadnezzar has set up. Whoever does not fall down and worship will immediately be thrown into a blazing furnace" (Daniel 3:4-6).

The music played, and everyone bowed down and worshiped the image that Nebuchadnezzar had set up – except Shadrach, Meshach and Abednego, the three friends of Daniel. Some in the king's company immediately reported this to the king, who was outraged to think that these high-ranking officials didn't respect him or his gods. Furious with rage, he brought these men before him and reminded them of his decree and the serious consequences if they didn't obey. He offered them a second chance, but they told the king that they served a greater King and would not bow down and worship his image. They told the king that they would rather die in his furnace than violate their faith in the sovereign God of the universe. It is interesting that they told the king that their God was able to rescue them from this fate (Nebuchadnezzar had just told them that no god could spare them) and that, if he didn't, it was all right with them. This is a great testimony of faithfulness in the face of death. It also underscores one of the sub-themes of the Book of Daniel: God will protect His own in every circumstance when they are obedient to Him. This doesn't mean that they will never experience consequences for their faithfulness and commitment to God. What it does mean is that no matter what men may do to us, God is always there, and His grace will sustain us through it all.

In his anger, Nebuchadnezzar ordered the furnace to be heated seven times hotter than ever before and the three men to be bound, fully clothed, by the strongest men in the king's army. For Nebuchadnezzar, there was no way that these men could survive this punishment. In fact, the heat from the furnace was so intense that the men who took Shadrach, Meshach and Abednego to the fiery pit to throw them in were consumed by the heat and died on the spot. However, God had other plans for these three Hebrew worthies. Once again, Nebuchadnezzar witnessed the awesome power of the living God. "Then King Nebuchadnezzar leaped to his feet in amazement and asked his advisers, 'Weren't there three men that we tied up and threw into the fire?' They replied, 'Certainly, O king.' He said, 'Look! I see four men walking around in the fire, unbound and unharmed, and the fourth looks like a son of the gods.' Nebuchadnezzar then approached the opening of the blazing furnace and shouted, 'Shadrach, Meshach and Abednego, servants of the Most High God, come out! Come here!' So Shadrach, Meshach and Abednego came out of the fire, and the satraps, prefects, governors and royal advisers crowded around them. They saw that the fire had not harmed their bodies, nor was a hair of their heads singed; their robes were not scorched, and there was no smell of fire on them" (Daniel 3:24-27).

Some people never get it. What does God have to do to prove His sovereignty and power? People are fickle and forgetful. We see His handiwork; we marvel at His grace; and we go on our way as if He didn't exist.

Nebuchadnezzar rehearsed what God had done and extolled the greatness of the living God, but he consistently forgot and worshipped other gods. Daniel 4 reiterates this truth.

THE MESSAGE OF THE METALLIC IMAGE

The vision given to Nebuchadnezzar in the second year of his reign is an outline of human history as seen through the governments of men from the time of Nebuchadnezzar to the end of human governments at the Second Coming of Jesus Christ. It is a complete pre-written chronology of human history. It is also important not to try to make more of the image than is actually revealed. The image is political in nature; it tells the story of world governments from the time of Nebuchadnezzar, King of Babylon, to the very end of the age. The message of this prophecy in Daniel 2 can be summarized in one sentence: The governments of men will someday come to an abrupt end, collapsing in ruin before the Kingdom of our Lord and Savior, Jesus Christ. Daniel made it clear to the king that the understanding of the dream and its meaning are from God alone (Daniel 2:27.)

There are four main sections to the image, representing four world empires. Each of these four world empires is represented by a metal that is inferior to the previous one. Gold is more valuable than silver. Silver is more valuable than brass. Brass is of greater worth than iron. As you move through the sections of the image from the head to the feet, the kingdom that is represented by the metal is correspondingly inferior to the preceding empire (Daniel 2:39). This inferiority may be represented by the divisions that increase as you move through the image. C.V. Tenney, writing more than 50 years ago, commented on this understanding when he said, "The tendency is to division and disintegration. For instance, Babylon, the golden head, was an absolute monarchy. The king was all-powerful. He could throw men into the fiery furnace. Medo-Persia was a divided monarchy. Its king was not a dictator. He had to consult his parliament, which passed laws that could not be changed. He could not save Daniel from the lions' den, though he tried hard enough. While Babylon was one kingdom, Medo-Persia was two kingdoms. Greece became divided into four kingdoms upon the death of Alexander the Great. Rome, at first a unit, later was divided into two kingdoms, east and west, and even later into approximately ten kingdoms which have developed into Modern Europe." The theory is that each succeeding empire was inferior in some sense due to the lack of an absolute monarchy.

Daniel addressed the meaning of the image by telling Nebuchadnezzar what the Lord revealed to him. He began with the head of gold. Daniel told Nebuchadnezzar, "You are the head of gold" (Daniel 2:38). Nebuchadnezzar was the logical one to receive this revelation as far as the intent of the prophecy is concerned. He ruled over a kingdom – Babylonia – that was the most powerful and wealthy kingdom in the Middle East. Nebuchadnezzar led his armies in conquest over Judea. He overran Jerusalem, ransacked the temple, and brought many captives to Babylon. This was the first exile of the Jews to Babylon. He had seemingly brought an end to the line of David. The era of national Israel had come to an end. It is important to mark this development as the beginning of "the times of the Gentiles" – an important understanding in Bible prophecy addressed by Jesus in Luke 21:24 as marking the season of the end. Nebuchadnezzar was the first to lay siege to Jerusalem and destroy it after David had become king, a period of about 700 years.

The Babylonian kingdom lasted from 605 BC to 538 BC, holding sway over the world of its day. In spite of its greatness, its days were numbered. Daniel had told Nebuchadnezzar that this kingdom would be superseded by another kingdom, inferior to Babylon, and history confirms the accuracy of this prophecy. Some Bible scholars identify the four kingdoms by the metals associated with their kingdoms. For instance, Babylon – symbolized by gold – made extravagant use of gold in the palace as well as throughout the empire. The Medo-Persian Empire is said to have made extensive use of silver, and the Greek Empire has been associated with the use of brass in its weaponry. While these comparisons can be made and substantiated, the main understanding is conveyed by the fact that each of the metals used in the image is inferior in value to the previous one. Daniel told the king that each of the kingdoms that followed him would be inferior.

The second section of the image – the breast and arms of silver – represented the kingdom of the Medes and Persians. In 539 BC, Darius the Mede conquered Babylon without a fight. Daniel 5 tells the story of how Belshazzar, King of Babylon, was holding a lavish banquet one night with a thousand of his nobles, drinking wine from the sacred artifacts his father Nebuchadnezzar had taken from the temple in Jerusalem. While engaged in this sacrilege, suddenly a hand appeared to be writing on the wall of the palace where this banquet was in progress. The king watched this take place, and he became so terrified that his knees began to knock and his legs grew very weak. His whole countenance reflected his fright. Immediately, he called his wise men, astrologers, enchanters and diviners to tell him what this writing meant. They were baffled by it all, and they drew blanks. This terrified Belshazzar even more. He was in a state of panic when the queen, overhearing the wailing and laments coming from the banquet hall, came in and told the king about Daniel and his special ability to interpret things like this. She reminded him of the time his father, Nebuchadnezzar, had a similar dilemma and how Daniel had given him the interpretation. Daniel was quickly summoned, and he appeared before Belshazzar with this statement: "O king, the Most High God gave your father Nebuchadnezzar sovereignty and greatness and glory and splendor. Because of the high position he gave him, all the peoples and nations and men of every language dreaded and feared him. Those the king wanted to put to death, he put to death; those he wanted to spare, he spared; those he wanted to promote, he promoted; and those he wanted to humble, he humbled. But when his heart became arrogant and hardened with pride, he was deposed from his royal throne and stripped of his glory. He was driven away from people and given the mind of an animal; he lived with the wild donkeys and ate grass like cattle; and his body was drenched with the dew of heaven, until he acknowledged that the Most High God is sovereign over the kingdoms of men and sets over them anyone he wishes. But you his son, O Belshazzar, have not humbled yourself, though you knew all this. Instead, you have set yourself up against the Lord of heaven. You had the goblets from His temple brought to you, and you and your nobles, your wives and your concubines drank wine from them. You praised the gods of silver and gold, of bronze, iron, wood and stone, which cannot see or hear or understand. But you did not honor the God who holds your life and all your ways in his hand. Therefore He sent the hand that wrote the inscription. This is the inscription that was written: MENE, MENE, TEKEL, PARSIN. This is what these words mean: MENE (God has numbered the days of your reign and brought it to an end); TEKEL (You have been weighed on the scales and found wanting); PERES (Your kingdom is divided and given to the Medes and Persians)" (Daniel 5:18-28).

That very night, Belshazzar, King of the Babylonians, was slain, and Darius the Mede took over the kingdom. With this conquest, the Medo-Persian Empire became the dominant world power. Cyrus was the leading figure of this empire, which ruled the world from 538 BC to 331 BC.

The third section of the image, the belly and thighs of brass, represent the Greek Empire, which ruled the world from 331 BC to 133 BC. Alexander the Great is the leading figure in the establishment of this third world empire. In a brilliant series of battles, he subdued the entire Persian world. However, his reign was short-lived; he died at the age of 32. The kingdom was divided among his four generals and, was subsequently conquered by the Romans in 133 BC. In each case of the establishment of these empires, leaders had a grandiose sense of their greatness, but God imposed a time limit on each one.

The legs of iron represent the Roman Empire that was the strongest and most brutal empire to have existed on the face of the earth, crushing all opposition. What the leaders failed to understand is that might doesn't make a nation great. The Roman Empire went the way of all the others, collapsing in ruin because of its moral and spiritual decadence. It wasn't conquered by another nation, but fell apart from within because of moral decay.

With the fall of the Roman Empire in AD 476, we come to the final section of the image – the feet, which were a mixture of iron and clay. There is a great deal of speculation about what is meant by this symbolism. Many Bible students understand this to mean a fifth empire, characterized by the strength of iron and the weakness of clay – an empire thought to be in the making but not yet having appeared on earth. In other words, this final world empire will be a coalition of nations established around a form of common government, but they will not be able to work together or live together, just as iron and clay do not hold together. Some elements of this final kingdom will be strong and some will be weak. Speculation is that this may be a reference to the European Union. Historically, the nations of Europe have not gotten along well with each other. Consequently, the European Union is a likely candidate to become the foundation of this final world kingdom as far as this thinking is concerned. Some go so far as to suggest that the feet – with the

10 toes – represent a revival of the Roman Empire in the last days, possibly growing out of the European Union, with 10 distinct parts, corresponding to the 10 toes. According to a certain group of Bible students, Rome qualifies uniquely as the capital city of a revived Roman Empire. More recently, the idea of a New World Order also fits with this thinking.

It is interesting that so much is made of the 10 toes, although other rudiments of the image – such as the two eyes, or the five fingers on each hand – do not have any specific meaning. One would expect that the image of a man, such as we have in Daniel 2, would have two eyes, a nose, a mouth and two ears. The hands would have five fingers on each one and the feet would have 10 toes. Why, then, do some Bible expositors find it necessary to assign specific meaning to the toes while overlooking the other features of the image? Similarly, we know that the Greek Empire was divided into four kingdoms on the death of Alexander the Great, but nothing in the third section of the image points to this division. The image isn't about body parts and their meaning. It is about metals and their meaning. Pushing the interpretation to these limits is unnecessary and unprofitable, since at no point is it even hinted at in the discussion of the image that the feet represent a kingdom at all. In the interpretation of the image of Daniel 2 and the beasts of Daniel 7, the reference is to four worldly kingdoms, not five. What we have here with the mention of the feet is a revelation about the political character of the last days prior to the Second Coming of Jesus Christ.

The late Dr. Clarence Hewitt, in commenting on this section of the image, wrote, "In the sense of world dominion, 'empire' died with the Caesars. We have passed beyond the days of empires. We have reached the twilight of the kings. This is the era of the common man, the proletariat, of democracy, and the socialist state."

It is my understanding that what is portrayed here is a period of time after the fall of the Roman Empire that would be characterized by political instability among the nations of the world. Some nations would be strong and some would be weak. Remember, this image is political in nature, tracing the course of human history from Nebuchadnezzar, King of the Babylonian Empire, through the governments of men until the intervention of God in human history at the Second Coming of Jesus Christ to establish His eternal Kingdom. According to what is revealed here, there were to be four world empires followed by a period of political instability, which is exactly what has transpired. For the last 1,500 or more years, no one nation has arisen on the scene of human history to dominate the world. That doesn't mean men haven't tried.

Muslim leaders came out of the east in the seventh century, with designs on world domination. They were fanatics to the core. They set out to conquer the world, and they almost destroyed the civilization of Western Europe, but they built no world empire. They are still a warring force in the twenty-first century, holding the West hostage with their huge oil reserves and committing acts of terror. There is a sense in which the iron will of Islam will continue to rain terror on every element of Christianity in the world today.

Napoleon was a man bent on conquering the world and setting himself up as a dominate figure. He was part of the iron referred to in the feet; but Napoleon built no world empire. Waterloo was his undoing. Hitler was another iron-like force to be feared in the early to mid-twentieth century, but Hitler also met his own Waterloo.

Later on in the twentieth century, Communism set out to conquer the world, but today it sits on the scrap heap of human history, having seen its dreams of world domination evaporate with the challenge of the West for global supremacy. The United States and the Union of Soviet Socialist Republics – at their strongest – represented two forces stronger than anything the world had ever seen in human history. In the twentieth century, we witnessed the clearest demarcations of iron and clay with the United States and the Union of Soviet Socialist Republics flaunting their power among the weaker nations of the world.

Near the close of the twentieth century, we saw what may be the last and strongest attempt at building a universal world empire since the fall of Rome in AD 476 AD in what was called the "New World Order." What was, to many, a promising experiment to unite the nations of the world under a common government – with a common court of law and a common monetary system – has virtually faded away. In 1991, President George H. W. Bush of the United States mentioned "The New World Order" in his State of the Union address. This New World Order would replace the systems of independent national governments with a vision of a global community of nations managed by an elite central government. At the time the thought was introduced, people from all walks of life felt optimistic. The New World Order would not only be comprised of a central government, but a world court system, world police force, world banking and currency, as well as a world church (possibly), with some universal-thinking theologians in charge of it. It sounds much like a fifth universal world empire, which is outside the parameters of the revelation in Daniel 2. The idea invented some new terms for our vocabulary – like "globalism" – which have become part of our thinking in the twenty-first century. The goal of the New World Order was to create a better world. Every generation has had leaders of human governments who have embraced this noble ideal without much success. Man has been an utter failure when it comes to creating an ideal world, free from all the distresses and troubles of society. His attempts to eradicate poverty, injustice, fear, war and disease have improved the quality of life for many, but have otherwise ended in utter failure.

If we have learned anything, it is that the governments of men are incapable of ever ruling in justice, peace and opportunity for all. Life is oppressive for some in even the world's best situations. For the most part, things are out of control. The history of human government is characterized by selfishness, greed, oppression and conflict.

The last period of human history is aptly symbolized in this image as iron mixed with clay – strength and weakness, rich and poor, good and evil – and that is precisely what has transpired over the past 1,500 years. The history of human government since the fall of the Roman Empire in AD 476 is one of strength and weakness. The iron-and-clay mixture in the feet represents the last days before the stone cut out of the mountain without hands falls on the kingdoms of men. It is a classic illustration of the political instability of world governments in our times. The four world empires have all come and gone in a period of about 1,100 years. We have been more than 1,500 years in this last phase of human government. It should be clear to everyone that we are living on the threshold of eternity.

The image concentrates on world history from the vantage point of human governments or empires. It is political in nature. What is missing here is any reference to the spiritual. God is at work among the nations, and He is sovereign over human governments. He sets up whomsoever He wills. No mention is made of what is going on in the world spiritually – especially during the lengthy period that follows the collapse of the Roman Empire. This is true even though we know that Christ was born during the time of the Roman Empire.

THE BOOK OF REVELATION COMPLETES THE STORY

It was obviously not the purpose of God to address what He would be doing in a spiritual sense during this time in this portion of Scripture. This is where the Book of Revelation is important. Just as Christ was born during the days of the Roman Empire, the Book of Revelation was written during the days of the Roman Empire.

If we didn't have the Book of Revelation, we would be at a great loss to understand the mystery of the past 1,500 years, about which Daniel is silent. Revelation fills in this blank.

It is interesting to note that both the Book of Daniel and the Book of Revelation come out at the same place. One traces the course of human history through the governments of men (beginning with King Nebuchadnezzar), and the other traces the course of human history through God's redemptive plan, which He instituted in Christ through the cross, resurrection and ascension of our Lord.

The image points to a time of divine intervention in the affairs of men when, symbolized by a stone cut out of the mountain without hands, Jesus comes in power and glory to establish the eternal Kingdom of God. Revelation climaxes with the glorious return of Christ, when He will subdue all forces that oppose God, destroy sin and Satan, and set up the eternal Kingdom of God.

The apostle Paul addressed the climax of human history in his letter to the church at Ephesus. "And he made known to us the mystery of his will according to his good pleasure, which he purposed in Christ, to be put into effect when the times will have reached their fulfillment – to bring all things in heaven and on earth together under one head, even Christ" (Ephesians 1:9-10). In Today's English Version, this verse reads: "God's plan, which he will complete when the time is right, is to bring all creation together, everything in heaven and on earth, with Christ as head."

The image of Daniel 2 culminates with a final kingdom – the Kingdom of God – bringing completion to God's great plan of the ages to create a people who would live in fellowship with Him in His Kingdom Paradise, for His glory forever. "In the time of those kings, the God of heaven will set up a kingdom that will never be destroyed, nor will it be left to another people. It will crush all those kingdoms and bring them to an end, but it will itself endure forever" (Daniel 2:44).

God will intervene in the affairs of men to bring their feeble efforts at creating a perfect world order to a decisive end. There is something more to life than world governments. There is something more to life than the oppression, injustice and conflict that we experience in life today. Things will not go on much longer as they are now. Soon, and very soon, the stone cut out of the mountain without hands will strike the feet of the image, grinding what is left of the governments of men to dust, and it will fill the whole earth with the glory of God.

There isn't anything more to the image. We are living in the last section – the feet – and have been there several centuries longer than it took for the four universal world empires to come and go. We are living today on the threshold of eternity.

PRACTICAL LESSONS FROM THE BOOK OF DANIEL

The overarching theme of the Book of Daniel is the sovereignty of God over the affairs of man and nations. This is first seen in the use of Daniel to accomplish God's purpose. He was a young man of noble birth, brought to Babylon as a teenager when Nebuchadnezzar overran Jerusalem. He was intelligent, as the incident relates; but, more importantly, he was devout. He was a committed servant of Jehovah God. He was primarily a statesman, not a prophet. He was never thought of as a prophet or even called to be a prophet in the usual sense. As a statesman, he was involved in the highest levels of government for both the Babylonian and Medo-Persian Empires, but God put him where He wanted him when He wanted him for the purpose for which He wanted him.

The lesson we learn from this development is that God can use anyone, anywhere, at any time, to accomplish His purposes. He is only looking for someone who is committed to Him and who is open to whatever God wants to accomplish through him.

The sovereignty of God can also be seen in the protective care that overshadows His people in all of life's distresses when they serve Him with the whole heart.

Three of Daniel's friends were thrown into a raging fiery furnace because they remained faithful to their God. They were bound securely, but after being thrown into the furnace they were seen by witnesses, including king Nebuchadnezzar, to be loosed and walking among the flames unharmed. They were brought out of the furnace, and they were found to be free of smoke. Not even a hair of their head was singed.

Later, Daniel was thrown into a den of hungry lions as punishment for his refusal to compromise his faith in the sovereign God of the universe. He was a man of prayer – a spiritual discipline that served him well in this experience. The lions acted as if he wasn't even there, going about their business as usual. This wasn't just a dip into the den of lions and a quick exit; Daniel was there all night. The king couldn't sleep; and, in the morning, when he rushed to the spot where Daniel was standing among the lions, he was astounded to see that Daniel hadn't been touched. Not even a scratch was found on his body.

The lesson that we learn from this development is that we may not ever face the threats these men faced as a challenge to their faith, but we will certainly be tested by Satan and the world from time to time. One thing that we can be certain of is that our God is still a God of miracles. He will protect and keep His people when they live for Him, whatever the danger or test they face. God protects and cares for His people.

Finally, the sovereignty of God is seen in the ultimate completion of His plan. His promise is certain, and His word is true. We are strangers and aliens in this land, even though we forget it most of the time. This world, as it is presently constituted, is not our home. What we learn from the Book of Daniel and the events that unfold here is that God is in control of history. In His own time, He will do away with the kingdoms of man, and, in their place, He will establish His own Kingdom with His own righteous government. The Roman Empire was not the end of the world. The current world condition is not all that there is. God, who has acted in the past, and is active in the world today in His great redemptive work, will intervene in the affairs of men, and He will set up the Kingdom for which we all yearn. His eternal purpose of a people living in fellowship with Him in His Kingdom Paradise for His glory, forever, will come to pass as He said it would.   Paul wrote a similar word of encouragement to the church at Ephesus when he said, "This was according to the eternal purpose that he has realized in Christ Jesus our Lord" (Ephesians 3:11).

Daniel, who wrote this book about 530 BC, after the fall of the Babylonian Empire, wrote it as a message of encouragement to his fellow Jews, who were in captivity. God revealed this outline of human history at this point in time to encourage His people not to give up hope. He was in control, even though circumstances didn't always appear that way. Everything they had learned from their prophets (and more) would come to pass as it had been revealed.

Life will not always be easy. At times, we may find ourselves in situations in which we wonder if God is there and if He understands. One thing we learn from the experiences that God's people passed through in the Book of Daniel is that God is always there. He always cares. He knows our circumstances and He is always able to meet our need. In fact, Ephesians 3:20 says that He is able to do immeasurably more than anyone can ask or think. Never give up or give in! Never lose hope! God is always there, and He loves and cares for His own!

QUESTIONS FOR DISCUSSION

1. What is the primary message of the Book of Daniel?
2. What are some examples of the rise and fall of powerful governments?
3. How is the Kingdom of God different from other kingdoms?
4. How was Daniel in a unique position to understand world history in advance of it happening?

5. What was the message conveyed by Nebuchadnezzar's dream in Daniel 2?
6. What parallels are there between the Book of Daniel and the Book of Revelation?
7. What are some practical lessons that we can learn from studying the Book of Daniel?

CHAPTER 4

THE GREAT DRAMA
OF THE AGES

It is difficult to understand the meaning of the times in which we live and to put life's developments into Biblical perspective. There seem to be as many end-times scenarios as there are prophetic teachers and writers. There is little agreement among Bible believing Christians in regards to end-time events. Subjects such as the Anti-Christ, the tribulation, and the millennium spark considerable debate and controversy. Current scenarios about the end-of-the-age range from the simplistic to the absurd. Jesus faulted the religious leaders of His day for not understanding what God was doing in the world. In Matthew 16:2-3, He said, "When evening comes, you say, 'It will be fair weather, for the sky is red,' and in the morning, 'today it will be stormy, for the sky is red and overcast.' You know how to interpret the appearance of the sky, but you cannot interpret the signs of the times." He seemed to be saying that if they paid better attention to what God had said and is doing, they would have a better understanding of the times.

The problem that we have in understanding the meaning of the times in which we live today is our interest in making more of developments around us than Scripture warrants. Some are obsessed with an eschatological frenzy, as if they are on a prophetic scavenger hunt. Gary DeMar refers to this obsession as "prediction addiction" as in pop-prophecy or newspaper theology. The Bible is rather clear when it comes to understanding God's purpose in history and the primary obstacle that He encounters in fulfilling His purpose. The Book of Revelation, written by John in AD 95, describes how God's purpose is worked out against great opposition from Satan and his demonic forces.

INTRODUCING THE BOOK OF REVELATION

The Book of Revelation was written in a time of intense persecution of Christians. Roman authorities were serious about enforcing the cult of emperor worship, holding that Caesar (not Christ) was Lord. There was a danger that some in the early church would lose faith in the teachings of Christ while facing increasing hostility and in view of the fact that Christ had not returned to establish His eternal Kingdom as many had believed that He would. It was important that they understand the nature of the great spiritual conflict between Christ and Satan – the fact that the victory of the cross and the grave didn't end the warfare. Satan had not been destroyed. He was still the god of this world (1 John 5:19). His ultimate purpose to dethrone God and rule in His place had not changed. The Book of Revelation is about the continuing conflict. It is the story of spiritual warfare – the last great effort of the evil one to achieve his purposes set over against God's redemptive activity in Jesus Christ.

The overarching theme or message of the Book is the sovereignty of God over the affairs of men, nations, rulers, principalities and dominions. The Book of Revelation differs from the Book of Daniel, which deals with God's sovereignty over worldly governments, by extending God's sovereignty over Satan and all demonic forces and strongholds. In Revelation, God's sovereignty is total – over all. Daniel traces the course of human history through the progression of worldly governments, while Revelation traces the course of human history through God's redemptive activity in Jesus Christ. Daniel's message is political. Revelation's message is spiritual. Both Daniel and Revelation come out at the same place: the intervention of God at the Second Coming of Jesus Christ.

The Church, which is composed of the redeemed in Christ Jesus, is the trophy of His grace. No matter what may happen – no matter what kind of Satanic opposition or threats she may encounter along the way – God will bring her to glorious victory. God is alive and well. He is in control, even though it may not always appear that way. In the end, He wins!

INTERPRETATIONS OF THE BOOK VARY

The Book of Revelation is the most confusing, controversial and complex of all the Books of the Bible. For that reason, one must not be dogmatic in respect to interpreting the message of the Book.

There are a variety of approaches to interpreting the Book. In the early centuries of the Christian church, all prophecy was future. Believers looked for the return of Christ, which – in their minds – was always imminent. The church viewed all prophecy as being fulfilled in history, in a time span beginning with Pentecost and ending with the Second Coming of Christ and the establishment of the eternal kingdom of God.

The first major development that influenced how the church looked at Revelation was St. Augustine's classic work, *The City of God*, in which he set forth the idea that the kingdom of God was a spiritual enterprise as opposed to a physical or earthly enterprise. This important work was written during a 13-year span, in response to critics who blamed the church for the sack of Rome by the Vandals in AD 410. Augustine contended that the city of Rome wasn't necessarily the issue and that God wasn't to blame. The city of God is where God reigns over His people – a situation that Augustine equated with the church, not the city of Rome.

Augustine's understanding appears to have been strongly influenced by the philosophical dualism of Plato. Plato held to a belief in two worlds: the ideal world and the real world. The ideal world was a place of beauty and perfection, whereas the real world was characterized by mud, hair and filth. Augustine's dualism involved two cities: the city of God and the city of man.

The city of God is the place where God rules over his people, and the city of man is ruled over by man.

Sparknotes.com summarizes *The City of God* as "a challenge to human society to choose which city it wishes to be a part of, and Augustine sees his task as clearly marking out the parameters of each choice. Augustine concludes that the purpose of history is to show the unfolding of God's plan, which involves fostering the City of Heaven and filling it with worthy citizens. For this purpose, God initiated all of creation itself. In such a grand plan, the fall of Rome is insignificant." Augustine's statement corresponds with the story line of the Bible – stated here earlier – that God is at work in society, forming a people who will live in fellowship with Him in His Kingdom Paradise, for His glory, forever.

Augustinian thought influenced the church until the time of the Reformation in AD 1517, when Historicism became a dominant eschatological interpretation. The Historicist manner of interpreting the Book of Revelation is to view the contents of the book as encompassing a period of time between Pentecost and the Second Coming of Christ. The primary feature of Biblical Historicism is that all prophecy is prewritten history. The Book is viewed as describing the conflict between God and Satan during the church age. While this system of prophetic interpretation was current during the early days of Christianity, the system became a dominant eschatological approach during the Reformation.

One of the features of Historicist interpretation is to identify the Antichrist of 1 and 2 John, the Beast of Revelation 13, the Man of Sin of 2 Thessalonians 2, the Little Horn of Daniel 7 and 8, and the Whore of Babylon of Revelation 17, with the Roman Catholic Church, the Papal system and each succeeding Pope. Martin Luther made that identification, a position that has been held by most Historicists since his day.

This identification caused the Roman church to create a counter-interpretation to shift the focus away from the church. A system which has become known as Preterism, was developed by a Roman Catholic priest named Luis de Alcazar. Preterism contended that all so-called prophecy was fulfilled with the fall of Jerusalem in AD 70 (or, in some cases, even before that event), which meant that the papacy couldn't possibly be identified as Antichrist. This system dated the Book of Revelation about AD 65. According to this understanding, prophecy is not predictive; it is history. This system never gained a great deal of momentum until fairly recently and has significant variations within. Among Preterists, there are two generally accepted schools of understanding – Partial Preterists and Full Preterists.

A system of interpretation more widely accepted of late was invented by another Roman Catholic prelate named Francisco Ribera. He is the father of the Futurist system of prophetic interpretation, which is very popular today. Futurism (as the name implies) puts off the fulfillment of the prophetic content of Revelation to some future period of time at the very end of the age. The first three chapters explain the history of the church during the church age. Everything from chapter four through to chapter 22 is in the future. This system does an injustice to the intention of the Book, which John said was a revelation of Jesus Christ in which things happening in the near future were revealed. The Futurist system leaves a huge chunk of history – 2,000 years and counting – unspoken to.

There are so many variations in each of these systems of interpretation that it is impossible to define any one of them in detail without doing an injustice to one of the variants. Not everyone who identifies with one of the systems of interpretation agrees on the meaning of the content uniformly.

The system that best fits the book – with the least amount of ambiguity and difficulty – is the Historicist approach. Historicists agree that the content of the Book is played out in history from the time of the first advent of Christ until His second advent and the establishment of the kingdom of God.

Historicists generally fall into three categories as I have chosen to identify them. My terminology simply clarifies the essence of these interpretations for the modern reader. There are those whom I identify as Sequential Historicists. People who hold to this system of interpretation look at the seals, the trumpets and the bowls as following after each other sequentially. Traditionally, this view has been referred to as Continuous Historicism. Another group sees these elements as occurring alongside of each other or at the same time. I would refer to this group as Concurrent Historicists. Traditionally, this view has been referred to as Parallel Historicism. A third group of Historicists takes an eclectic approach to the Book. They tend to agree that the content of the Book is played out in history, but they borrow from different systems of interpretation to explain the content. This view might best be identified as Accommodating Historicists.

The Book of Revelation is not a story built chapter upon chapter, as we normally understand a book, with each chapter being connected to the previous chapter and based on it as an expansion of the story. Rather, it describes events and developments occurring between the first and second advents of Jesus Christ. These events and developments are described by visions, symbols and images. It is not a sequential history of this time period, but rather a large portrait of it with the various events illustrated that are common to each generation. It tells the story of God's plan of world redemption being carried out among the nations through the proclamation of the Gospel with Satan's opposition expressed in a variety of forms throughout the time frame until he is finally defeated and destroyed at the second coming of Jesus Christ.

REVELATION AN APOCALYPTIC BOOK

Revelation is an apocalyptic book, meaning that the message of the book is encoded in symbols and images, which don't necessarily relate to specific events in history. The message of the book is more like looking at something from a distance in order to get the big picture. You can't always read about something and assign it to an historical development, although many people try to do this and get lost in the imagery and symbolism of the book, which is easy to do.

Western minds tend to struggle with understanding apocalyptic literature. We are accustomed to reading a story in which each chapter of the story builds on the previous chapter until we reach the conclusion. Apocalyptic literature isn't structured that way.

There is a story to Revelation, but it is not necessarily sequential. It is the story of God's redemptive activity during the last days, centered in Jesus Christ, His finished work on the cross and His triumph over death and the grave – the ultimate conquest. Through the preaching of the Gospel among the nations, God is creating a new humanity to fulfill his eternal purpose. Satan's opposition to the work of the Gospel is illustrated by images and visions until he is finally defeated at the Second Coming of Jesus Christ and the establishment of the Kingdom of God. It is a story of spiritual warfare, with God ultimately victorious.

Revelation is a book of mystery and intrigue. There are images of horses of varying colors galloping across the landscape. There are frightening beasts rising out of the sea. The sun turns black and the moon turns red like blood while stars are falling from heaven. There is imagery of hail and fire mixed with blood falling to the earth. There is a great pit resembling a giant smoking furnace, out of which issues a mass of devouring locusts. One image is of a pregnant woman before whom is crouched a great red dragon, poised to spring on the child and devour him the moment that he is born. Evil spirits like frogs are said to come out of the mouth of the dragon, the beast and the false prophet, flooding the whole earth with their evil exploits. There is a scarlet beast with seven heads and 10 horns with a woman riding on the beast and the name "Babylon the Great" emblazoned on her garments. Revelation is a book of mystery and intrigue. It has become the playground for prophetic sensationalists who – in every generation – have not hesitated to attempt to identify these bizarre images and assign them to some historical event, current event, or events supposedly on the horizon of history.

The problem that most people have in reading the Book of Revelation is in trying to make it say more than God ever intended it to say. How one reads the Book determines whether or not it fulfills the purpose that God had in giving it or leaves the reader hung up somewhere on the horn of a beast. First and foremost, it is the revelation of Jesus Christ. We make a major mistake when we approach Revelation for any other reason than to see Jesus Christ as God has chosen to reveal Him. G. Campbell Morgan has said, "Any study of Revelation, which does not concentrate upon Christ, and does not view all else in relation to Him, must bring the reader into an inextricable labyrinth." (See Revelation 1:1.)

This is the last chapter in the story of God's redemptive plan and purpose, now centered in Jesus Christ as the last Adam creating the new people of God, who will live in fellowship with Him in His kingdom Paradise, for His glory, forever. The book covers developments in the church age (or gospel age), culminating in the Second

Coming of Jesus Christ and the establishment of God's eternal Kingdom Paradise.

The Book of Revelation describes the struggles of good and evil in a series of apocalyptic visions that precede the ultimate triumph of God. With the appearance of Jesus Christ on the scene of human history, the curtain is lifted on the final act of the great drama of the ages this side of eternity. It is important to always keep in mind the purpose of God in human history, which is the formation of a people who will live in fellowship with Him in His Kingdom Paradise, for His glory, forever. History tells the story of how God has been working to accomplish this purpose in every generation from the time of creation.

THE PLAYERS IN THE GREAT DRAMA OF THE AGES

One would think that this goal would be an easy thing for an all-powerful, sovereign God of the universe (who created everything that exists) to accomplish. It was He who merely spoke the word, and the worlds came into being. By His word, He hung the stars in place. Every aspect of creation was spoken into being. So, how is it that His goal of forming a people to live in fellowship with Him in His Kingdom Paradise, for His glory forever, is still not a reality? One might wonder, "Is God incapable of achieving His purposes? Did He start out to do something that He can't finish?" What is the problem?

The problem is the presence of the adversary of God and man known as Satan. As Job 27:2 and Ephesians 2:2 show us, Satan was created by God, as a member of the spirit realm of being. There are four realms of being. The first is the realm of deity. God is unique in the universe and is the creator of everything that exists (Isaiah 66:1-2). He alone is God, beside whom there is none else. God is spirit (John 4:24). He is the ground of all being (Colossians 1:15-17). Everything began with God and finds its purpose and fulfillment in Him. The second realm of being is the spirit realm. While God is Spirit, the spirit realm is distinct from God and was created by Him (John 1:1-3). This realm consists of angels, both fallen and elect. The third realm of being is the human realm, and the fourth realm is the realm of other living things.

Satan was created by God as part of the spirit realm (or the angelic realm). Every angel that God created was holy. Satan was possibly the highest-ranking angel as an anointed Cherub (Ezekiel 28:12, 14, 16). In his original position, he was part of the hierarchy of heaven (Isaiah 14:12-15 and Ezekiel 28:11-19). Satan possesses great power – so much that Michael the archangel viewed him as a powerful foe (Jude 9). The realm of spirit beings is a supernatural realm. The term "supernatural" is used in this context to mean that the powers of spirit beings are greater than or beyond what we experience in the natural realm as human beings.

Satan is not an ordinary creature. He is a superhuman spirit being, who was created by God but is also subject to God (Zechariah 3:1; 1 Chronicles 21:1; Job 1-2). It appears from Scripture that his power is limited and that when it comes to his desire to inflict harm and injury on the people of God, he may act only within God's permissive will. You can't blame everything that Satan does on God, but you can credit God with keeping His people within His permissive will when Satan would otherwise destroy them.

Satan rules over a kingdom of wicked angels (Matthew 8:24, 9:34. 12:25-29; Luke 11:18-19; John 12:31, 14:30, 16:11; Revelation 12:9, 20:3, 7). Scripture indicates that a time came in his lofty estate that he became proud and coveted the place of God. I suspect that what he coveted was the place of Jesus Christ as he watched the creation of all material things (John 1:3). He led a rebellion against God and was cast out of heaven. Scripture says, "There was war in heaven" (Revelation 12:7-9). It is intriguing to think about warfare in the realm of spirit beings. What was going on, and what did it look like? When did it actually occur? From Satan's prominence in the heavens, he held a powerful influence on other angels and succeeded in seducing one-third of all the angelic beings to join him in this rebellion. We have no idea how many angelic beings were created by God, but all evidence points to an inordinate number. In Matthew 26:53, we are told that when Jesus was betrayed by Judas and arrested in the garden, He told those around Him that they really had no power over Him and that the Father could send 12 legions of angels to deliver Him if He so chose. Twelve legions of angels would total 72,000. The Bible uses the term "hosts of heaven" to signify the innumerable realm of spirit beings (Psalm 103:21 and Psalm 148:2).

Satan and all his fallen angels are part of the hosts of heaven, and they now form an evil force of spirit beings (demons) who, with Satan, work against the purposes of God in the human realm. His influence is universal (Isaiah 2:4 and Matthew 4:8). I am not sure that nominal believers (of which there are many) fully understand the nature of the enemy that is arrayed against us, or the power of the evil with which we must contend.

The apostle Paul, while addressing the church at Ephesus in the first century, noted that we contend for our very lives against the rulers, authorities and powers of this dark world and against the spiritual forces in the heavenly realms (Ephesians 6:12). There are several significant understandings referred to in this text. Paul mentions rulers (or principalities), authorities, powers and forces of evil in the heavenly realms. Some commentators interpret these stations as referring to human governments opposed to Christianity, but the general consensus is that Paul is talking here about different groupings or orders of evil spirits under the control of Satan, who (with him) militate against the purposes of God in the work of the Gospel.

Life isn't easy. We struggle in the normal affairs of life. There are broken relationships, mean-spirited beings, financial setbacks, disappointments, diseases and failures. There are storms and troubles that we all face as part of our ordinary existence. What the Apostle is talking about here has nothing to do with these distresses and trials that are part of our everyday existence. He states clearly that our struggle is not against flesh and blood (the ordinary circumstances of life). Paul is talking about a totally different battleground – the stuff of spiritual warfare. The battle is not against the day-to-day common struggles of life, but against an unseen, powerful enemy who seeks to destroy us. This is an area of warfare that we know very little about, but it is nevertheless very real. Principalities, rulers, authorities and the like are obviously organized groupings of evil spirits (demons), holding immense power and control over the human realm. One might question, "Where did these principalities come from?" Interestingly, Colossians 1:16 says that all things were created by Christ, visible and invisible, including (and mention is made specifically to) thrones, or powers or rulers or authorities. In Ephesians 3:10, Paul makes reference to the rulers and authorities in the heavenly realms. What he was saying is that God has made known His purpose and plans through the Church, so that even these groupings in the heavenly realm understand. Another interesting reference is made to these same groupings in Colossians 2:15, where Paul says that Christ (in the cross/resurrection event) has, in effect, disarmed the powers and authorities. I assume that Scripture is speaking of the same things in these references.

My sense is that as Satan held a prominent position in the spirit realm prior to his rebellion and the creation of the universe, so, too, there probably were other groupings of angels (such as powers, principalities and authorities), who, in these groupings, held specific functions of service to the Creator in ways that we don't understand. Some of these groupings may have joined Satan in his rebellion, and they were cast out of the presence of God. Paul refers to these groupings in Ephesians 6:12, where he tells us that they form a mighty, evil force, opposing the work of Christ. They war against believers in this age. Principalities, rulers, authorities and the like are obviously organized groupings of evil spirits (demons), holding immense power and control over the human realm.

The warfare is real, but Jesus Christ is greater than all the forces arrayed against us. The Lordship of Jesus Christ is stated by Peter in 1 Peter 3:21-22: "by the resurrection of Jesus Christ: Who is gone into heaven, and is on the right hand of God; angels and authorities and powers being made subject unto Him" (KJV). 1 Corinthians 15 which establishes the fact of the resurrection of Christ makes reference to what His resurrection means in respect to the spiritual warfare in which we are engaged. In that conquest of Satan's dominion Christ has destroyed the hold these evil groupings have. The power of the resurrection is seen in that the reign of Christ (His Lordship won via the resurrection Romans 1:4) makes even these evil groupings subject to Him. 1 Corinthians 15:24 reads, "Then the end will come, when He hands over the Kingdom to God the Father after He has destroyed all dominion, authority and power."

We don't know a great deal about the spirit realm (or angelic realm). Both good and bad angels are obviously a formidable force, as can be seen by the numerous references to them in the Book of Revelation. We know that angels are distinct from men. They appear to have some characteristics in common with men (such as emotion and will), but they lack reproductive ability. In Matthew 22, Jesus answered the question of the Sadducees, who thought that they could trick Him by questioning whose wife one would be who had several husbands. Matthew 22:28-31 reads, "Now then, at the resurrection, whose wife will she be of the seven, since all of them were married to her? Jesus replied, 'You are in error because you do not know the Scriptures or the power of God. At the resurrection, people will neither marry nor be given in marriage; they will be like the angels in heaven'" (NIV). From this statement, it would appear that the angelic realm is very distinct from the human realm. The angelic realm was created by God, so it was originally "good and holy" (Mark 8:38). They are called "sons of God" in Job 1:6 and 2:1. They have super-human powers and characteristics.

The Bible speaks of Satan as the god of this world (2 Corinthians 4:4), and John wrote that the whole world lies in the control of the evil one (1 John 5:19). Satan is a monumental source of cosmic trouble, conflict, heartache and turmoil.

We are in mortal combat with the flesh, the world and the devil. This triple threat is actually one threat, because the only problem that we have with the flesh (or the world) is the corruption of the same by the devil. Satan has corrupted man's thinking. He has messed up our sense of values, truth and reason. Our enemy, the devil, is known as the evil one. There is no good in him whatsoever. Scripture reveals his character in derogatory terms. There isn't anything good said about Satan in Scripture. One prominent aspect of his character is that he is a liar (John 8:44). Becky Nicoll, writing a monthly devotional for women, says, "I have been home sick for the week, and watched every day a show called 'Meet the Browns.' I very much enjoy this show. Yesterday, Mr. Brown said, 'The Devil is a LIAR,' and it all came together for me. Everything God had been putting in my mind to share with you for the first of this year is about that. The Devil IS a LIAR." In this powerful devotional, she goes on to share how Satan lies to people about their sexual orientation; about their marriage vows and commitment; and about their self-worth. She describes how the Devil's lies keep people in a state of confusion; how he demeans people by reminding them of past sins; and how his lies blind a person to the truth of God's word. One prominent characteristic of Satan, which trips us all up, is his lying and scheming. Satan is a liar, and there isn't any truth in him whatsoever.

Scripture further describes Satan as an enemy (Matthew 13:39), an adversary (1 Peter 5:8), a deceiver (Revelation 12:9), the tempter (Matthew 4:3; 1 Thessalonians 3:5), an accuser (Revelation 12:10), a destroyer (Revelation 9:11), the evil one (John 17:15; 1 John 5:18), the prince of demons (Matthew 12:24; Luke 11:15), the prince of the power of the air (Ephesians 2:2); the prince of this world (John 12:31; 16:11) and the prince of the power of darkness (Luke 22:53). It is significant that Satan is called the prince of the power of darkness. When Satan was cast out of heaven, he was cast into the earth, which (according to Genesis 1) was originally without form and void – covered in darkness. This was the perfect location for Satan, the prince of darkness. It is difficult to know when and how he was dismissed from the glories of heaven, but Scripture is clear about where he was cast down. One can only imagine that the timing of this ejection was consistent with the pre-creation account.

The darkness of evil is further illustrated by what happened when Jesus died on the cross for the sins of the world. Something very interesting happened, affecting the whole realm of nature. Luke tells us, in his gospel account of the crucifixion, "It was now about the sixth hour, and darkness came over the whole earth until the ninth hour, for the sun stopped shining." Notice what this says: "Darkness came over the whole earth, and the sun stopped shining." This is an important description of what was going on. The sins of the world were placed on Jesus, the sinless one. The moment that this happened, God made it clear to the whole world that Christ had taken on himself the penalty of our sin. Darkness is associated with evil. When Christ became sin for us, light turned to darkness. This was God's exclamation point on the meaning of the cross. Sin is darkness. Satan is darkness. Evil is darkness. Notice what happened after Jesus died. Once He had completely paid the penalty for our sins, the sun came back out.

Satan must have rejoiced when he saw the sun turn to darkness while Christ was on the cross. I wonder what he might have felt when he saw the sun come back out. He rules over a kingdom of darkness. There is a kingdom of darkness, and there is a kingdom of light. There is a kingdom of evil, and there is a kingdom of righteousness. There is a kingdom of death, and there is a kingdom of life. There is the kingdom of Satan, and there is the kingdom of God. We understand life to be a battle of kingdoms in conflict. This war has been raging since the foundations of the world.

The twelfth chapter of the Book of Revelation provides some insights into this warfare.

Revelation 12 says, "A great and wondrous sign appeared in heaven: a woman clothed with the sun, with the moon under her feet and a crown of twelve stars on her head. She was pregnant and cried out in pain as she was about to give birth. Then another sign appeared in heaven: an enormous red dragon with seven heads and 10 horns and seven crowns on his heads. His tail swept a third of the stars out of the sky and flung them to the earth. The dragon stood in front of the woman who was about to give birth, so that he might devour her child the moment it was born. She gave birth to a son, a male child, who will rule all the nations with an iron scepter. And her child was snatched up to God and to his throne. The woman fled into the desert to a place prepared for her by God, where she might be taken care of for 1,260 days. And there was war in heaven. Michael and his angels fought against the dragon, and the dragon and his angels fought back. But he was not strong enough, and they lost their place in heaven. The great dragon was hurled down – that ancient serpent called the devil, or Satan, who leads the whole world astray. He was hurled to the earth, and his angels with him. Then I heard a loud voice in heaven say, 'Now have come the salvation and the power and the kingdom of our God, and the authority of his Christ. For the accuser of our brothers, who accuses them before our God day and night, has been hurled down. They overcame him by the blood of the Lamb and by the word of their testimony; they did not love their lives so much as to shrink from death. Therefore rejoice, you heavens and you who dwell in them! But woe to the earth and the sea, because the devil has gone down to you! He is filled with fury, because he knows that his time is short.' When the dragon saw that he had been hurled to the earth, he pursued the woman who had given birth to the male child. The woman was given the two wings of a great eagle, so that she might fly to the place prepared for her in the desert, where she would be taken care of for a time, times and half a time, out of the serpent's reach. Then from his mouth the serpent spewed water like a river, to overtake the woman and sweep her away with the torrent. But the earth helped the woman by opening its mouth and swallowing the river that the dragon had spewed out of his mouth. Then the dragon was enraged at the woman and went off to make war against the rest of her offspring — those who obey God's commandments and hold to the testimony of Jesus."

Two signs are given: the woman and the dragon. The woman represents the work of God, and the dragon is the symbol for Satan. Some Bible scholars identify the woman with Israel and some make the identification with the church. The Bible talks about the last days as days of spiritual warfare. That's what the Book of Revelation is all about. Satan, with his host of fallen angels, is in mortal combat with the ministry of the Spirit and the work of the Gospel. Spiritual warfare is very active today, as it has been in the entire life of the Church, which is the real battleground.

SATAN'S STRATEGIC ATTACKS ON THE CHURCH

Satan's long, unrelenting warfare against the church has been distressful, but never truly successful – partly due to the fact that he isn't as smart as he thinks he is. Consider, for instance, how over the centuries Christians have been severely persecuted and martyred. History has clearly demonstrated that the blood of martyrs is the seed of the church. You should have known better, Satan!

The letters to the seven churches of Asia Minor, recorded in Revelation 2 and 3, reveal for us how Satan opposes the work of the Gospel and attacks the church. Each of these letters is couched in the overall theme of the book, which is the sovereignty of God over the forces of evil arrayed against Him and His eternal purpose. In each of these letters, there is reference to the presence of Satan, as he seeks to hinder the work of the gospel. There is a clear outline or description of Satan's plan of attack illustrated in the seven letters. This is the way he seeks to defeat the Church and keep God's eternal purpose from ever being realized. This Satanic strategy is employed by the evil one in every age, in different ways and in different places. Herbert Lockyer, in his book, *All About the Second Coming: The Drama of the Ages*, has said, "Satanic opposition, as mentioned in John's record of the seven churches, has never ceased." His presence and activity creates problems for the believer. We are told that in some cases, believers lose the excitement and commitment of their relationship to Christ; others experience persecution attributed to Satan; some get mixed up doctrinally; and some suffer martyrdom. For some, Satan has deceived them into tolerating his presence, leading God's people into sin. Spiritual death has occurred for some, and others have been weakened by compromising the Word of God. Satan is an effective adversary who never gives up in his warfare against the church. He is always attacking, but never wins more than a skirmish here or there. In each situation or spiritual conflict, the Lord triumphs and believers – who are referred to as overcomers – receive the rewards of their faithfulness.

There is an impressive list of blessings awaiting those who overcome. Notice the quality and extent of the blessings promised! These are not superficial promises. For instance, in the letter to the church at Ephesus, a blessing is promised in light of the fact that Satan has brought many hardships on the believers, causing them to lose their spiritual zeal. Spiritual warfare takes different approaches, always engaging the believer, in an attempt to lead him from his faith and commitment to Christ. Jesus tells them that if they will repent and rediscover their first love, He will "give the right to eat from the tree of life, which is in the Paradise of God."

The significance of this blessing is staggering. For one thing, the overcomer is rewarded with a new residence: the Paradise of God. This is not like moving across the street (or from downtown to a suburb), but to a totally new place of existence. The Paradise of God is a reference to the fulfillment of God's original Kingdom plan. This assures the believer that what God has promised from the beginning will come to pass as He said it would in His own time. The Paradise of God is a prepared place. According to John 14:2, it is the place that Jesus went to prepare for His new creation after the cross/resurrection event.

A second aspect to this blessing is the reference to the "tree of life." The tree of life was part of God's original creation. The Book of Genesis, which describes the elements of the garden Paradise in which Adam and Eve were placed, makes reference to the fact that in the midst of the garden was "the tree of life" (Genesis 2:8-9.) We don't know a great deal about this special home given to man except that man did not apparently have the right to eat from this tree of life. God had given man full authority over every created thing. He was to live and reign as king over the created order. Everything was made for him (Genesis 1:28-30).

The original creation required a test of man's will to the ultimate rule of God. God was still sovereign God of the universe, and man was merely the caretaker. The test of this submission was the prohibition to not eat of the tree of the knowledge of good and evil as we read in Genesis 2:16-17. Adam was explicitly told that to disobey this divine prohibition would result in his death.

It goes without saying that Adam did not possess the right to eat from the tree of life either, because (as a consequence of his disobedience) the Lord banished him from the Garden of Eden (Genesis 3:22) so as to prevent him from eating of the tree of life and living forever. This banishment presumes that once man ate from the tree of life, he would be immortal. Death and life are not synonymous. If Adam had been given the right to eat from the tree of life, the death warning would have been an empty threat.

However, in the end-time vision, John sees man restored to his Paradise home, where the tree of life is located, but in this context he is now given the right to eat from the tree of life. This understanding is consistent with the testimony of Scripture that at the Second Coming of Jesus Christ and the wrap-up of human history, there is a resurrection to eternal life for those who have overcome by the blood of the Lamb. The reference to the tree of life in the Paradise of God is simply a testimony to the credibility of the promise of God that this mortal shall put on immortality and this corruptible shall put on incorruption. Eternal life will be given to all who trust Christ for their salvation.

Revelation 22 speaks of this: "Then the angel showed me the river of the water of life, as clear as crystal, flowing from the throne of God and of the Lamb down the middle of the great street of the city. On each side of the river stood the tree of life, bearing twelve crops of fruit, yielding its fruit every month. And the leaves of the tree are for the healing of the nations. No longer will there be any curse. The throne of God and of the Lamb will be in the city, and his servants will serve him. They will see his face, and his name will be on their foreheads. There will be no more night. They will not need the light of a lamp or the light of the sun, for the Lord God will give them light. And they will reign forever and ever." The reference to the tree of life, bearing twelve crops of fruit, yielding its fruit every month is simply a way of stating that we will live forever in that city called Glory. Days, months, and years are part of how we reckon time now. In our future home, time will be no more.

For the church at Smyrna, spiritual warfare takes the form of Satan establishing his own synagogue within the fellowship of believers. He has a corner of their house from which he operates. He has designs to put some of them in prison to test them as well as to subject them to severe persecution. As believers, we must understand that the household of faith is not immune from satanic attack. But the promise to one who overcomes is: "He who overcomes will not be hurt at all by the second death." The significance of this promise is that in spite of what we go through as we live out our faith – sometimes falling and sometimes failing – forgiveness is greater than our sin. Even though we may deserve to be destroyed in the fires of hell, the salvation of our Lord delivers us from the guilt, power and consequence of our sin. The second death will not touch the believer who puts his trust in Christ.

For the church at Pergamum, Satan's attack is very direct. In fact, Satan has established his throne among them, from which he controls what is going on. Spiritual warfare, for Pergamum, results in martyrdom and leads others to embrace false doctrine – making them comfortable in their sin. Again, the promise to the one who overcomes is noteworthy. Believers who overcome Satan's schemes will be blessed with the promise of hidden manna. This is a reference to the sustaining power of the Lord. Believers are living in the midst of Satanic rule, suffering his attacks and deceptions, but what is being promised is the sustaining power and keeping power of the Lord, which only those committed to Christ can experience. Also, a white stone will be given them with a new name written on it, which only those who receive it will know. This blessing is significant in that the Lord is assuring these believers that He knows who they are and has absolved them of any guilt through the cleansing power of the blood of Christ. The white stone is a symbol of being judged righteous. He has given them a new name and written it down in glory. When the roll is called, everyone with the white stone will hear his name and will recognize it as he is welcomed into the glories of the Lord.

Satan is also at work in the church at Thyatira. No fellowship of believers in any age or in any location is ever free from the onslaughts of the enemy. In this instance, his activity is to use his deceptive schemes to cause the believers to be weak on sin. This is a common deception. He works in such a way as to make us think, "This isn't any big sin." There is a reference to his deep secrets. Everything that Satan does is a deep secret. If he was forthright and up front on things, no one would buy into what he does. He makes black look gray and white look gray so that there isn't any great distinction between right and wrong. Such is a life of toleration. While there are many who are influenced by Satan's deep secrets, some remain faithful and true to the Lord. It is important to remember that while Satan is at work in every fellowship of believers in every age and in every place, he is never fully successful. God always has a remnant who remain faithful to Him.

To those in Thyatira who overcome, the Lord promises they will rule and reign with Him over the nations. This promise reminds us that even though Satan may be the god of this world now, there is coming a day when the kingdoms of this world will become the Kingdom of our Lord and He will reign forever and forever (Revelation 11:15). As believers, we share in His triumph.

In Sardis, the work of Satan again focuses on deception. He pumps his spirit into things to make them appear living when in fact they are dead. Spiritual satisfaction is a deceptive trick of Satan. The believer can never become complacent in his walk with the

Lord. That's exactly where Satan does his most damaging work. In Sardis, they have heard the gospel, and they know what the Lord requires, but they have fallen asleep. The Lord challenges them to wake up. Satan has a way of putting us to sleep so that even though we know what we should be and do, it never occurs to us that there is a problem.

There are those in Sardis who are awake and who overcome in the power of the Lord. To those who overcome, the promise is that they will be dressed in a white robe, and their names will never be blotted from the Book of Life. This is an interesting statement. The robe of white is a reference to the day when we stand, as those who overcome, dressed in the robes of His righteousness. All of our righteousness is as filthy rags, according to Scripture. However, in that final day, we will not stand in our righteousness, but we will be dressed in His righteousness, which alone makes us worthy. The blotting out of a name from the Book of Life suggests that our salvation may not be as eternally secure as some think. If a name that is written in the Book of Life (which name only God can write) can be erased, it would suggest that anyone who names His name and subsequently persists in his sin could conceivably lose what he thought was his salvation. The seriousness of this should not be passed over lightly by any professing Christian. However, the promise to the committed believer is that his name would not be erased from the Book of Life. This is great news.

The next letter that John records appears to be an exception among the seven letters in that the Lord of the church finds no fault with this fellowship of believers. It isn't that Satan isn't active here, since a reference is made to the synagogue of Satan. Where this is we do not know, but we can assume that it has a presence of some sort among them, although they are not partakers of it. Satan has a pew or two in every assembly of believers. His goal is to disrupt the work of the gospel; but, as this letter illustrates, his power to accomplish his work is limited. Only words of commendation and encouragement are given. Satan has not been able to deceive these believers even in the midst of adversity and trial. They may be weak; but, in the strength of Christ, they are made strong. This is a wonderful encouragement to all believers who find that they are struggling against forces of evil that threaten to consume them.

The promise to the overcomer is a promise of great blessing. Jesus reminds them that He is coming again and that, when He does, things are going to change. The believer will be given a place of security in the Kingdom of our Lord and will be identified as belonging to the Lord by the new name that is written on him. The idea of a new name is an intriguing idea in Scripture. It signifies ownership. We belong to the Lord. We are His children and share in the glories of His eternal Kingdom.

The final letter in this series is addressed to Laodicea. The spiritual warfare experienced by the church at Laodicea is typical of what has been referred to in other settings. Different terms are used to describe it, but the result and activity are the same. Lukewarmness is a deceptive scheme of Satan. It is the state of spiritual self-satisfaction – the "I'm all right" state of mind. The most dangerous state of mind spiritually is the lukewarm state. The Lord wants followers who are on fire for Him. "Neither hot nor cold" is a Satanic state, which displeases the Lord. This type of thinking is one of Satan's most successful ploys. The promise to the overcomer centers on the right to sit with Christ in His Kingdom as one who reigns with Him.

In each of these seven letters, the theme of the Book of Revelation – the ultimate triumph of Christ over the forces of evil – is underscored. The church will be subjected to spiritual warfare, but the resources of the Lord will enable her to overcome and share in the glories of His ultimate triumph.

The church is engaged against the enemy, Satan, who is at work in society to control the destiny and outcome of all things. We feel his effects in our day-to-day life. The Church of the twenty-first century is not immune from his attacks.

For one thing, today's Church has to deal with the secularization of society, which began in earnest in the 1960s. This is an insidious, calculated, Satan-inspired strategy to remove the influence of Christian teaching from all aspects of life. We are in the midst of a moral revolution fueled by the secularization of society. It affects every area of life, and no one knows where it will end.

Jesus indicated (in His teaching about the last days) that we would experience great difficulty in respect to the nature of life. Matthew 24:21 reads, "For then there will be great distress, unequaled from the beginning of the world until now, and never to be equaled again." In other words, the last days would be uniquely distressful, violent and troublesome. Almost all of the trouble that we are experiencing can be traced to this breakdown of moral values. This generation has experienced a major cultural shift from a strong Judeo-Christian moral influence that had characterized society for generations to a basic amoral society practically devoid of any Biblically based values.

The days of moral absolutes are passed. This generation doesn't know the difference between right and wrong. In fact, in respect to moral values, the terms "right" and "wrong" have no clear meaning. In a survey conducted by the Barna Group among a representative sample of American adults, it was discovered that most Americans consider themselves to be Christians, despite the fact that very few adults base their moral decisions on the Bible, and surprisingly few believe that absolute moral truth exists. Even more startling is the fact that only three out of 10 people who claim to make moral decisions based on specific principles named the Bible as the source of those principles. One of the first signs of the last days is a moral revolution replacing the Biblical standards of right and wrong with an attitude of permissive personal indulgence.

Jesus talked about a last-days apostasy in Matthew 24:10 and following. He indicated that many would turn away from the faith. This deadening of spiritual sensitivities – this moral and spiritual deterioration of society – opens the door for Satan to carry out his campaign of evil.

A radical moral shift has taken place in our culture in one generation, creating a crisis of hope. We don't know the difference between right and wrong which leaves us perplexed about the great issues of life that confront us on a daily basis.

The pervasiveness of evil has rotted away the moral foundations of our culture. This is a generation that has lost its way in respect to moral values.

Consider, if you will, the following points:

1. This is the generation that has opened the closet door to life-styles specifically identified Biblically as sin.

2. This is the generation that has legalized same-sex marriage – an obvious abomination to God.

God didn't make us this way or for this purpose. It isn't evil for two men or two women to live together in a Christian relationship; however, if they engage in sexual activity with each other or live together as a married couple (with all that implies), it is wrong in the sight of God. Genesis 1:26-27 reads, "Then God said, "Let us make man in our image, in our likeness, and let them rule over the fish of the sea and the birds of the air, over the livestock, over all the earth, and over all the creatures that move along the ground." So God created man in his own image, in the image of God he created him; male and female he created them." He went on to say that His purpose was that they should be fruitful and multiply. Reproduction (God's plan) is biologically impossible in a same-sex marriage. God's creative purpose can only be fulfilled when a man is truly a man and a woman is truly a woman – two distinct individuals functioning as male and female. It is clear from what's happening that our generation isn't guided by the teaching of the Word of God. The same-sex movement has been gaining nationwide momentum, and only time will tell how far it will go.

3. This is the generation that has sanctioned the taking of innocent life. There have been more than 50,000,000 reported legal abortions in the United States since 1973, the year in which the Supreme Court legalized abortion. There were 3,600 abortions per day in 2000 – 149 per hour – about one every 24 seconds. In contrast, the combined number of military deaths in all of America's wars from the Revolutionary War to the present time is about 1,200,000.

4. This is the generation that has seen the judicial system rewrite laws that had helped give the nation a moral conscience, so that today our culture is characterized as amoral – nearly devoid of any Biblically based values. It's as if the judiciary has a private agenda to eliminate God from the arena of public life.

5. This is a generation that has worshipped Satan as deity. There have always been witches and evil expressions of the occult, but worship Satan as deity? Satan worship has become an official religion. There is a Church of Satan with a Satanic bible – with priests and priestesses – which boasts of living in a cosmos which is permeated and motivated by the Dark Force which they call Satan. They speak of themselves as being their own gods. Wikipedia (the free encyclopedia) says, "The Church of Satan is an organization dedicated to the acceptance of the carnal self, as articulated in *The Satanic Bible*, written in 1969 by Anton Szandor LaVey." It was reported recently in an evangelical church prayer chain that a small church built over 100 years ago was experiencing problems with occult practices on their property. The church has a graveyard next to the church, and the graveyard is not gated. The problem the church is having is with local people practicing a voodoo religion in the graveyard. Those people are performing curse rituals there and are trying to desecrate the church area. What makes this even more astounding is that this is happening in the most advanced, enlightened age of human civilization. We are living in a different time, an age of godlessness, in which Satan carries out his program of evil uninhibited.

6. As recently as September 14, 2006, a federal judge declared the reciting of the Pledge of Allegiance in public schools unconstitutional. In June of 2002, a federal appeals court in California ruled that reciting the Pledge of Allegiance in public schools is an unconstitutional "endorsement of religion" because of the addition of the phrase "under God" in 1954 by Congress. The Supreme Court rejected that ruling on procedural grounds. The court did not rule on the merits of the argument. The same atheist who brought the argument to the court in 2002 is behind this new ruling by the federal judge in California. The Supreme Court will likely be forced to deal with this issue again, and we have all learned that the court is a product of the secularization of society.

The buzzword of this generation is "tolerant" – meaning "equal in value and veracity." While I believe that Christians must be gracious and respectful of other divergent groups, it flies in the face of Biblical understanding to suggest that other divergent religious groups are equal in value and veracity to Biblical Christianity. Jesus made the claim that He is the way, the truth, and the life. Acts 4:12 says, "Salvation is found in no one else, for there is no other name under heaven given to man by which we must be saved." The claim of Christianity is exclusive. The greatest challenge facing the Church today is in communicating the truth of the gospel in a culture where all truth claims are perceived to be equal. This places the Church in a position of standing outside the culture, beckoning to the culture to consider the claims of Jesus and leave the broad way that leads to destruction. Satan has done an effective job of duping modern man into thinking that all roads lead home.

The secularization of society is one of Satan's most troubling schemes. It makes the work of the Church a constant battle. Spiritual warfare is something that we must contend with, and the Book of Revelation sets it all in context. Revelation – the revelation of Jesus Christ – opens with a vision of the risen, exalted and enthroned Lord, the conqueror of all forces that oppose God, including that final barrier to the completion of God's glorious plan of world redemption – the barrier of death.

CHRIST IN THE BOOK OF REVELATION

The Book of Revelation, which is the revelation of Jesus Christ, revolves around a series of visions showing Christ as triumphant Lord. The late Dr. Edwin K. Gedney divided the Book of Revelation into seven visions of Christ.

Vision and Activity of Christ	Chapters	The Related Series
I. Christ, the Man among the Lampstands (The heart and power of the Church)	1 – 3	The seven letters
II. Christ, the Triumphant Lamb (Administering the plan of God)	4-8:1	The seven seals
III. Christ, the Intercessory	8:2-11	The seven

High Priest		trumpets
(Transmitting the prayers of Saints)		
IV. Christ, the Hope of	12-14:5	The seven
the Ages		Personages
(The Child made Ruler)		
V. Christ, the Great Reaper	14:6-16	The seven
(Preparing for Judgment)		Bowls of God's wrath
VI. Christ, the Conquering	17-20	The seven
Logos		dooms
(Destroying the great enemies of God)		
VII. Christ, the eternal King	21-22	The seven new
(The light and center of the new Cosmos)		things

I have found that the Book naturally falls into three major divisions, each one opening with a vision of Jesus Christ.

1. The first is Jesus Christ, Reigning Lord of the Church (Chapters 1-3).
2. The second is Jesus Christ, Overcoming Lamb/Redeemer, Author of Salvation, Head of a New Creation (Chapters 4-18).
3. The third is Jesus Christ, Triumphant Lord, King of kings and Lord of lords (Chapters 19-22).

JESUS CHRIST, LIVING LORD OF THE CHURCH

The Book opens and closes on a note of victory. In Chapter 1, John receives a vision of the risen, ascended and exalted Christ. This is a glorious revelation, because it assures John – in his present state of distress – that God is on the throne and that the future that He has planned for His people will come to pass as certainly as He said it would. John has been exiled to the island of Patmos as a consequence of his faith in Jesus Christ. He is an old man, sentenced to a life of oppression because he is a believer in Christ. Revelation

1:9 says that John was a prisoner "on account of God and the testimony of Jesus." Patmos was a small, rocky island in the Aegean Sea, about 15 miles west of Ephesus. The island of Patmos was not a resort where people went to vacation. According to Nelson's Bible Dictionary, the island was desolate and barren – the perfect setting for Rome to banish criminals who were sentenced to hard labor in the mines and quarries of the island. Christians were treated as criminals by the Roman emperor, Domitian, which meant that the apostle John undoubtedly suffered severe physical persecution while he was held as a prisoner of Rome. It was here in this setting that the Lord gave him this Revelation of Jesus Christ, which must have made the experience that he suffered fade in comparison with the glory of the revelation that he received.

God sent His angel to John to show him what God was going to do in the future. Patmos was not the end. As gloomy as John's situation may have seemed, God announces victory in the person of His Son, Jesus Christ. This assurance came to John in a vision of the risen Christ, in all of His glory, reigning over the Church as Lord. All aspects of the vision have significance, but the key to victory for John, which is illustrated here, is the key of death and the grave in Christ's hand. It is a statement of consummate victory. Satan has attempted to defeat God's redemptive plan in Christ since the day that Christ was born in Bethlehem of Judea. Throughout the public ministry of Jesus, Satan was a constant adversary, coming against Christ at numerous times and in numerous forms, but always without success. The ultimate test is the cross/resurrection event, in which Satan's power has been crushed. It's as if you can hear Jesus saying to John, "Look – here in my hand – what do you see? Keys! These are the keys of death and the grave. I have defeated this enemy of man and now own access to the place of death, where my people were once held captive. I have burst open the gate that sealed the grave and held men captive. I am victor. Rejoice! Don't ever fear what man can do to you! I will raise you up in the last day."

The revelation of the risen, ascended and exalted Christ is a statement of victory, which gives the believer courage and confidence as he journeys through life buffeted and troubled by evil. The outcome of the great drama of the ages has been determined even though there are still battles and skirmishes to be fought.

Nothing that Satan does can stop the program of redemption centered in the person of Jesus Christ, the Lamb of God, slain for the sins of the world. John is given a vision of this in the fourth and fifth chapters of the Book of Revelation. The great drama of the ages has reached its final phase this side of eternity. The cross/resurrection event is history. Christ has ascended to the right hand of the Father, and He presides over the redemptive work of the gospel as the church launches its global mission of gospel witness.

JESUS CHRIST, AUTHOR OF SALVATION

The vision given to John in Revelation 4 and 5 shows the centrality of Christ to the future of God's redemptive plan. This vision is one of the most compelling scenes in all of Scripture. John is caught up by the Spirit into heaven, where he is to be shown the next phase of God's redemptive program – "what must take place after this." He first observes a throne and One sitting on it, with a rainbow encircling the throne.

This vision of the hierarchy of heaven showed the throne of God surrounded by 24 other thrones with "elders" sitting on them. These elders were robed in white, with gold crowns on their heads.

As John watched, he noticed flashes of lightning coming from the throne, with rumblings and peals of thunder. Seven lamps were blazing before the throne, which are said to be the seven spirits of God. Additionally, before the throne, he observed what appeared to be a sea of glass, clear as crystal. I can't imagine how John must have felt as he was immersed in such glory, but there was more.

In the center, around the throne, were four living creatures, and they were covered with eyes, in front and in back. The first living creature was like a lion, the second was like an ox, the third had a face like a man, and the fourth was like a flying eagle. Each of the four living creatures had six wings and was covered with eyes all around, even under his wings. Day and night they never stop saying, "Holy, holy, holy, is the Lord God Almighty, who was, and is, and is to come."

Whenever the living creatures give glory, honor and thanks to him who sits on the throne and who lives forever and ever, the 24 elders fall down before him who sits on the throne, and worship him who lives forever and ever. They lay their crowns before the throne and say, "You are worthy, our Lord and God, to receive glory and honor and power, for you created all things, and by your will they were created and have their being." A truly awesome scene! But, there is more.

John saw, in the right hand of him who sat on the throne, a scroll with writing on both sides and sealed with seven seals. A mighty angel cried out in a loud voice, "Who is worthy to break the seals and open the scroll?" No one, either in heaven, or on earth, or under the earth, was found worthy to open the scroll.

John was overcome with sorrow, since it appeared, from what has transpired, that what appeared to him to be a glorious scene would now end in terrible defeat. He began to weep profusely over these developments. He must have had an understanding that what he observed represented the only hope for mankind to ever share in God's eternal purpose. Did this mean that all hope was gone? What was he to think?

At that time, one of the elders spoke to him and told him that he didn't need to weep. "Look!" he said. "The Lion of the tribe of Judah, the root of David, has triumphed. He is able to open the scroll and the seven seals." John looked, and what he saw was a Lamb – not just any lamb, but a Lamb that appeared to have been slain at some point. It was obvious that this Lamb had been engaged in mortal combat. The battle scars were obvious.

What followed gave John great hope, for the Lamb took the scroll from the right hand of Him who was seated on the throne. John described what he saw: "Then I saw a Lamb, looking as if it had been slain, standing in the center of the throne, encircled by the four living creatures and the elders. He had seven horns and seven eyes, which are the seven spirits of God sent out into all the earth. He came and took the scroll from the right hand of him who sat on the throne. And when he had taken it, the four living creatures and the 24 elders fell down before the Lamb. Each one had a harp, and they were holding golden bowls full of incense, which are the prayers of the saints. And they sang a new song: 'You are worthy to take the scroll and to open its seals, because you were slain, and with your blood you purchased men for God from every tribe and language and people and nation. You have made them to be a kingdom and priests to serve our God, and they will reign on the earth.'" This is a great word of assurance concerning God's eternal purpose, which will be accomplished.

"Then I looked and heard the voice of many angels, numbering thousands upon thousands, and 10,000 times 10,000. They encircled the throne and the living creatures and the elders. In a loud voice they sang: 'Worthy is the Lamb, who was slain, to receive power and wealth and wisdom and strength and honor and glory and praise!' Then I heard every creature in heaven and on earth and under the earth and on the sea, and all that is in them, singing, 'To him who sits on the throne and to the Lamb be praise and honor and glory and power, forever and ever!' The four living creatures said, 'Amen,' and the elders fell down and worshiped."

This vision of the triumphant Lamb of God, the Lord of Salvation, is engaged to carry out God's program of redemption throughout the time that follows until He is seen in His final triumph as conquering Lord, coming at the end of the age victorious over all forces that offend. He has been exalted to this place of supreme authority. He is the Lord of the new creation. Everything that follows through Revelation 18 illustrates how, in every circumstance of life, God's program succeeds, and Satan is defeated.

Warfare is taking place, as can be seen by the description of the seals, trumpets and bowls – and, in the end, Jesus triumphs. What the seals, trumpets and bowls depict is where most Bible students get bogged down and struggle to interpret. The problem with our interest in precise identification and interpretation is to think that these symbols refer necessarily to a precise historical development. They are snapshots of developments that are common to all generations of the Church in this period between the ascension of Christ and His return in power and glory. They represent the spiritual warfare that goes on between Satan and the Church in every age. These are real situations, but they are not necessarily limited to a particular time and place.

The idea that each seal, trumpet or bowl corresponds to one specific historical development may be stretching the point. I suspect that inquiring minds in every generation since the revelation was given to John could find something in their generation that would fit the description given. The problem that we have is that we want everything to add up so that we can count down and know when the day of His appearing is at hand. Prophecy isn't given as a timepiece that we can follow to know the precise hour of human history. There is enough revealed to know that we are living in the last days.

The significance of the seals, the trumpets and the bowls is that they characterize life in the last days – the period between the first and second advents of Jesus Christ. When Christ was born in Bethlehem of Judea, God initiated His plan of redemption in Christ, the second or last Adam. This development triggered Satan's aggressive activity in opposition to what God was doing. Satan would not let God go about recovering His lost creation without an attempt to disrupt and (if possible) defeat this plan. The Book of Revelation tells the story of how things happen in the last days.

A summary of what is going on as based on the seals, the trumpets and the bowls reveals the character of life in the Gospel Age. On the one hand, the global spread of the Gospel is illustrated; and, on the other hand, warfare, famine, pestilence, persecution and moral decay are illustrated. Interestingly, these are the things that Jesus said would characterize the last days in His description of the same in Matthew 24.

Satan's massive assault on the work of the Gospel as illustrated here in the seals, trumpets and bowls is described in chapters 2 and 3, where he is seen as the adversary of Christ and His Church. Everything spoken of in those chapters recurs in these apocalyptic images of the seals, trumpets and bowls. In each descriptive event, Christ is illustrated as conquering. He is the Author of salvation, and nothing that Satan does can defeat God's redemptive plan.

CHRIST, THE CONSUMMATE CONQUEROR AND KING (CHAPTERS 19-22)

The final vision of Christ begins in chapter 19. It portrays Him as consummate victor over the forces of evil, with which he has contended from the time of Satan's rebellion and subsequent fall from fellowship with God.

The scene opens with heavenly rejoicing. The time has come for putting an end to the controversy between God and Satan. Satan's time is up. God is ready to complete His glorious Kingdom goal of forming a people who will live in fellowship with him in his kingdom Paradise for his glory, forever. Rejoice! The Lord is King!

The picture of the throne room of God corresponds with the vision that John had in chapter 4. This time, it is a scene of celebration. All the angelic personages of heaven are shouting and singing. This is the culmination of all that has been going on during the church age. The marriage supper of the Lamb is come.

Christ is portrayed coming in conquest over all the forces that have been arrayed against Him. Everything described here is conquest. It's been a long time coming, but the hour has dawned, and God's Kingdom goal is about to be realized.

No wonder there is rejoicing! Consider the heartache, the pain and the trials that humanity has experienced as a result of living in a world ruled by the enemy, where death has reigned from Adam until now! But, it's over for Satan. The day of his conquest has arrived. He is about to be destroyed, obliterated and consumed – never to be heard from again!

Kingdom building is now Kingdom realized. Paradise restored! Perfection, beauty, joy, peace and unending life in the Kingdom of glory!

SUMMARY

The message of the Book of Revelation is threefold and is contained in the three major visions of Christ described in the Book:

1. Christ as Reigning Lord of All

God will complete His eternal plan of forming a people who will live in fellowship with Him, in His kingdom Paradise, for His glory, forever. We know that because of the finished work of Christ in His first advent. He announced the coming of the Kingdom of God; He called men to repentance; He provided a means of forgiveness of sin and opened the door of salvation; He destroyed all barriers to the completion of God's eternal plan by His conquest of death and the grave. His position as reigning Lord over all was achieved in the cross/resurrection event (Romans 1:1-6). God has highly exalted Him and bestowed on Him the name that is above every name (Philippians 2:8-11).

2. Christ, the Author of Salvation

Having provided the complete sacrifice for sin, He ascended to the right hand of the Father, where He presides over the work of the Gospel in bringing men to salvation. The church age or Gospel age is a period of Kingdom building. There are three components of this period of Kingdom building:

a. The Word of the Gospel;
b. The person and work of the Holy Spirit;
c. The human messengers who bear witness to the saving power of the Gospel.

The enemy of God and man, Satan, is very active during this period of Kingdom building, providing fierce opposition. He and his demonic forces disrupt the work of the Gospel by inflicting wounds on God's chosen people, agitating the assembly of the saints, persecuting believers and even causing some to fall away. His attacks are vicious and pervasive. The time between the first and second advents of Christ is not a pretty period of human history; but, in spite of the severity of Satan's attacks, God's Kingdom plan moves forward to fulfillment.

3. Christ, the Consummate Conqueror, King of Kings and Lord of Lords

The ultimate triumph of Christ over Satan and the forces of evil is dealt with in chapter 6 of this writing.

The Book of Revelation is the revelation of Jesus Christ. Whatever else you may make of it, don't miss Jesus as He is revealed here in the Book of His revelation!

QUESTIONS FOR DISCUSSION
1. Under what circumstances was the Book of Revelation written?
2. What is the main theme of the Book of Revelation?
3. Name and describe some of the systems by which the Book of Revelation has been interpreted.
4. What are some of the lies that Satan uses to deceive people?
5. What blessings are promised in Revelation 2 & 3 to those who overcome?
6. What are some examples of the moral shift that has taken place in modern times?
7. Discuss the author's depiction of the three major divisions of the Book of Revelation. How might this analysis affect one's interpretation of the various details given in the Book?

CHAPTER 5

LIFE'S FUNDAMENTAL QUESTIONS

Any discussion of personal eschatology begins with the questions, "What is man? Who am I? Where did I come from, and why am I here?" These questions are fundamental to the greater questions, "What does the future hold for me? Is there an afterlife? What happens to me when I die?"

There are different theories about the origin of human life. The most plausible understanding in respect to man's origin and destiny comes from the Bible. The Bible answers the question of man's origin by stating that man is the creation of God.

The early chapters of the Bible tell the story of how God created man as the crowning glory of His creation consistent with His eternal purpose to form a people who would live in fellowship with Him in His Kingdom Paradise, for His glory, forever. Many people struggle with the idea of creation, choosing rather to believe in the theory of evolution.

THE THEORY OF EVOLUTION

The theory of evolution is the most popular concept of how life came about and has reached its current state. This theory – taught in most colleges and universities as the explanation for living things – has come under closer scrutiny in this generation, mainly due to the fact that it is indefensible scientifically. There are major gaps that defy explanation.

A Swedish geneticist, Dr. Heribert Nilsson, professor of Botany at the University of Lund in Sweden – although not a creation scientist – has stated, "My attempts to demonstrate evolution by an experiment carried on for more than 40 years have completely failed. At least, I should hardly be accused of having started from a preconceived antievolutionary standpoint."

Evolution explains the existence of human life as an ongoing process in which "what is" evolved from a simple, basic life form. Where that simple basic life form came from is never satisfactorily answered. Nothing ever remains what it is but is continuously changing into a different and usually more complex life form.

Natural selection is the engine that drives evolution. According to this understanding, natural selection can cause an organism to change into a totally different form of life. This idea is called macro-evolution, which is defined as transition from one kind of plant or animal into another. What is so perplexing about this concept is that the change is indistinguishable even over extraordinarily long periods of time. You can't observe the change because no one lives long enough and because no scientific data exists to prove it.

Micro-evolution is defined as variation within a kind. Creationists tend to have less of a problem with micro-evolution – the idea of change within a kind – because it is consistent with the Biblical record of creation, according to which everything that was created reproduces after its kind. We know that changes occur over periods of time, but never outside of the kind. This is a critical understanding that is borne out historically.

Micro-evolution can only occur when something already exists. You can't have variation within a kind unless that kind exists. Creation, then, can give micro-evolution a level of credibility.

Evolution is not an exact science (as some assume). It takes as much faith (if not more) to accept the theory of evolution as it does to believe the Biblical account of creation.

The story is told of an atheist philosophy professor who (at the expense of a young Christian in his class) decided to prove his theory that God doesn't exist by engaging the innocent student in a debate about the existence of God on philosophical grounds. The young student didn't fare very well with the experienced professor, admitting that he had no scientific evidence to prove the existence of God but accepted it on faith, which the professor ridiculed. Subsequently, another Christian student in the class rose to the defense of his brother and began to question the professor on the same premise that the professor had used to discredit the other student. The conversation went along these lines:

"Tell me, professor, do you believe that we have evolved from a monkey?"

"If you are referring to the natural evolutionary process, young man, of course I do."

"Have you ever observed evolution with your own eyes, sir?" The professor makes a sucking sound with his teeth and gives his student a silent, stony stare.

"Professor, all previous attempts to explain how the process works have failed. Since no one has observed the process of evolution at work and no one can even prove that the process is an ongoing endeavor, are you not teaching your opinion, sir? Are you now not a scientist, but a priest?"

"I'll overlook your impudence in the light of our philosophical discussion. Now, have you quite finished?" The professor hisses.

"So, you don't accept God's moral code to do what is righteous?"

"I believe in what is – that's 'observable science'!"

"Ah! SCIENCE!" The student's face splits with a grin. "Sir, you rightly state that science is the study of observable phenomena. What you call 'science' is a premise that is flawed."

"Science is flawed?" The professor sputters. The class is in uproar.

The Christian remains standing until the commotion has subsided. "No, sir; I mean that your view of science is flawed. To continue the point that you were making, earlier, to the other student – May I give you an example of what I mean?" The professor wisely remains silent.

The Christian looks around the room. "Sir, the basic law of physics says that matter can neither be created nor destroyed; yet you, in spite of that, believe in 'spontaneous generation' of the entire physical universe. Spontaneous generation of vermin was disproved centuries ago. Talk about straining out the gnat and swallowing the camel! Sir, biogenesis is 'observable science,' as you say – life has only been observed to come from other life of like kind – yet, you apparently still believe that that is exactly what happened – in spite of science – that life somehow came from non-life and that animals gave birth to children of other kinds!"

"Young man," the professor began tersely, "I believe that science will eventually...."

"That science will eventually prove that matter can be created – that life can come from non-life," interrupted the young Christian. "Sir, that's not science; that's Faith! What you believe is the exact opposite of 'observable science'! Your faith is in what you are calling 'science' – my faith is in God who created 'science.' Make no mistake, professor, we're both operating from faith."

The real question is: "Does it make any sense to put one's faith in an irrational system of belief as opposed to accepting the Biblical account of creation?" History has proven the God of the Bible to be exactly who the Bible says that He is.

THE CHRISTIAN UNDERSTANDING OF ORIGINS

The Christian understanding of origins comes to man by divine revelation in the Word of God. Dr. Edwin K. Gedney – a trained scientist – commenting on origins, says, "In the Book of Genesis, we have an account of the origin of man that is simple, reasonable, believable, and the only one that can be harmonized with current scientific fact and with many scientific theories. The early part of the Book of Genesis is not given to us as a scientific treatise on the origin of the earth and man. If it had been so written, no one could have understood it until the last 100 years. It is given to us as a reasonable and brief summary of the beginning that would:

a. Satisfy the inquiring human mind through the pre-scientific era,
b. Be harmonious with true scientific concepts when these concepts would be discovered, and

c. Answer the basic questions regarding the meaning, purpose, nature and destiny of man that science and philosophy cannot resolve in any age."

In respect to the origin of human beings, no one was there when it all began to happen. Consequently, thinking people – who have always pondered the question of origins – are left to theorize what indeed happened. Throughout the six or so millennia of human history, several myths have evolved, either religiously based or through scientific speculation. The other alternative to the question of origins is to believe the divine revelation as recorded in Scripture.

Man is the product of intelligent design. God knew what He was doing when he created man. From the beginning, He had a plan and purpose for man. Believing the Biblical account of man answers the fundamental questions of the I am and the why I am.

The first mention of man is made in Genesis 1:26-27, which reads, "Then God said, 'Let us make man in our image, in our likeness, and let them rule over the fish of the sea and the birds of the air, over the livestock, over all the earth, and over all the creatures that move along the ground.' So God created man in his own image, in the image of God he created him; male and female he created them."

The Psalmist, speaking of the greatness and majesty of God, ponders the meaning of man by asking the question, "What is man that you are mindful of him, the son of man that you care for him? You made him a little lower than the heavenly beings and crowned him with glory and honor" (Psalm 8:4-5).

Two important understandings are established in these Scriptures. The first is that man is a created being, created by God as opposed to some chance happening. He has not always been. He has a certain beginning and ending. There is a time when he becomes and a time when he is no more. Also, there is man and there is woman, two distinct aspects of humanity necessary for the fulfillment of God's creative purpose.

THE MORTALITY OF MAN

We speak of man as being a mortal being, meaning that he will die at some point in time. The question arises as to the nature of man in creation. One could say that he was created as a mortal being because he did experience death. Some contend that man was created as a candidate for immortality. By this it is understood that if man was obedient to the restrictions placed on him in the garden he would have lived forever.

What we do know is that man was created in the likeness of God, but what that likeness entails is subject to question. It was not a material likeness, since God is spirit. It was not a likeness in respect to the attributes of God; otherwise, man would have been totally self-sufficient – not dependent on anyone or anything for his existence.

My sense is that man may have been created in a unique state, neither mortal nor immortal. The fact that he died proves that he was capable of dying, but there is no indication in the Biblical record that he was a dying creature before his disobedience and the pronouncement of the death sentence. Neither was he immortal, as is evident from the fact that in his Paradise home was a tree of life, access to which he was deprived of by his eviction from the garden Paradise following his sin, lest he eat of that tree and live forever.

No one knows with any certainty what it meant to be truly human in the sense in which Adam was created. What we do know is that once sin entered into the world and the death sentence was pronounced, man's state of being is one of mortality.

The idea that man was created as an immortal soul existing in a fleshly shell that is his terrestrial home to be discarded at death, releasing the true self to go to its celestial abode, is a misunderstanding of Scripture. Darren King, in a review of N. T. Wright's book, *Surprised by Hope*, says, "Wright begins *Surprised By Hope* by giving us the *Reader's Digest* version of the conclusions that he draws in his epic work, *The Resurrection of the Son of God*. Namely, Wright exposes as false the idea that our Christian hope for the afterlife should be a disembodied, eternal bliss spent amongst the clouds and angels of heaven."

The idea of the separation of body and soul at death – the body being buried in the ground and the soul being released to some celestial abode – is untenable for a number of reasons. For one thing, the idea that the soul, as an invisible, immortal entity, can do all the things that man did before death – such as talk, sing, bow in worship in heaven, or feel pain while suffering eternal torment in hell fire – without the physical mechanisms that he had in life to experience these emotions and sensations, is absurd.

Furthermore, if man is naturally immortal, then, at death, he moves to another location – heaven or hell – where he will exist forever, because that's what "immortal" means. The idea of a permanent location as hell – with never-ending suffering, torment, weeping, wailing and gnashing of teeth – is inconsistent with the nature of God as revealed in the Bible.

Furthermore, the thought of natural immortality is totally unbiblical. Nowhere in Scripture is it even hinted that man was created an immortal being. Any immortality apart from God is derived or bestowed. Scripture clearly teaches that only God has immortality. First Timothy 1:17 mentions immortality and ascribes it to God. More importantly, 1 Timothy 6:16 states that only God has immortality. If God alone has immortality, the obverse is true: man doesn't have it.

Every description of man in Scripture positions him as a creature dependent on a source outside himself for life. In the original garden Paradise, man is provided with food to eat, which he needs to sustain life. He will not automatically continue to live from a source within. As long as he eats what God provides for him, he can live.

Mention is also made of a tree of life in the midst of the garden Paradise, the fruit of which man is forbidden to eat. This is obviously a source of life that God doesn't want man to touch until he has passed the test of obedience to the command of God. The fact that there is a tree of life clearly illustrates that man is dependent on a source outside himself for life. After man disobeys God, and the consequence of his disobedience is announced, man is expelled from the garden Paradise, and the only reason the Bible gives for his expulsion is, "lest he eat from the tree of life and live forever" (or, become immortal).

The other fruits and vegetation continue to be available to man after he is expelled from the garden because he needs this food to survive. The difference between the condition in the original state and after his expulsion is that man now must sow and harvest his food by the sweat of his brow.

The Bible also speaks of immortality as something that man will "put on" as opposed to something that he naturally possesses. According to Scripture, this is a change in the nature of man that takes place in the resurrection of the last day. If man is already immortal, what is this change spoken of regarding his putting on of immortality (1 Corinthians 15:51)?

THE UNITY OF MAN

Man was created as fully man, in the image of his Creator. He was not created as a work in progress. He was created as a complete, distinct and unique individual. There is only one you!

The other understanding is that man is essentially a two-part being. Man is the sum total of his parts. Man is not completely man in any single part of his being. Both the material and the immaterial existed independent of each other and did not constitute man until God put them together and the body that He had created became a living being. An important Biblical understanding has to do with the unity of man.

Moses C. Crouse, commenting on the nature of man, says, "Man is a unitary organism. He is not a disproportionate compound of an undying soul and a dying body. Such dualism is contrary to the Scriptures."

Man is physical matter, and he is non-matter – the breath of life, also called the spirit. This truth is clearly stated in the creation account in Genesis 2:7, which reads, "The Lord God formed man of dust from the ground and breathed into his nostrils the breath of life, and the man became a living creature ('soul' – KJV)."

Some people think of man as an immaterial being living in a body of flesh, which is his house or shell. For those who hold to this understanding, the body (or material part of man) is simply where one lives during the time/space period of his existence. His true being is the spirit dimension of his being. This begs the question of how we define man in the present stage of his existence. Speaking of man as soul, N.T. Wright says that man is "a whole human being living in the presence of God." The idea that man is essentially a spirit being, living in a temporary shell or physical body, is a gross oversimplification of reality. Medical science understands that very well. When diagnosing a person for some ailment, doctors do not draw air out of some bodily cavity for analysis. Rather, they draw blood, which is a material substance. Man is basically a material being. Somehow, who I am is intrinsically intertwined with my material or physical being. As far as human beings are concerned, no one exists as a human being apart from a body.

There is a difference between a spirit being and a human being. There are spirit beings, and there are human beings, but they are not the same thing. They belong to different realms of creation. In fact, Jesus said to His disciples on one occasion, "A spirit does not have flesh and blood, as you see that I have" (Luke 24:39).

When one thinks about another person, they think of body as being. For instance, when you say, "I saw so-and-so today," what you mean is that you saw a physical being. When one talks about feeling ill, he is talking about how his body feels. When he has a fever, his temperature reading is taken from his body. When one talks about having a pain or an ache, he is talking about a physical sensation.

When you seek to define a man – to say what he is – you look at his DNA. This is what a person is. Everything that he is is in his DNA, and DNA is material. According to *Genetics Home Reference*, a service of the U.S. National Library of Medicine, "DNA, or deoxyribonucleic acid, is the hereditary material in humans and almost all other organisms. Nearly every cell in a person's body has the same DNA. Most DNA is located in the cell nucleus (where it is called nuclear DNA), but a small amount of DNA can also be found in the mitochondria (where it is called mitochondrial DNA or mtDNA). The information in DNA is stored as a code made up of four chemical bases: adenine (A), guanine (G), cytosine (C), and thymine (T). Human DNA consists of about 3,000,000,000 bases, and more than 99% of those bases are the same in all people. The order, or sequence, of these bases determines the information available for building and maintaining an organism, similar to the way in which letters of the alphabet appear in a certain order to form words and sentences."

It baffles me that people talk about the real man as being the immaterial part of his being. It is true that man is more than material being. He possesses the breath of life, an immaterial life-giving element.

According to Genesis, when God made man, he began with material (the dust of the ground), and he breathed into his nostrils the breath of life (immaterial), and man became a living being. In other words, God took the material that He had made, and by adding the breath of life (the life principle), everything God created man to be (DNA) was energized and began to live. I think of that action like a match being struck to light a fire. You could have all the elements in place to have a great fire, but it needs ignition. That is precisely what happened in creation, when God breathed life into the body that He had made. The unity of man is an important Biblical understanding. Man is only truly man in his completeness.

Clio Thomas, writing in the West Valley Advent Christian newsletter several years ago, said, "The Biblical understanding of human beings is not that they have bodies, but that they are bodies. When God made Adam, He did it by slapping some mud together to make a body and then breathing some breath into it to make a living soul. Thus, the body and soul which make up human beings are as inextricably part and parcel of each other, like the leaves and flames that make up a bonfire. When you kick the bucket, you kick it 100% – all of you. There is nothing left to go marching on with."

E. Earle Ellis, in "Let the Reader Understand: Temple and Eschatology in Mark," in Kent E. Browner and Mark W. Elliot, ed., *Eschatology in the Bible and Theology: Evangelical Essays at the Dawn of the New Millennium* (Downers Grove, Illinois: IVP, 1997), p. 211, says: "The Scriptures, both Old and New Testament, represent individual personality as a complex and totally mortal monism, a unity that can be viewed from different perspectives, but that cannot be broken into separate parts. The Biblical view is compatible with an outer/inner distinction or even matter/thought or matter/will distinction, as long as both aspects are recognized as mortal and as a part of the present fallen creation thus subject to the natural death process."

Dr. David Dean speaks to the matter of human nature when he says, "In contrast to the ancient Greek philosophical idea that the immaterial soul is the real person, the Bible insists on the organic unity of all human beings. God created the first man out of the dust of the ground so that the human body is an essential part of the real person. God created not just immaterial souls but whole people. He saves whole people and raises whole people in the resurrection of the last day. However many parts God may have made us with, all parts are essential to human nature and belong together in an organic unity." Dean goes on to say, "Presbyterian theologian Mike Williams has argued that this is the Biblical view of human beings: 'While the question of body and soul is a most vexing one from a biblical perspective, one thing is clear: Scripture envisages human beings as psychosomatic unities. Human beings are created as total beings.' {and then he quotes John Murray that} 'The body is not an appendage. The notion that the body is the prison-house of the soul and that the soul is incarcerated in the body is pagan in origin and anti-biblical; it is Platonic in origin and has no resemblance to the biblical conception.'"

Wikipedia (the free online encyclopedia) speaks of Aristotle's philosophical ideas about souls and the nature of living things: "The notion of soul used by Aristotle is only distantly related to the usual modern conception. He holds that the soul is the form, or essence of any living thing; that it is not a distinct substance from the body that it is in; that it is the possession of soul that makes an organism an organism at all, and thus the notion of a body without a soul or of a soul in the wrong kind of body, is simply unintelligible." It would appear that even Aristotle believed in the organic unity of man.

As one seeks to explain origins, the most plausible and satisfactory explanation is to attribute all origins to God. He is the ground of all being. All being emanates from God. There isn't any being apart from God.

Being exists in four realms – the realm of deity, the realm of spirits, the realm of humans, and the realm of other living things. The realm of spirit beings, the realm of human beings and the realm of other living things are all the creation of God and are dependent on him for being. God is the ground of all being and the source of all being.

By accepting the fact of creation, man is placed in a position of accountability to a sovereign God. Life is a gift from God and is intended to be lived out in a manner that pleases God and glorifies Him.

THE FACT OF DEATH

Man lives from day to day with the understanding that the life he lives may be interrupted by death at any time. Death is the common lot of all peoples, in all of time and in all places. Life is a march toward death. Death never takes a vacation in any generation. Everyone will die at some point in time, regardless of one's rank or status in life. Death is real. Without the reality of death, resurrection has no meaning. There are no guaranties about tomorrow. Death is the inevitable stalker of life. The Bible says, "It is appointed unto man once to die."

As you travel across the face of our planet, the one thing that is common to almost every culture and civilization is a cemetery. Burial traditions may vary from one culture to another, but death is common to all peoples.

DEATH A PUNISHMENT FOR SIN

The Bible establishes the fact that death was introduced into the human condition as a punishment for sin. Some might argue, "OK, if death is a punishment for sin, and everyone therefore suffers death, why, then, in the resurrection at the last day, are not all people raised to eternal life in God's Kingdom? If one pays the penalty for his sin by dying, what more must he do?" That is a reasonable question. The answer is that when the Bible says that the soul that sins must die, it is not talking only about natural death; it is talking about the second death. There are two deaths mentioned in the Bible – natural death and the second death. I believe that it was D. L. Moody who once said, "Born once, die twice. Born twice, die once." Natural death, which comes to all, is a temporary state of being, from which all (good and bad alike) will be raised to face divine judgment.

DEATH AS CONSEQUENCE AND DEATH AS PUNISHMENT

Natural death is not so much a punishment for sin as it is a consequence of sin. The second death, which follows the judgment, is the real punishment for sin. It is reserved for those who have not availed themselves of God's gracious offer of salvation in Jesus Christ. It is final, complete and permanent. Natural death is but an interruption of life. The second death is the termination of life – a state of non-being.

It is important to understand what we mean by natural death. Lack of understanding in this regard opens one's imagination to a host of fanciful ideas.

DEFINING DEATH

The most common understanding is that death is the cessation of life – the permanent cessation of all vital bodily functions. According to MedicineNet.com, "The common-law standard for determining death is the cessation of all vital functions, traditionally demonstrated by an absence of spontaneous respiratory and cardiac functions."

In 1980, the National Conference of Commissioners on Uniform State Laws formulated the Uniform Determination of Death Act. It states: "An individual who has sustained either (1) irreversible cessation of circulatory and respiratory functions, or (2) irreversible cessation of all functions of the entire brain, including the brain stem, is dead. A determination of death must be made in accordance with accepted medical standards." This definition was approved by the American Medical Association in 1980 and by the American Bar Association in 1981.

Interestingly enough, every definition of death describes death as complete in respect to all that a person is. No reputable medical authority that I am aware of has ever even hinted that in death, something about man survives the experience.

Defining death can be a complicated matter, but the fact of death is not at all complicated. Death comes to everyone at some point in their existence. It doesn't matter who we are, when we are, where we are or what the circumstances of our lives are. We all meet death, at some point in time, from one cause or another.

Many people die prematurely (before reaching old age). The leading cause of death among the young is by accident. In addition to accidents (mainly, auto accidents), many young people die from suicide or disease (cancer, for example). As one grows older, the more likely cause of death is disease. Cancer and heart disease are leading causes of death.

Interestingly enough, some people actually die from fear, a psychiatric disorder known as Catatonia. Uncontrolled fear can lead to death. Still others die from the stress of a broken heart caused by the death of a loved one or a broken relationship. Grief can create sufficient trauma to actually cause one to die. Whatever the cause, death is the common lot of all.

From the moment in which one is given life, he is moving toward death. Life is a process of dying. It sounds paradoxical, but it is true. No person since Adam has known what it means to be fully alive. When a person is born, the death sentence is already on that person because of the sin nature that he inherited. Death is the consequence of sin of which everyone partakes. That is why life is such an uneven journey. Some people never get out of the birthing stage, while others die in infancy or meet death at an early age.

But, even if one survives the common and not-so-common diseases and lives to a ripe old age, the whole process of aging is a process of dying. It doesn't take very long for the aging signs to show up. We experience bodily changes; our abilities to do things change; our appearance changes. Growing old is not a pleasant experience. Life expectancy is a fictitious statistic. Death is the inevitable outcome of life.

Death was introduced to the human condition in the Garden of Eden. God told Adam and Eve that they could eat from everything that had been created for them, except that they could not eat from the tree of the knowledge of good and evil, for in the day in which they ate, they would surely die. They ate the forbidden fruit, and they died. This act of disobedience placed the entire human race into a state of disobedience, since Adam and Eve were the entire human race at this point in time, and they could not possibly birth an offspring more righteous than themselves. Who they were – including their sinful nature – was passed on to their posterity.

The sentence of death was passed on to the race of human beings in that death is a consequence of sin and sin is a constant of human experience. "All have sinned and come short of the glory of God" (Romans 3:23). "There is none righteous, no not one" (Romans 3:10).

The Bible clearly states the reality of death for all men:

"For all can see that wise men die; the foolish and the senseless alike perish and leave their wealth to others" (Psalm 49:10).

"There is a time to be born and a time to die, a time to plant and a time to uproot" (Ecclesiastes 3:2).

"For the living know that they will die, but the dead know nothing; they have no further reward, and even the memory of them is forgotten. Their love, their hate and their jealousy have long since vanished; never again will they have a part in anything that happens under the sun" (Ecclesiastes 9:5-6).

"But see, there is joy and revelry, slaughtering of cattle and killing of sheep, eating of meat and drinking of wine! 'Let us eat and drink,' you say, 'for tomorrow we die'!" (Isaiah 22:13).

"For as in Adam all die, so in Christ all will be made alive" (1 Corinthians 15:22).

"Just as man is destined to die once, and after that to face judgment, so Christ was sacrificed once to take away the sins of many people; and he will appear a second time, not to bear sin, but to bring salvation to those who are waiting for him" (Hebrews 9:27-28).

Death is the inevitable outcome of life. It is not only stated Biblically; it is experienced humanly.

UNDERSTANDING DEATH

The real question that everyone ponders is this: "What is death? Is it the end? And, what happens to a person when he dies?"

It should be noted that death is the antithesis of life. As darkness is the absence of light, so death is the absence of life. Death and life are not the same thing. The terms are contradictory. "This day I call heaven and earth as witnesses against you that I have set before you life and death, blessings and curses" (Deuteronomy 30:19).

Consider the death sentence that was imposed on Adam. When God established the boundaries for Adam and told him that if he crossed the boundary he would die, He wasn't suggesting that Adam would continue to live in a better place. What could be better than the Eden Paradise? Furthermore, the appeal of the forbidden fruit to Adam (as suggested by Satan) was that his eyes would be opened and that he would be as God. Of course Adam would like to be like God! After all, he had intimate fellowship with God in the garden Paradise. If you carry the thought a little further, if death ushered Adam into the presence of God, in what manner could it be considered a punishment for sinning against God? Adam wanted to be like God, but being with God would be even better. The idea of death being a continuation of life in the presence of God is irrational.

Death is death, and life is life – two distinct opposites! But, this is difficult for man to grasp. Dr. Linden J. Carter writes, "There is something about the solemn presence of death, the still, cold form, the open grave, these partings with our kith and kin, that make us think. And it is not surprising that dying men grasp at every straw and build towering castles of hope – sometimes, on sinking sand." We say that we know what death is, but we have a tendency to slip into a state of romanticizing when facing the death of a loved one. For some strange reason, death becomes the gateway into a greater and better life. For those who think along these lines, death is a continuation of life, not the cessation of life.

If the dead don't really die, but survive the death experience as a real person (a disembodied spirit) – with greater capacities than when imprisoned in a body of flesh – it seems strange that they do not communicate with us to tell us what the experience is really all about. I, for one, would like to know from someone who's been there. However, no human being has ever come back from the dead to describe the experience or otherwise sent us a communication from beyond the grave.

We live in a world of modern medical marvels. From time to time, we hear stories of how someone died and came back to life. On September 2, 2009, the news carried a story of a Brooklyn, New York, man who had died and come back to life. The article read: "A Brooklyn dad, whose heart stopped beating for an incredible 45 minutes, was released from the hospital Tuesday – perhaps the luckiest man in New York. Joseph Tiralosi was raised from the dead by a team of doctors at New York Presbyterian Hospital Weill Cornell after he went into sudden cardiac arrest two weeks ago. His doctors and other experts are calling his case a miracle." A remarkable story, to be sure; but, was he "raised from the dead by a team of doctors"? I don't think so. Stories like this are fascinating; they may border on the miraculous; but, this isn't resurrection – it's resuscitation.

There are some who were raised from the dead as recorded in Scripture. Lazarus of Bethany was one. The Bible says that he had been dead for four days when Jesus raised him from the dead. That certainly is long enough to get a good understanding of what the death experience is all about. I would like to know what Lazarus experienced. I can hear him now. "Wow! That was great! I don't know what happened to me, but it was awesome. I saw Jesus and many of the Old Testament saints. The beauty of the place was indescribable. The sun was always shining. The flowers were beautiful. I saw the river of the water of life flowing down the center of the city. There was joy, happiness and excitement beyond imagination. Why did you bring me back to this sinful, cruel old world with all the pain, disease and death?" However, in fact, Lazarus never mentioned what happened to him during those four days, because he was in the sleep of death (as Jesus said), and he didn't have a clue as to what was going on. He had nothing to say because he wasn't aware of what was going on outside the tomb.

I know that some people say that they communicate with the dead. They tell us about how Uncle Ted (or Aunt Sarah) spoke with them through a medium or necromancer. Some people conduct séances, and they supposedly communicate with the departed, but these so-called experiences are not what we think they are. There is possibly communication in the spirit world, but what we are communicating with are demonic spirits who represent our loved ones.

Satan is the god of this world, and a host of demonic spirits work with him to deceive the unsuspecting. He knows everyone who has died. He worked with them, controlled them and knows all about them. It is not a difficult thing for him to represent them in order to deceive us into thinking that we are actually communicating with them. We aren't. The dead don't know anything in the silence of the grave. Their memory has ceased, their being is asleep in death.

Solomon spoke these words of understanding in Ecclesiastes 9:3-6: "This is the evil in everything that happens under the sun: The same destiny overtakes all. The hearts of men, moreover, are full of evil and there is madness in their hearts while they live, and afterward they join the dead. Anyone who is among the living has hope—even a live dog is better off than a dead lion! For the living know that they will die, but the dead know nothing; they have no further reward, and even the memory of them is forgotten. Their love, their hate and their jealousy have long since vanished; never again will they have a part in anything that happens under the sun."

I have discovered that most people don't believe in death. There is a great deal of confusion about the nature of man. For most people, because of the notion that you go to heaven when you die, man is essentially an immortal being living temporarily in his fleshly shell, waiting for emancipation. Most people think that you never die, but that you continue to live in some form and place even after this life has ended. According to a 2003 Harris Poll, 84% of Americans believe in the survival of the soul after death. To these people, the soul is the real person, and it continues to live as a disembodied spirit. This theory robs death of its sting, and it is in direct contradiction with the Biblical teaching that man is a mortal being in need of immortality if he is ever to live anywhere forever.

A.A. Phelps, A.M., Late Free Methodist Minister, U.S.A. [Bible Standard, No. 2, November, 1877, pp12-14.] says, "For many years, I tenaciously clung to the dogma of natural immortality. At length, I so far laid aside my prejudice as to give the whole subject a thorough investigation. I became intensely in earnest to know the truth, whatever might befall my preconceived opinions. This investigation resulted in a radical revolution of sentiment in regard to man's nature and the sinner's destiny. I have been compelled by an overwhelming array of Scripture evidence, to reject and repudiate the current doctrine of natural immortality. I subjoin a few reasons, very briefly stated, for this rejection.

1. The doctrine of natural immortality has a very unfavorable origin. It can be traced back through the Romish Church to the Pharisees, and from them to the heathen philosophers and idolatrous Egyptians, who advocated it. They probably received it by a sort of

Satanic mesmerism; for the old Serpent first published the doctrine amid the lovely bowers of Eden in these words: 'Ye shall not surely die' (Genesis 3:4). A dogma that was invented by the Devil, received by Pagans, nurtured by Papists, and adopted by Protestants, ought to be looked upon with some suspicion.

2. It is at variance with the inspired record of man's creation. His origin is succinctly stated thus: 'And the LORD God formed man of the dust of the ground, and breathed into his nostrils the breath of life; and man became a living soul' (Genesis 2:7). There is not the faintest intimation here of an invisible, intangible, imponderable, immaterial, immortal conscious entity, without length, breadth, or thickness, without exterior or interior, capable of thinking, knowing, and feeling, independent of the body, and destined to live through all the years of God.

3. It clashes with the Biblical account of man's fall. Adam was placed on probation. A simple test was applied. Obedience would have brought immortality, while disobedience would as certainly result in mortality. The penalty was thus briefly stated: 'in the day that thou eatest thereof thou shalt surely die (or, "dying thou shalt die")' (Genesis 2:17). When a term is used for the first time, it ought to be used in a plain, natural, literal sense. It was so used in Eden. If the penalty in Eden was moral death, then the doctrine of Universalism is true; 'For as in Adam all die, even so in Christ shall all be made alive' (1 Corinthians 15:22). Adam sinned. He at once became a dying man. He was driven out of Paradise "lest he put forth his hand, and take also of the tree of life, and eat, and live forever' (Genesis 3:22). It was the hand of love that pushed fallen and sinful man aside; that shut him away from the tree of life, and thus cut off all possibility of his becoming immortal in sin and misery.

4. It renders the execution of the sinner's penalty impossible. God allowed the race to be propagated under the malediction of physical death, yet coupled with provisions for the future. Adam's disobedience lands all his progeny in the grave; but Christ's obedience lifts them all out of it. The whole human family shares so fully in the atonement of Jesus as to have secured to them an unconditional resurrection from the Adamic death. Every man must now stand or fall for himself. Whoever will come into the glorious plan

will be eternally saved. Whoever refuses must die for his own sins. This awful doom awaits the impenitent, after the judgment verdicts shall have been pronounced. In various phrases do the Scriptures teach the final extermination of the wicked in the 'lake of fire.' They shall 'die.' They shall 'perish.' They shall be 'destroyed.' They shall be 'consumed.' They shall be 'burnt up, root and branch.' Such a destiny would be impossible, if man possessed an immortal soul.

5. Immortality is never ascribed to man. In our common version [the KJV] the term 'immortal' occurs only once, and is then applied to God (I Timothy 1:17). The term 'immortality' is found five times; from which we learn: (1) that God only possesses it (1 Timothy 6:16); (2) that Christ brought it to light in the Gospel (2 Timothy 1:10); (3) that we are to seek for it (Romans 2:7); and (4 and 5) that Christians are to put it on at the resurrection (1 Corinthians 15:53-54). Such terms as 'undying soul,' 'deathless soul,' never-dying spirit,' though so common in theology, are nowhere to be found in the Bible. So far from teaching that immortality is a birthright possession, the Scriptures everywhere hold it up as a priceless boon to be sought – a blessing for which we are entirely dependent upon Jesus Christ, the great Life-giver.

6. The doctrine of natural immortality supersedes the necessity of a resurrection. The difference between Church theology and Biblical theology is this: the former predicates a future life upon the assumed fact of inherent immortality; the latter predicates it upon a resurrection from the dead. There is a natural antagonism between the two positions. Hence it is that the glorious doctrine of the resurrection, so conspicuous in the teaching of Christ and the Apostles, has fallen into disrepute. Many popular divines utterly repudiate it. Others habitually ignore it. In the Churches generally, very little stress is laid upon it. Indeed, why should there be if the prevailing notions are correct? If death is a grand emancipation, coming with a friendly hand to open our prison and let us go free, if 'death is the gate to endless joys,' if the dead are not really dead, but more fully alive than ever; then a resurrection is entirely superfluous, and ought to be rejected.

7. It reduces the judgment scene to a nullity. If the current view is correct, that the real man is immortal, 'shuffling off this mortal coil'

and entering upon his reward at death, surely a judgment day would be entirely useless. Consistency demands that we should either give up the idea of a coming tribunal or cease to believe that man can be rewarded before he is judged. Popular theology would have us believe that Christians are continually flying up to heaven, and sinners sinking down to hell! That the one class are already crowned with glory, and the other class already cursed with the pangs of their merited doom, but that there is still a day of judgment, when the saints are to be rallied from their abode of blessedness, and sinners are to be brought out of prison of despair; that they are to receive their formal sentence, and then be sent back to their former abodes of blackness or bliss! Can anyone seriously believe that God's administration will ever be so absurd?

8. It subverts the doctrine of Christ's second coming. If men are rewarded and punished in a 'disembodied' state, there is no need of Christ's coming to raise the dead. If the destinies of men can be adjusted at death, there is no need of Christ's coming to judge the world. If the saints are to live forever in heaven, there is no need of Christ's coming to renew the earth and to set up His kingdom upon it; for it would be a lovely reign with every saint in heaven, and every sinner removed to a distant hell. Surely there is no adequate reason why Christ should ever return to earth if the prevalent ideas of man's nature and destiny are correct. Is it any wonder that so little stress is laid upon the doctrine of Christ's personal coming? The traditions of men have displaced this glorious truth, and turned the whole system of revealed religion into a terrible moral chaos!

9. The dogma of natural immortality is the fruitful source of dangerous error. It has given birth to a hateful progeny. It is the foundation of the worst religious developments that have ever cursed the earth. The intelligent reader will hardly venture to deny that Mormonism, Mahometanism, Swedenborgianism, Shakerism, and Spiritualism are built upon the assumed fact that man is immortal. It is the boasted mission of Spiritualism, indeed, to teach that 'man has an immortal soul.' The whole system depends upon it. And yet it is but a natural and logical outgrowth from what the Churches generally advocate as 'orthodoxy.' Spiritualism is 'orthodoxy' gone to seed. Nor can we with any consistency pour out denunciations upon

a class of religionists for having travelled legitimately to certain conclusions from the premises that we have so generously granted to
them. Who does not know that Mariolatry and Purgatory are based
upon the assumption that dead folks are alive? Let the Scriptural
fact that 'the dead know not anything' be established, and there will
be no more money paid to have departed friends prayed through the
pains of Purgatory. Let the whole Catholic Church be convinced that
the virgin Mary is now dead, and she will cease to be an object of
worship. The horrid doctrine of eternal torment would never have
found a place in the Church of God but for the antecedent notion
of natural immortality. This granted, the other is a logical necessity,
unless it can be shown that all men are to be saved. But the doctrine of endless misery is so foul a slander on God's character that
many have been compelled to repudiate it. Assuming that man is
immortal, the only alternatives are eternal torment and universalism.
The latter is a natural rebound from the former. If men are to exist
eternally, they must exist in a state of happiness or misery. The one
being rejected, the other must be accepted. The consequence is, that
the dogma of unending agony is making men Universalists and infi-
dels on a large scale. Universalism and endless misery are both built
upon the foundation of inherent immortality. They are the dangerous
extremes. The truth lies between them. But, enough! The bitterness
of the fruit attests the badness of the tree."

SATAN'S LIE

If you were to ask a person on the street what happens to a
person when he dies, they would probably say that he has gone to be
with the Lord. They will hold a funeral service of some type – often
referred to as a Celebration of Life – and what they mean by that is
that the person in question has really gone on to live in some better
place or form. The traditional view of death is not consistent with
Biblical teaching. Instead, it amounts to a redefinition of death as a
continuation of life.

The idea that death is not really death, but a continuation of life,
goes back to the Garden of Eden, when Satan appeared to Eve in the
form of a serpent and told her (regarding God's sentence of death),
"You will not surely die." In his beguiling manner, Satan incarnated

himself into the serpent, and he sought to cause Eve to disobey God by suggesting that the fruit of this tree was actually good for her and that it would make her more like God. Satan is a liar and the master deceiver. In her innocence (since she had not yet seen death), it was easy to believe that death was not real. "You shall not surely die" was Satan's lie. The whole world lies under the control of the evil one according to 1 John 5:19. Is it any wonder, then, that his lie – which denies the reality of death – is so universally believed? The idea that death is a continuation of life is Satanic in origin.

VIEWS OF THE AFTERLIFE

There are three prominent ideas about what happens to a person when he dies. These three understandings can be summed up by the words Reincarnation, Relocation and Resurrection. There are also a few professing atheists who deny any continuing existence for man after death or any accountability for life, and there is a smattering of materialists who contend that this life is all that there is, although there are some materialists who believe in a resurrection at the last day.

REINCARNATION

Reincarnation may be the most widely believed theory about the afterlife held by man. It is a common tenet of the religions that are popular in the East, where the world is most densely populated. According to a 2003 Harris poll, 23% (that figure is probably higher today) of the people in North America hold to this theory. This is not surprising, given that the belief in reincarnation is a prominent element of New Age thinking, which celebrates the deification of man.

It is difficult to understand how educated, intelligent, sophisticated beings can subscribe to such a primitive and irrational system of belief as reincarnation. Apparently, the desire to live is so powerful that it overrides logic and reason.

According to the teachings of the First Spiritual Temple (which was founded in 1883), "The fact of reincarnation makes more sense – and is more in line with natural law – than the myth of it is." Here are the reasons they give:

"a. Reincarnation follows the universal Law of Cycles.
b. Reincarnation is a wonderful demonstration of God's grace and our ability to correct that which needs to be corrected.
c. It seems inconceivable that we can master the lower aspects of the personality in one earthly lifetime.
d. Reincarnation helps explain the appearance of evil in a world guided by a loving God."

Reincarnation contends that when a person dies, he doesn't really die (sound familiar?), but continues to live in another form in another place. The change, which is experienced in death, may be progressive or regressive (depending in part on the character of one's life). Interestingly enough, all theories of the afterlife reflect back on the character of the present life. The ultimate goal of reincarnation (which may occur an infinite number of times) is the purification or perfecting of the soul until one has attained ultimate bliss (nirvana).

For one who believes in reincarnation, life as we know it now is not the beginning of your existence, but a step in your passage to perfection and oneness with God. You were someone else (or something else) before you became what you are now, and you will become someone else or something else after you are through being what you are now.

According to Wikipedia, "Belief in reincarnation is an ancient phenomenon. This doctrine is a central tenet within the majority of Indian religious tradition and was also entertained by some ancient Greek philosophers. Many modern pagans also believe in reincarnation, as do some New Age movements, along with followers of Spiritism, practitioners of certain African traditions and students of esoteric philosophers."

Wikipedia goes on to say, "Reincarnation is once again attracting the minds of intellectuals and the general public in the West. Millions of Westerners are joining the more than 1,500,000,000 people who have traditionally understood that life does not begin at birth or end at death."

The belief in reincarnation as an explanation of being is totally contradictory with the Biblical understanding of "being" in respect to both origins and destiny. The theory of reincarnation is the creation of Satan, who is the Prince of Darkness. There is no light in him at all. He leads people to buy into his lie so that they forsake the truth of God. He seeks to create what he thinks will inspire men to follow his thinking as opposed to accepting the truth of God. The goal of reincarnation is ultimate bliss. Everyone is promised this destiny through all the stages of incarnations. This is a theory of darkness.

The story is told of a pastor who was visiting an elderly woman to speak with her about the hope that is ours in Christ, to which she responded, "I don't believe any of that. When I die, I will go into a dark, deep pit." I can't imagine what she thought would happen to her in that deep, dark pit, but it couldn't be good. Jude spoke about a place of darkness when he said, "And the angels who did not keep their positions of authority but abandoned their own home – these he has kept in darkness, bound with everlasting chains for judgment on the great Day."

The theory of reincarnation has its roots in Platonic philosophy. Plato taught that there were two worlds – the ideal world and the real world. The ideal world was a place of perfection, and the real world consisted of mud, hair and filth – a corruption of the ideal world. Between these two worlds ran a stream of soul stuff, from which everyone born in the real world partook. It was the source of being (or life). Plato taught that the real you came from the soul stuff (disembodied spirit), inhabited some material form for a time and, subsequently (at death), returned to the stream of soul stuff.

It would be like taking a glass and dipping it into a stream to fill it with water. What you now have is a particular body of water in a glass. While the water is in the glass, you can do any number of things with it without changing the fact that it is a particular body of water in a glass. You can heat it, freeze it or color it; but, all the time, it is in the glass – it is the same body of water whatever form or color it takes. Once you dump the water back into the stream from which you took it, you can never recover that same glass of water. You can dip the glass into the stream and fill it up again, and you will have another particular glass of water. Every time you dip it into the stream, you will have a new body of water in the glass – which, when you are done with it, can be dumped back into the stream. It is still water, but it is not the same glass of water. That is reincarnation.

What is significant about the idea is the concept of incarnation. In pagan thought, incarnation is a natural order of things, occurring *ad infinitum*. For Christians, incarnation is unique; it has special meaning in respect to the understanding that the Sovereign God of the universe incarnated human flesh in the birth of the Messiah, Jesus Christ. This is a fundamental truth, on which Christianity stakes its claim of being the only true religion. No other world religion has a god who comes to man to save him from the guilt and consequence of his sin. In other world religions, man is seeking his god to find favor and salvation (whatever that means). In Christianity, God came to man in the person of Jesus Christ – the God-man, the last Adam, through whom God creates a new humanity – who alone fulfills His eternal purpose of a people who will live in fellowship with Him, in His Kingdom Paradise, for His glory, forever. Jesus Christ is God incarnate.

But, also, in Christian teaching, there is the understanding that Satan – as a spirit being – has the capacity to incarnate human beings. We refer to this as demonization. He can assume different forms in different settings.

RELOCATION

The pagan theory of reincarnation has influenced the Christian view of man as a soul (immaterial consciousness) living in a body of flesh. The goal of life is to escape this prison house and fly away to one's celestial abode. This view is called the theory of relocation. It is widely held in the communion of Christians around the globe. Those who believe in the theory of relocation view death as a gain. They are done with this life with all its heartache, trouble and sorrow.

According to the Harris poll cited earlier, 84% of Americans believe in the survival of the soul after death. What is meant by that is the idea that the real person exists in the immaterial part of a person (understood to be the soul), which is a disembodied consciousness. The body (the house in which one lives) may die and be buried, but the real you survives death (sound familiar?). Like reincarnation, this is a continuation theory that denies the reality of death. The basic difference between reincarnation and relocation has to do with the identity of the deceased. In reincarnation, the person may have existed in different forms or species prior to his existence as a person. The matter of personal identity is difficult if not impossible to maintain. In the theory of relocation, the deceased continues to be the same person, retaining his identity. Unlike reincarnation – in which you can never get the same glass of water out of the stream once it has been poured back – in relocation, you do get the same glass of water. Identity remains in relocation.

There is a striking similarity between the theory of reincarnation and this theory of survival beyond death that is held by most Christians. The similarity has to do with the idea that the real man is a disembodied spirit incarnating material and that death is not really death. It is simply another phase of life.

The theory of relocation is held by many Christian groups. The belief is that at death, the deceased has gone home to be with the Lord. Death is thought of as a graduation ceremony, in which one is elevated to eternal bliss in the presence of the Lord. Unlike reincarnation, the relocated person bypasses the multiple stages of incarnation and is thought to have gone on immediately to live in the big house with all the departed saints of the ages. It is a time of reunion with loved ones who have predeceased the departed.

Interestingly enough, I have never heard anyone spoken of at a funeral service as having gone to hell to begin being punished in the fires of hell, although we know that hell is the alternative destiny for man. Somehow, everyone goes to the better place to be with the Lord.

Relocation is not a Biblical position. No human being has ever died and gone to heaven as is commonly believed – not even Jesus! In fact, when Jesus was discussing eternal truths with Nicodemus, he told Nicodemus, "And no man hath ascended up to heaven, but he that came down from heaven, even the Son of man which is in heaven" (John 3:13, KJV). This statement is clear.

All Christians believe that Jesus died, having been crucified by Roman authorities in the first century, but Jesus didn't die and go to heaven. As He was expiring on the cross, one of His last words was, "Father, into thy hands I commit My spirit." It is important to notice what He said in this moment. Only a short time prior to this, He had prayed that the Father would glorify Him with the glory that He had with the Father before He came to earth (John 17:4-5). One might expect that in His dying moment He would have reminded the Father of His prayer. But He did not say, "Father, I am coming home to be with you." "I am coming home to be glorified." Instead, He confirmed what happens at death. Death is a separation of the life-giving spirit from the body of dust, into which it was breathed, but it is not the person. Just as Adam was a body fashioned from dust until God breathed into it the breath of life (spirit), so, in death, the spirit (breath of life) returns to God, Who gave it. There are those who might want to debate where Jesus went when He died on the cross. 1 Peter 3:18-19 makes reference to His going and preaching unto the spirits in prison. This is a powerful understanding. The only prison referred to in this text is the prison house of death. Death is a place of captivity. It holds the dead in its prison. The writer of Hebrews understood this when he said, "Since the children have flesh and blood, He too shared in their humanity so that by His death He might destroy him who holds the power of death – that is, the Devil – and free those who all their lives were held in slavery (in prison) by their fear of death" (Hebrews 2:14-16, NIV). Jesus went into that prison and broke open the gates. In His resurrection, He delivered a profound message to those held in the prison house of death (Revelation 1:18).

Jesus was buried in a tomb and was resurrected on the third-day morning, the first fruits of them that slept. Easter, the celebration of the resurrection of Christ, is an important holiday for Christians. The resurrection of Christ is the cornerstone of Christian faith. Jesus is now in heaven, sitting at the right hand of the Father, reigning as Lord of the church; but, He didn't gain this position at death. Following His resurrection, He appeared to His disciples; then, after forty days, He ascended to the Father. This Biblical teaching – accepted by all true Christians – is death, resurrection and ascension.

In the popular view of death as continuation (or going to heaven), the Rev. A.J. Gordon, the late distinguished pastor of Clarendon Street Baptist church in Boston, said, "Death has very largely usurped the place that belongs to resurrection" (see Hebrews 11:39-40). E.A. Stockman, who wrote in the late nineteenth century, made the observation, "To say that dead men are living men is to destroy the meaning of language."

The Bible never speaks of anyone dying and being relocated to heaven or hell. The Bible talks about some who were translated, but they did not die in the normal sense of that word. In respect to those of whom this is true – Enoch, for example – the Bible clearly states that he was translated (caught up) so that he would not see death. If death was a passage into the presence of the Lord, why not just die and fly away? Enoch did not die. He was translated.

Death is a definite stage of being. According to the Bible, there are two distinct deaths – the first death and the second death. The difference between the two deaths is dramatic. The first death is a discontinuation of life; the second death is a destruction of life. We will speak to the matter of the second death subsequently.

Most people have difficulty facing the reality of death; in an attempt to cope with their grief, they tend to redefine it. One does not need to fear death. It may be an enemy, but it is not the final end of being. It will continue to invade our ranks as long as human beings live, but it will one day release its captives and be destroyed. 1 Corinthians 15:26 says, "The last enemy to be destroyed is death" (NIV).

I remember following the hearse along the road that leads into the cemetery for the burial of my brother, Raymond. It was a sad and sobering reminder that the final moment of separation had arrived. As the hearse passed different gravestones before arriving at the gravesite that had been prepared for my brother, the thought came to me that this road into the cemetery was not a dead-end street. It was just a rest stop on Raymond's pilgrimage to the city called glory!

Separation is difficult, but it is not forever. Brent Ross refers to this rest stop as the "Advent Nap."

So, what is death, and how are we to understand it? When facing the loss of a loved one, questions arise as to their whereabouts.

When death comes, our first response is to deny that death is what it really is. Our inherent desire (to live in a state of blessedness and peace) causes us to create scenarios that respond to that desire.

It isn't a planned response; rather, it is something that arises naturally in our subconscious minds.

In an article in *Signs of the Times*, March 2007, Maylan Schurch says, "Death is so unsettling to us that if we don't have facts about what happens next, we quickly invent some." For many, even though we know differently, we still resort to some unreal hyperbole. For many, death is unreal. This approach to death is a form of denial.

The late Dr. James Kennedy, in a sermon preached on the Trinity Broadcasting Network on April 7, 2007, said, "I am never going to die – sorry about you, but I am not going to die! No one will shovel dirt on my face. I will never be in the casket. I will never be in the grave. I am not going to die. I know that my body may be there, but I won't be there. I will step out of this body into Paradise. People will stand around that hole in the ground, and maybe shed a few tears, but I will be in heaven, watching it all." Unfortunately, Dr. Kennedy spoke for many people with those words. You can deny death, but it doesn't alter the reality of death.

Everyone has questions; everyone wants to know what really happens. When facing the loss of a loved one, questions arise as to their whereabouts.

I remember thinking about my brother, Vincent, who passed away at the age of 70 from cancer. Vincent and I were close, and my heart was pained watching his demise and subsequent death.

I am a trained theologian. I know what the Bible teaches about death. However, thoughts about him haunted my imagination at times. I stood by his grave and watched the cemetery workers lower his casket into the ground and fill the cavity with the dirt that they had dug out to make the burial spot.

In this moment of separation, the human tendency is to question where he is. Has he gone forever, like the dew that evaporates in the morning sun? Is his spirit alive somewhere, wandering through a celestial Paradise? Is he aware of my comings and goings? Are my actions causing him sadness or joy?

I've thought about wanting him to get in touch with me and give me the scoop on what it's like so that I can write an exciting story to enlighten the world. I'd like to know, but I'm Biblically literate enough to know that I won't find out from someone who has predeceased me, and I'm not ready to learn about it personally.

Why do we have so much trouble understanding and accepting death for what it really is? I've come to the conclusion that our problem with death stems from the fact that we were created for something better. A desire to live forever in fellowship with God in His kingdom Paradise – a place of perfection, beauty, happiness, peace and life – was planted in everyone's heart by our Creator when He first created man. Death prevents the fulfillment of this desire – at least, for the moment.

DEATH AS SLEEP

The best understanding of death is the understanding that the Bible gives, which is to speak of death with the synonym "sleep." The idea of death as sleep does not originate with any religious group or denomination; it comes from the Bible – more specifically, from Jesus Himself (John 11:11-14). It would be unwise for one to dismiss this matter lightly simply because it doesn't fit with one's preconceived understanding of death. This term, "sleep," is the common Biblical description of death. Linden J. Carter says that the synonym "sleep" is used "in no less than 17 Books of the Bible and in no less than 66 texts of Scripture" to refer to death. Job 7:21 reads, "And why dost thou not pardon my transgression, and take away mine iniquity? For now shall I sleep in the dust; and thou shalt seek me in the morning, but I shall not be" (KJV). "Look on me and answer, O Lord my God. Give light to my eyes, or I will sleep in death" (Psalm 13:3, KJV).

A further illustration of this terminology is the statement made in 1 Kings 2:10, referring to King David's death. "Then David slept with his fathers, he was buried in the city of David." Obviously, the term "slept" meant that he died, because he was buried.

Throughout the history of the Church, this understanding has been the basic belief of the Church, as can be seen in a statement attributed to Martin Luther: "We shall all sleep until He comes and knocks on our little grave, saying, 'Dr. Martin, get up!' Then I shall rise up in a moment, and I shall be eternally merry with Him."

John Bunyan, in his classic poem, *Pilgrim's Progress*, says of Pilgrim, "The Pilgrim they laid in a chamber whose window opened towards the sun rising; the name of that chamber was, Peace, where he slept till the break of day."

Dr. Gardiner Spring said in a sermon, "We die, but intervening ages pass over those who sleep in the dust. There is no plate there on which to count the hours of time – its flight no longer noticed by the event perceived by the sensor, for the ear is deaf and the eye is closed. The busy world of life, which wakens each morning and ceases every night, goes on above them; but, to them, all is silent and unseen. The greetings of joy and the voice of grief, the revolution of the empires, and the lapse of ages, send no sound within the narrow cell. Generation after generation are brought and laid by their side; the inscription on their monumental marble tells the centuries that have passed away; but, to the sleeping dead, the long interval is unobserved."

Martin Luther, commenting on Ecclesiastes 9:10, says of death, "Another proof that the dead are insensible! Solomon thinks, therefore, that the dead are altogether asleep and think of nothing. They lie not reckoning days or years, but when awakened will seem to themselves to have slept scarcely a minute."

There is but a moment between the hour when the eye is closed in the grave, and when it wakes to judgment. When a person falls asleep in death, their next conscious moment will be in the presence of the Lord even though decades, years or even millennia shall have passed since the enemy, death, overtook them.

The most accurate way of speaking of death is with the Biblical synonym for death, which is sleep. This is consistent with the Biblical idea of resurrection. Death is a temporary state of being, after which one is raised to life. Sleep, as we experience it, is a temporary state of being. When one goes to sleep, the expectation is that he will awaken at some point, like taking a nap.

But, how are we to understand that term? What does it mean to fall asleep in death? N. T. Wright, commenting on the term "sleep" says, "When one sleeps, one is still alive, albeit (as we sometimes say) 'dead to the world.'"

Scripture doesn't have much to say about it – supposedly, because we know what sleep is – or do we? It is important to understand words in their common or usual meaning as opposed to redefining terms to fit our preconceived notions.

Charles Spurgeon, in his book, *Pictures From Pilgrim's Progress*, comments on the state of a sleeping Christian. He gives extensive commentary on the following characteristics:

a. When a man is asleep, he is insensible.
b. Again, sleep is a state of inaction.
c. The man who is asleep is also in a state of insecurity.

When thinking of sleep in the usual sense of that term, several understandings come to mind:

1. Sleep is a state of unawareness. During the period of sleep, the person asleep is not aware of developments around him.
2. Sleep is a state of insensitivity. The normal intellectual or bodily functions are turned off.
3. Sleep is a state of temporary rest. We sleep; but, at some point, we awaken.

Mark Curtis, a hospital pharmacist, says that there are 6 stages of sleep:

"Stage one is when you start to doze off, and any little sound, etc., can awaken you.
Stage two is very similar to stage one, but fewer things will awaken you. The difference between stage one and stage two is determined by the brain waves with an EEG.
Stage three is the time when we dream and go into REM (rapid eye movement).
Stage four is the time of deep sleep and the time when the body works the hardest on healing, repairs and converting short-term memory into long-term memory.
Stage five is not a natural stage, but is used during surgery. In this stage, you are not awakened by even painful stimulus.

Stage six is death, which is a different sleep, insensitive to any stimuli except the voice of God.

The body, during rest, will cycle through these stages (1-4). Stages one and two are very brief at the beginning of sleep, and stage four takes up most of the early hours. As the night goes on, stage three begins to dominate the sleep (with times that we go to stage two) and later on cycle to stage one. Near the end of our sleep we cycle more and more to lighter sleep until we awaken."

In this state of death – temporary rest – one is unaware of things, insensitive to things, but at some point will awaken. It is a temporary state.

The main difference between natural sleep and the sleep of death is that in natural sleep any number of stimuli can awaken you. However, in the sleep of death, only His voice can reach the slumbering souls (John 5:28).

I have often used these stanzas from an anonymous poem titled, "Sleep," at a graveside service:

"He sees when their footsteps falter, when their hearts grow weak and faint;
He marks when their strength is failing, and listens to each complaint;
He bids them rest for a season, for the pathway has grown too steep;
And folded in fair, green pastures, He giveth his loved ones sleep.
All dread of the distant future, all fears that oppressed today,
Like mists that clear in the sunlight, have noiselessly passed away;
Nor call nor clamor can rouse them from slumbers so pure and deep,
For only His voice can reach them, who giveth His loved ones sleep."

One may sleep the sleep of death, but the grave is not the destiny of the believer. Death may be spoken of Biblically as an "enemy," but it is not the victor. The Bible's answer to the problem of death is resurrection. The only person who can truly view death as gain is the one who has lived his life for Jesus and has accepted Jesus as his personal Lord and Savior from sin and its horrible consequences. For that person, death is a rest from all the trials and adversities of life. He rests in the safe and secure keeping of Jesus, who will raise him to eternal life at His coming again. For this person, death is truly gain.

RESURRECTION

On the occasion of the death of His friend, Lazarus, Jesus made the statement: "I am the resurrection and the life. He who believes in me will live, even though he dies; and whoever lives and believes in me will never die. Do you believe this?" (John 11:25-26)

To believe in resurrection, one must accept the fact of an omnipotent God, Who is able to do immeasurably more than can be imagined. From a medical, scientific or rational point of view, the idea of resurrection of the body is a difficult understanding to embrace. It just doesn't make sense. We know that, in death, the body decomposes and returns to dust. The Biblical record is confirmed by observable phenomena. The Bible says that, in death, the body returns to dust. "You are dust, and to dust you shall return" (Genesis 3:19). "When you take away their breath, they die and return to their dust" (Psalm 104:29). "All are from the dust, and all return to dust again" (Ecclesiastes 3:20).

In some cases, the process is accelerated by cremation. I once preached the funeral sermon for a distinguished, godly pastor who had died at the age of 96 years. The decision was made to have his body cremated. I stood with the family and friends of the deceased as his ashes (contained in a small box) were buried in the ground. This was once a tall man, weighing 200 pounds, now reduced to a few ashes. My faith told me, "He will rise again! These ashes will reform into his body – not just a body, but a resurrection body, real and substantial with identity." At the same time, my rational mind said, "There had better be a real God with power to raise the dead, because that is the only way that he will ever rise again."

You can see how from a pathological, scientific or rational point of view, the idea of resurrection is difficult to embrace. Without God, death is final.

Matthew records an incident in the life of Christ when He was confronted by the Sadducees, a Jewish sect, who didn't believe in the resurrection. They thought that they could trick Him with a question about marriage at the resurrection. It was a clever question, which they thought would embarrass Christ and prove their point that there isn't any resurrection of the dead. Jesus silenced them by his reply, saying, "You are in error because you do not know the Scriptures or the power of God" (Matthew 22:29). Notice His reference to the power of God! The key to belief in the resurrection is the power of God. What is there that God cannot do? He has demonstrated His power over every force in the universe, including death (Ephesians 1:19).

I believe in the resurrection of the dead because the Bible says so. In fact, resurrection is the foundational truth of Christianity. Resurrection is the only door to a future life. The grave is a place of captivity. Without a literal, personal resurrection, no one has any hope of a future life. Those who place their hope in the theory of reincarnation or relocation suffer an illusion, lacking any substance for their hope. The resurrection of Jesus Christ is the substance of hope for the Christian.

The resurrection of Jesus Christ out from among the dead demonstrated God's power over death and the grave so that it can be said, "Death has no dominion over him." Christ went into the grave – into this place of captivity, into this domain of Satan – and He planted the Christian flag there, claiming the grave for God. Satan was dealt a decisive defeat. The resurrection of Jesus Christ was Satan's most stunning defeat. The grave is where the battle of the ages was fought. No resurrection – no future. Resurrection – Paradise.

The apostle Paul said, "When you were dead in your sins and in the uncircumcision of your sinful nature, God made you alive with Christ. He forgave us all our sins, having canceled the written code, with its regulations, that was against us and that stood opposed to us; He took it away, nailing it to the cross, and having disarmed the powers and authorities, He made a public spectacle of them, triumphing over them by the cross" (Colossians 2:13-15).

Hebrews 2:14-15 says, "Since the children have flesh and blood, He too shared in their humanity so that by His death He might destroy him who holds the power of death, that is, the devil and free those who all their lives were held in slavery by their fear of death."

Still, Satan has not given up. He must believe that he still has a chance, because death continues to reign. Perhaps he thinks that

Christ was an exception. After all, he was the Son of God. God may have won that battle, but it is not over in Satan's mind. People still die. Good people still die. Believers still die, and as long as there is death, Satan still thinks he has a chance.

The reason why death is so important to Satan is that it represents his dominion over man and all things earthly. Man is of the earth. A believer is a new creation in Jesus Christ, but he can never be what God created him to be without resurrection. Death is the antithesis of life. Contrary to popular opinion, it is not the same as life. Death prevents man (even a believer) from ever experiencing the glories of God's Kingdom Paradise. Without resurrection, there isn't any future for man.

Without a literal, personal resurrection, Christianity has no legitimacy. Without belief in resurrection, those who believe in Christ are suffering a delusion and have an empty faith (1 Corinthians 15:12-19).

The resurrection of the dead is a crucial and certain doctrine. P. Brett Morgan, in his book, *Outlines of Eschatology*, says, "The resurrection stands out in the Bible with a boldness and an emphasis second to no doctrine in the Scriptures." All through Scripture, the resurrection in the last day is set forth as the hope of the people of God. Speaking of how God will swallow up death forever, Isaiah said it well: "On this mountain, the Lord Almighty will prepare a feast of rich food for all peoples, a banquet of aged wine – the best of meats and the finest of wines. On this mountain, he will destroy the shroud that enfolds all peoples, the sheet that covers all nations; he will swallow up death forever. The Sovereign Lord will wipe away the tears from all faces; he will remove the disgrace of his people from all the earth. The Lord has spoken" (Isaiah 25:6-8, NIV).

The certainty of the resurrection is established on Biblical and logical evidence. The concept of a future resurrection goes back to God's eternal purpose for His creation in the formation of a people who would live in fellowship with Him, in His kingdom Paradise, for His glory, forever. Without a literal resurrection of the dead at some point in time, the prospect of His eternal purpose ever being realized is nil.

The Bible is explicit in reference to a resurrection of the dead. Jesus told His hearers, as recorded in John 5:28-29, "Do not be amazed at this, for a time is coming when all who are in their graves will hear his voice and come out – those who have done good will rise to live, and those who have done evil will rise to be condemned." The fact of resurrection is referenced many times in the Bible. Isaiah wrote, "But your dead will live; their bodies will rise. You who dwell in the dust, wake up and shout for joy! Your dew is like the dew of the morning; the earth will give birth to her dead" (Isaiah 26:19, NIV). An impressive list of passages speaking to the certainty of the resurrection could be cited here, but how many times does the Bible have to state something for it to be true?

While the Bible explicitly states the fact of resurrection, the human mind wrestles with the possibility of resurrection. After all, there isn't any historical documentation of resurrection ever taking place apart from the special incidents recorded in Scripture. Resurrection just doesn't occur. It is natural, then, for the human mind to question the probability or even the possibility of resurrection.

When the apostle Paul was defending himself before King Agrippa, he told the king that Jews had always believed in the promise of resurrection as God's answer to the problem of death. Job, in his trials, understood that no matter what came his way, there was a future. He made an astounding statement considering that he lived and wrote millennia before Christ. His words, as recorded in Job 19:23-27, were, "Oh, that my words were recorded, that they were written on a scroll, that they were inscribed with an iron tool on lead, or engraved in rock forever! I know that my Redeemer lives, and that in the end he will stand upon the earth. And after my skin has been destroyed, yet in my flesh I will see God; I myself will see him with my own eyes – I, and not another. How my heart yearns within me!" That is the language of resurrection.

Daniel 12 also reflects the belief of the Jews that God had a future planned for them and that the future required resurrection. Daniel 12:1-4 says, "At that time, Michael, the great prince who protects your people, will arise. There will be a time of distress such as has not happened from the beginning of nations until then. But at that time your people – everyone whose name is found written in the book – will be delivered. Multitudes who sleep in the dust of the earth will awake: some to everlasting life, others to shame and everlasting contempt. Those who are wise will shine like the brightness of the heavens, and those who lead many to righteousness, like the stars forever and ever."

Since King Agrippa knew the beliefs and expectations of the Jews concerning the coming Messiah and His Kingdom, Paul asked him, "Why is it thought impossible by anyone that God should raise the dead?" One reason that it might be thought impossible is because of what happens to a person when he dies. We know that in death there is decomposition and decay. As stated earlier, man returns to the dust of the ground. It is preposterous to presume that, once a living being dies and returns to dust, that dust can be resurrected to a living being again.

That is especially true when considering that the ashes of some have been thrown to the wind, and the bodies of some who have died tragically have been consumed by animals or by fish of the sea, which, in turn, have been consumed by other creatures. Where are these remains, and how can they ever be recovered?

Modern science has attempted to preserve a corpse through freezing or other measures with the expectation and hope that when a cure for the disease that caused death was discovered, the corpse would be thawed out, treated and returned to life healthy. Grandiose idea, but not going to happen!

The fact that decomposition occurs at death is no reason to deny the possibility of resurrection. With God in the equation, anything is possible.

Consider what happened in creation! According to the creation account in Genesis 1 and 2, God spoke everything (except man) into existence by the word of His mouth. For instance, the record says, "And God said, 'Let there be light,' and there was light." Everything that exists, (with the exception of man) was spoken into existence by the sovereign God of the universe.

After the creation of all other things was complete, Genesis 1:26 says of the creation of man, "Then God said, 'Let us make man in our image, in our likeness, and let them rule over the fish of the sea and the birds of the air, over the livestock, over all the earth, and over all the creatures that move along the ground.' So God created man in his own image, in the image of God he created him; male and female he created them."

A further understanding of how God made man is given in Genesis 2: "Thus the heavens and the earth were completed in all their vast array. By the seventh day, God had finished the work that he had been doing; so, on the seventh day, He rested from all His work. And God blessed the seventh day and made it holy, because on it He rested from all the work of creating that He had done. This is the account of the heavens and the earth when they were created. When the Lord God made the earth and the heavens – and no shrub of the field had yet appeared on the earth, and no plant of the field had yet sprung up, for the Lord God had not sent rain on the earth and there was no man to work the ground, but streams came up from the earth and watered the whole surface of the ground – the Lord God formed the man from the dust of the ground and breathed into his nostrils the breath of life, and the man became a living being."

It is important to notice here that God didn't speak man into existence by the word of His mouth. Instead, He created man by the works of His hand out of what He had already created – the dust of the ground.

This understanding has profound implications for man – of the earth, out of the earth, for the earth! The earth is God's laboratory of life. It is the source of life for all living things – vegetation, fruits, trees, etc. The earth gives life to everything that man depends on for living. Without the earth, even the animals couldn't survive, since the earth is their primary food source.

The connection of man with the earth is profound. It serves God's purpose for man, but it also speaks to the ultimate destiny of man in resurrection.

In death, man returns to the dust of the ground – the same substance from which man was originally created. Consider Paul's question to King Agrippa: "Why should anyone question whether or not God can raise the dead?"

God created man from the dust of the ground, and He can recreate man from the dust of the ground. The earth is God's laboratory of life.

God's answer for the problem of death is resurrection. There are several resurrections mentioned in the New Testament, but they are dissimilar to the resurrection in the last day in that those who were raised returned to mortal life only to die again. Christ is the only first-fruits of the resurrection to immortality.

Listen to what the apostle Paul says in 1 Corinthians 15:20-27: "But Christ has indeed been raised from the dead, the first fruits of those who have fallen asleep. For since death came through a man, the resurrection of the dead comes also through a man. For as in Adam all die, so in Christ all will be made alive. But each in his own turn: Christ, the first fruits; then, when he comes, those who belong to him. Then the end will come, when he hands over the kingdom to God the Father after he has destroyed all dominion, authority and power. For he must reign until he has put all his enemies under his feet. The last enemy to be destroyed is death" (NIV).

Resurrection is God's answer to the problem of death, and it will occur for all at the end of the age at the Second Coming of Christ. The apostle Paul wrote these words of encouragement and hope to the church at Thessalonica: "For the Lord himself will come down from heaven, with a loud command, with the voice of the archangel and with the trumpet call of God, and the dead in Christ will rise first. After that, we who are still alive and are left will be caught up together with them in the clouds to meet the Lord in the air. And so we will be with the Lord forever. Therefore encourage each other with these words" (1 Thessalonians 4:16).

The Second Coming of Jesus Christ triggers the resurrection. Christ comes with a shout (or loud command), with the voice of the archangel and with the trumpet call of God. These eschatological signals announce God's ultimate triumph over death and the grave. The last enemy is destroyed. The shout (or loud command) is simply a call to wake up. One word often used for resurrection in the New Testament is a Greek word, which means, "to awaken and rise up." The shout isn't the calling out of an individual's name (as was the case with the resurrection of Lazarus), but a universal call to wake up and rise from the dead. The resurrection spoken of in Scripture is universal in nature. Everyone – all 100,000,000,000 people (or more) who have ever lived – will be raised from the dead. John 5:28 says, "Do not be amazed at this, for a time is coming when all who are in their graves will hear his voice and come out – those who have done good will rise to live, and those who have done evil will rise to be condemned."

There are some Bible scholars who believe that the Bible teaches two separate resurrections separated by a period of 1,000 years. This idea is based on an obscure passage in the Book of Revelation, a highly symbolic book, which mentions some of the dead not being raised to life for this long a period of time. The problem with this idea is that resurrection (wherever it is mentioned in Scripture) is set in the context of the Second Coming of Jesus Christ, and no mention is ever made in the Bible to a third coming of the Lord. Furthermore, all the references to the resurrection speak of the resurrection of the just and the unjust as if they occur at the same time, or as understood in connection with the same event. Only one Second Coming of the Lord, one resurrection of the dead and one judgment are spoken of in Scripture.

The resurrection of all the dead occurs at the Second Coming of Jesus Christ, not before it or after it. Matthew 13:40-43 reads, "As the weeds are pulled up and burned in the fire, so it will be at the end of the age. The Son of Man will send out his angels, and they will weed out of his kingdom everything that causes sin and all who do evil. They will throw them into the fiery furnace, where there will be weeping and gnashing of teeth. Then the righteous will shine like the sun in the kingdom of their Father. He who has ears, let him hear."

In this passage, Jesus is describing an "end of the age" development. The "then" in verse 43 refers to the eschatological moment when the judgment of God falls on the unrighteous and when sin and evil are destroyed. "Then shall the righteous shine like the sun in the kingdom of their Father" – not before, but then (or at the end of the age). Paul's understanding is that resurrection is necessary to future life. We do not die and relocate. We are raised out from among the dead, not brought back from some celestial abode (Philippians 3:11). The resurrection of all the dead at the end of the age will be the most stupendous event to take place on planet earth since the original creation.

THE RESURRECTION BODY

A further question arises as to how the dead are raised up: "With what body do they come forth?" Can you imagine what it will be like to be driving past a cemetery when the trumpet sounds? According to the best estimates, more than 100,000,000,000 people have been born on planet earth over the past six plus millennia. They aren't all buried neatly in cemeteries around the world, but many are. It will be one spectacular sight when all the graves are opened at the sounding of the heavenly trumpet.

According to Scripture, the dead will be raised with the same identity that they had when they died – however long ago that may have been – but with a different body. The apostle Paul addressed the question of how the dead are raised up in 1 Corinthians 15:35-54, where he said, "But someone may ask, 'How are the dead raised? With what kind of body will they come?' How foolish! What you sow does not come to life unless it dies. When you sow, you do not plant the body that will be, but just a seed, perhaps of wheat or of something else. But God gives it a body as he has determined, and to each kind of seed he gives its own body. All flesh is not the same: Men have one kind of flesh, animals have another, birds another and fish another. There are also heavenly bodies and there are earthly bodies; but the splendor of the heavenly bodies is one kind, and the splendor of the earthly bodies is another. The sun has one kind of splendor, the moon another and the stars another; and star differs from star in splendor. So will it be with the resurrection of the dead. The body that is sown is perishable, it is raised imperishable; it is sown in dishonor, it is raised in glory; it is sown in weakness, it is raised in power; it is sown a natural body, it is raised a spiritual body. If there is a natural body, there is also a spiritual body. So it is written: 'The first man, Adam, became a living being;' the last Adam, a life-giving spirit. The spiritual did not come first, but the natural, and after that the spiritual. The first man was of the dust of the earth, the second man from heaven. As was the earthly man, so are those who are of the earth; and as is the man from heaven, so also are those who are of heaven. And just as we have borne the likeness of the earthly man, so shall we bear the likeness of the man from heaven."

This is the fundamental difference in our body in the resurrection. In Adam, we had a body of flesh, fashioned out of the dust of the ground. In the resurrection, we will have a hybrid type of body – not flesh and blood as we now have, but a body fashioned like the resurrection body of Christ, bearing marks of identity with the old body, but not restricted to the functions of the old body.

Paul went on to say, "I declare to you, brothers, that flesh and blood cannot inherit the kingdom of God, nor does the perishable inherit the imperishable. Listen, I tell you a mystery: We will not all sleep, but we will all be changed – in a flash, in the twinkling of an eye, at the last trumpet. For the trumpet will sound, the dead will be raised imperishable, and we will be changed. For the perishable must clothe itself with the imperishable, and the mortal with immortality. When the perishable has been clothed with the imperishable, and the mortal with immortality, then the saying that is written will come true: 'Death has been swallowed up in victory.'"

There are some things that we cannot know with certainty until we experience them. That is the case with the resurrection. Paul gives us a clue about the body with which we are raised, but that is all it is – a clue. What we know beyond a shadow of a doubt is that we shall be changed. The change involves a body that is subject to corruption being changed to a body that is incorruptible – that sounds good. From a body that is perishable to a body that is imperishable – that sounds good. From bearing the likeness of a human being to bearing the likeness of Jesus – that sounds phenomenal.

Christ will change us into those who are fit to live forever in His Kingdom Paradise – a change we don't fully understand but enthusiastically embrace. I can't wait; how about you?

The words of Mary A. Kidder express it well:

"We shall sleep, but not forever, there will be a glorious dawn!
We shall meet to part no never, on the resurrection morn!
From the deepest caves of ocean, from the dessert and the plain,
From the valley and the mountain, countless throngs shall rise again.

When we see a precious blossom that we tended with such care
Rudely taken from our bosom, how our aching hearts despair!
Round its little grave we linger, till the setting sun is low,
Feeling all our hopes have perished with the flower we cherished so.

We shall sleep, but not forever, in the lone and silent grave:
Blessed be the Lord that taketh; Blessed be the Lord that gave,
In the bright eternal city, death can never, never come!
In His own good time He'll call us, from our rest, to home, sweet
home.

QUESTIONS FOR DISCUSSION:
1. Compare and contrast the theory of evolution with the Christian understanding of origins.
2. What does the Bible say about man's "mortality" and "immortality"?
3. What does the Bible say about man's "unity"?
4. Discuss some of the problems in the theory of natural immortality.
5. How do you understand the terms Reincarnation, Relocation and Resurrection?
6. What reasons can you give for why resurrection is such a critical doctrine?
7. What do we know about resurrected bodies?

CHAPTER 6

FORECASTING THE FUTURE

Today, people seem to be more interested in what the future holds than they were in recent generations. This is partly due to heightened awareness of a possible divine intervention in human history.

Some have thought of the first decade of the 2000's as the decade of selling the Apocalypse. Certainly there were numerous developments that focused on this possibility. For instance, Hollywood produced more than 25 feature-length movies highlighting end-of-the-world scenarios.

In addition to movies, end-of-the-world books were prevalent – most notably, the *Left Behind* series, by Tim LaHaye and Jerry Jenkins. This series sold more than 60,000,000 copies worldwide.

The Apocalyptic frenzy that characterized the first decade of the 2000's was triggered by the Y2K millennial hype that warned that the transition to a new millennium could possibly bring on Armageddon. The transition came about without incident, but a new development surfaced on September 11, 2001, with the terrorist attack on the World Trade Center in New York City. The world suddenly awakened to the realization that a group of religious fanatics were part of our global community. From this point on, life would never be the same. This realization is a major aspect of the Biblical end-times scenario.

On December 31, 2009, Bruce Watson posted this statement on America On Line: "For much of the last decade, the battle hasn't been between right and left, liberal and conservative: rather, it has been framed as a steel-cage match between God and Satan, patriotism and treason." People everywhere are worried about the future, and the ominous nature of life in the early stages of the twenty-first century only heightens that fear.

It is difficult to know with any certainty what tomorrow might bring, but that doesn't stop people from conjecturing or forecasting. If you log on to the internet and search the question, "What does the future hold?" you will come up with 48,800,000 websites. Apparently, a lot of people have an opinion about what the future holds – most of which is frightening.

THE WORLD FUTURE SOCIETY

One organization that specializes in forecasting the future is the World Future Society. If you want some fascinating reading (science fiction?) you will find it in their publications and on their website. A few of the forecasts for 2010 and beyond are:

1. The era of brain-to-brain telepathy dawns.
2. Ammonia may become the fuel of choice for cars by 2020.
3. Algae may become the new oil.
4. Radical methods of altering the planet may be the only way to prevent the worst effects of climate change.
5. The existence of extraterrestrial life will be confirmed or conclusively denied within a generation.

Forecasting the future has been a staple of society, especially since the days of Nostradamus, who published his famous projections in 1555. Today, many futurist-oriented organizations are eager to project their scintillating ideas onto a gullible public. However, there is only one source of reliable projections about the future, and that is the Bible.

THE BIBLE AND THE FUTURE

There is a future that is not incorporated in this present age, and the event that marks the transition to that future is the Second Coming of Jesus Christ. This event brings the present age to an end and inaugurates the age to come.

John, the author of the Book of Revelation said, "Then I saw another mighty angel coming down from heaven. He was robed in a cloud, with a rainbow above his head; his face was like the sun, and his legs were like fiery pillars. He was holding a little scroll, which lay open in his hand. He planted his right foot on the sea and his left foot on the land, and he gave a loud shout like the roar of a lion. When he shouted, the voices of the seven thunders spoke. And when the seven thunders spoke, I was about to write; but I heard a voice from heaven say, 'Seal up what the seven thunders have said and do not write it down.' Then the angel I had seen standing on the sea and on the land raised his right hand to heaven. And he swore by him who lives forever and ever, who created the heavens and all that is in them, the earth and all that is in it, and the sea and all that is in it, and said, 'There will be no more delay!' ('Time shall be no more' - KJV)" (Revelation 10:1-7).

Life as we know it – with all the heartache, suffering, pain and death – will give way to the new order of life in the glorious paradise of God. Revelation 21:1-5 says, "Then I saw a new heaven and a new earth, for the first heaven and the first earth had passed away, and there was no longer any sea. I saw the Holy City, the new Jerusalem, coming down out of heaven from God, prepared as a bride beautifully dressed for her husband. And I heard a loud voice from the throne saying, 'Now the dwelling of God is with men, and he will live with them. They will be his people, and God himself will be with them and be their God. He will wipe every tear from their eyes. There will be no more death or mourning or crying or pain, for the old order of things has passed away.' He who was seated on the throne said, 'I am making everything new!'"

That is the promise – everything new! The old order of things passes away. Everything changes at the Second Coming of Jesus Christ.

THE SECOND COMING OF CHRIST

Some people contend that the idea of a second coming of Christ is just a wish or a hollow expectation without any basis in reality. Many hope that that is true because the idea of the return of Christ in power and glory to execute judgment is a frightening scenario. In spite of what people think, the Bible clearly establishes the fact that Jesus will return just as he went away – personally, purposefully and powerfully! (See Acts 1:11.)

The Biblical references to the Second Coming of Christ are numerous. John Mason, after an extended study of the New Testament, said, "There are 318 references in the New Testament to the Second Coming of Jesus Christ." Albert Barnes, author of *Notes on the New Testament*, said, "Let us look for the coming of the Lord: all that is hoped for depends on His reappearing." The Second Coming of Christ will result in resurrection, rewards and restitution.

HE WILL RETURN PERSONALLY

Jesus Christ will come again personally. Following the cross-resurrection event, He was taken up from His disciples bodily and personally. Angelic messengers told His disciples, "This same Jesus, who has been taken from you into heaven, will come back in the same way you have seen him go into heaven" (Acts 1:11).

Numerous references speak of His return in a personal sense. For instance, in John 14, He told His followers, "In my Father's house are many rooms; if it were not so, I would have told you. I am going there to prepare a place for you. And if I go and prepare a place for you, I will come back and take you to be with me that you also may be where I am." It is important to notice the reference to the personal pronoun "I." Jesus was telling His followers that He would return personally to them at some future time. He would go away for a time, but He would come back. He had already told them that where He was going, they couldn't follow him; but He tells them that it's OK – because, while they cannot follow Him, He will return to take them where He is. We need Jesus to come again because, on his own, no man can go to where He is.

The apostle Paul emphatically stated, "For the Lord himself will come down from heaven, with a loud command, with the voice of the archangel and with the trumpet call of God, and the dead in Christ will rise first. After that, we who are still alive and are left will be caught up together with them in the clouds to meet the Lord in the air. And so we will be with the Lord forever" (1 Thessalonians 4:16-17). Again, there is a strong emphasis on the fact that the Second Coming of Christ will be personal in nature.

We are to understand from Scripture that the Second Coming will be a noticeable event. It will not occur in secret. Some people understand Scripture to teach a secret coming of Christ at the end of the age to gather His people out of the pending distress and tribulation. Everything in Scripture teaches that the Second Coming of Christ will be personal and visible. There is nothing secretive about it. His message to His followers is, "So, if anyone tells you, 'There he is, out in the desert,' do not go out; or, 'Here he is, in the inner rooms,' do not believe it. For, as lightning that comes from the east is visible even in the west, so will be the coming of the Son of Man" (Matthew 24:26-27). The teaching is meant to emphasize the fact that no one who is alive at the time of the return of Christ will miss it, any more than you could miss a thunder and lightning storm that suddenly arises.

FALSE CHRISTS AND THE ANTICHRIST

Jesus went on to say, "For false Christs and false prophets will appear and perform great signs and miracles to deceive even the elect – if that were possible. See, I have told you ahead of time." In the last days, characters will appear on the stage of life, speaking great things and possibly even doing great things. People will wonder, "Where did this messiah come from? Who is he? Could he be the one to lead us out of the chaos and trouble of this life?" As we near the end of the age, the deceptions of Satan will be very powerful.

The subject of antichrist figures prominently in end-times Biblical prophecy. The idea is that a personality will appear on the stage of human history at the end of the age who – by his speech and actions – will command a large following.

The Bible speaks about an antichrist in four distinct passages – all written by John – but John never identifies who the antichrist is.

The four passages are 1 John 2:18, 1 John 2:22, 1 John 4:3 and 2 John 7. The appearance of this figure is said to be between the first and second advents of Christ, and John suggests that there will be many. However, the sense that one specific antichrist may rise to power during the end times is also conveyed by the passages in 1 John. It is said that he will deny that Jesus is the Christ as well as deny God the Father. He will be a liar and a deceiver (sound familiar?). From Genesis through Revelation, the Bible consistently speaks of Satan as a liar and a deceiver who covets the place of God.

Popular prophetic speakers – especially television evangelists – have suggested a number of possible candidates for the title, including presidents of the United States, other heads of state, religious leaders (including the pope), or almost any figure who comes on the scene of life with a godless agenda and an attractive personality or charisma.

John uses the term "antichrist" to describe this figure, while other writers of Scripture use different names but seem to be speaking of the same character. For instance, Paul (writing in 2 Thessalonians 2) speaks of the appearance of a "man of sin" or "son of perdition." The term "antichrist" doesn't appear in the Book of Revelation. However, some Biblical teachers believe that the beast mentioned in Revelation 13 and the false prophet mentioned in Revelation 16 are references to the same figure.

Some Bible teachers see the antichrist in Daniel's vision of the four beasts (Daniel 7:1-8), corresponding with the image of Daniel 2. In the vision of Daniel, there is a little horn that rises out of the fourth empire (identified as Rome), whose characteristics correspond to what is stated elsewhere about the antichrist or man of sin.

Whatever you understand about who or what the antichrist is, the Bible is clear about the character of antichrist. He is a liar and a deceiver.

For one thing, Scripture defines "antichrist" as anyone who doesn't believe in the deity of Jesus Christ and passionately teaches against Christ. John said that at the time of his writing there were already many antichrists in the world. Imagine what he might say about the twenty-first century!

Everything that I read in Scripture points clearly to Satan as the primary antichrist. From the time of his rebellion in heaven, he has been against (anti) Christ and the purposes of God. He is the only "anti" being specifically named in Scripture. Satan is a super-human spirit being who – from the time of his rebellion in heaven – has been at work in God's creation to exalt himself as God (Isaiah 14:12-14), opposing Jesus Christ and making war on the Church. He is a pseudo- deity. His character strikingly corresponds to every-thing that the Bible says about antichrist. He is the master deceiver.

The reason why John can say that there were already many antichrists in the world is because Satan rules over a host of fallen angels and is capable of demonizing human beings. Because Satan is the primary antichrist with superhuman powers, controlling the time/space continuum (1 John 5:19), he may indwell a person, a system of government or a religious order that take on his character and do his bidding. As the days grow shorter and he knows his time is running out, his deceptions may become more grandiose and his demonic activity more personal.

UNDERSTANDINGS ABOUT THE SECOND COMING OF CHRIST

When Jesus returns in power and glory at the end of the age, there won't be anything secret or quiet about it. He will be visible to all and recognized by all. No one will be standing around asking, "Who is this?"

Not everyone believes in a one-time, personal and visible return of Christ. The simple Biblical view of the personal, visible and glo-rious return of Christ at the end of the age has been corrupted over the years by well-meaning teachers of Scripture who have reinter-preted the teaching by adding colorful but erroneous ideas.

Some have taught that the Second Coming of Christ is a spiritual event, in which Christ "comes" to live in a person's heart through faith. Jesus does come to live in a person's heart through His Holy Spirit, but the coming of Christ in conversion is not what the Bible means when it speaks of the Second Coming of Christ.

Still others contend that the Second Coming occurs at death when the Lord "comes" to take the deceased believer home. Going home to be with the Lord is thought to be the Second Coming. This popular idea is not what the Bible teaches about the Second Coming of Christ.

Another of today's widely held teachings is that the Second Coming of Christ is a multi-staged phenomenon. According to this theory, the first stage of the Second Coming is an event known as "the rapture." This theory is held by the majority of Christians in the twenty-first century, largely influenced by the writings of Hal Lindsey and – more recently – by popular televangelists and the writings of Tim LaHaye and Jerry Jenkins. Their greatest contribution to fueling this position is in the fictional *Left Behind* series.

Those who believe in the rapture of the Church believe that Christ will come suddenly and unexpectedly, secretly snatching all living Christians up into heaven to escape the imminent tribulation coming on the earth. This cataclysmic event will be unlike anything that has ever occurred in the history of the universe. People will suddenly disappear without warning or announcement, leaving behind a few billion unbelievers to endure the outpouring of God's wrath in the tribulation. There will be global confusion as millions are unaccounted for without explanation. Few will know what has happened.

The concept is mind-boggling and bizarre. A jet airliner, flying at 41,000 feet between Paris and New York, is suddenly left with an empty cockpit as the pilot has been raptured. No one is able to explain what happened to the plane or the 376 passengers on board, some of who also mysteriously disappeared.

A major league baseball game is in the ninth inning at Yankee Stadium. The Yankees are at bat, needing a run to win the game. The bases are loaded, with two outs and two strikes on the batter. The pitcher winds up and delivers a fastball towards home plate. In the split second that it takes for the ball to reach the catcher's mitt, the batter disappears – raptured! The umpire behind the plate is baffled. Is it strike three? Is it a no pitch? How does he call it? No one called time out. If it's strike three, who struck out, since there wasn't anyone in the batter's box?

A worship service is taking place at a large church in Chicago. Parishioners are enthusiastically engaged in singing and clapping as the worship band leads in worship. Suddenly, almost everyone disappears, while a few in the congregation are wondering what happened. Where did everyone go so quickly? The few that are left behind are confused, trying to make sense of everyone's disappearance.

The idea of a secret rapture of the Church is a popular teaching even though the word "rapture" does not appear in the Bible. The idea associated with the use of the term is to describe a catching up, which is a teaching of the Apostle Paul in 1 Thessalonians 4:17, which reads, "After that, we who are still alive and are left will be caught up together with them in the clouds to meet the Lord in the air. And so we will be with the Lord forever."

In the context of this verse, the Apostle Paul was speaking of a sequence of events that culminate in being caught up. The events that Paul describes here are spectacular and earthshaking – a global phenomenon. The personal return of Christ to earth is accompanied by a shout, a loud command and a trumpet blast. The resurrection takes place, after which we who are alive and remain will be caught up with them to meet the Lord in the air as part of His glorious victory parade.

To the best of my knowledge, this is the only place in the Bible that addresses this subject, and there isn't anything secretive about it. Jesus will come again – once and for all, personably, visibly and powerfully – and every eye shall see Him.

RECOGNITION OF CHRIST

One may wonder how we will know Christ from other heavenly luminaries. I am convinced that there will be distinguishing characteristics. For one thing, following His resurrection with a post-resurrection body, His identity was made known by the fact that He could show His scars (from the crucifixion) to His followers. "On the evening of that first day of the week, when the disciples were together, with the doors locked for fear of the Jews, Jesus came and stood among them and said, 'Peace be with you!' After He said this, He showed them His hands and side. The disciples were overjoyed when they saw the Lord" (John 20:19-20).

"Now Thomas (called Didymus), one of the Twelve, was not with the disciples when Jesus came. So the other disciples told him, 'We have seen the Lord!' But he said to them, 'Unless I see the nail marks in his hands and put my finger where the nails were, and put my hand into his side, I will not believe it'" (John 20:24-27).

A week later, His disciples were in the house again, and Thomas was with them. Though the doors were locked, Jesus came and stood among them and said, "Peace be with you!" Then He said to Thomas, "Put your finger here; see my hands. Reach out your hand and put it into my side. Stop doubting and believe."

Jesus will be identifiable because of the uniqueness of His body. He alone is the Savior. He alone paid the penalty for our sins, and this feature means that we will never forget it throughout eternity.

However, His uniqueness is not confined to His bodily features. As our Redeemer, He will be enthroned in a glory that only He possesses. Paul referred to this in 2 Thessalonians 1, in discussing His triumph over the forces of evil. "God is just: He will pay back trouble to those who trouble you and give relief to you who are troubled, and to us as well. This will happen when the Lord Jesus is revealed from heaven in blazing fire with His powerful angels. He will punish those who do not know God and do not obey the gospel of our Lord Jesus. They will be punished with everlasting destruction and shut out from the presence of the Lord and from the majesty of his power on the day He comes to be glorified in His holy people and to be marveled at among all those who have believed. This includes you, because you believed our testimony to you" (2 Thessalonians 1:6-10). The "glorification" that Paul spoke about means that Jesus will be distinguishable by this special aura reserved for the Redeemer.

There is a glory – or brightness – that belongs exclusively to the realm of deity. One classic passage is found in Exodus 33. Moses had been chosen by God to lead His people out of captivity, but Moses was concerned that the project could be a catastrophe if he tried to do this awesome thing on his own. God and Moses were engaged in conversation about how Moses could be assured that God would lead him and go with him. The Lord had assured Moses that His presence would go with him, but Moses wasn't satisfied with that assurance. God had told Moses that He even knows his name. After all, this was the baby that was miraculously spared at birth, and God had been with him throughout his life. He had met the Lord at the burning bush in the desert and seen His glory. Now he asks the Lord to show him His glory.

What follows in the Exodus passage demonstrates the awesomeness of His glory. God tells Moses that he will pass by him, but – because no one can see Him and live – He will hide Moses in a cleft of a rock while His glory passes by, after which Moses will be permitted to see the afterglow. The glory of God is illustrated by a consuming brightness.

We talk about the glory of God – and about doing things to the praise of His glory – but, for the most part, it is language that we use without a great deal of understanding. The term "glory" is used in different ways in Scripture. In the New Testament, as in the Exodus passage, its meaning has a sense of brightness, brilliance or splendor when used about the presence of God. At the transfiguration (Luke 9:28ff), a supernatural brightness was observed when Jesus took Peter, John and James to the mountain to pray. It was on this occasion that the appearance of His face was changed and His clothes became dazzling white. In this connection, Peter and the others were said to have seen His glory. Similarly, when the angel appeared to the shepherds in the field on the occasion of the birth of Jesus (Luke 2:9), there was the presence of a great brightness or glory associated with the appearance of the angel.

Matthew 16:27 makes reference to Christ coming in the glory of His Father. This is obviously a statement about a glory belonging to the realm of deity that man can only talk about. When Jesus came to earth as our Savior, He laid aside this glory, which He had before the world was created. Philippians 2:7 describes how he "emptied himself" of this glory when he left the portals of glory. John records the prayer of Jesus in John 17, in which Jesus prays that the Father will clothe Him in the glory that He previously had with the Father.

There is a glory of deity that Christ will exhibit when He comes again to be glorified in the redeemed (2 Thessalonians 1:10). The Second Coming of Jesus Christ will be a glorious spectacle accompanied by brightness so strong as to destroy Satan and all his demons and all the works of evil (2 Thessalonians 2:8).

Everyone who has ever lived will see Jesus coming on the clouds of glory. Revelation 1:7 reads, "Look, he is coming with the clouds, and every eye will see him, even those who pierced him; and all the peoples of the earth will mourn because of him. So shall it be! Amen."

Matthew 24:29-31 says, "Immediately after the distress of those days the sun will be darkened, and the moon will not give its light; the stars will fall from the sky, and the heavenly bodies will be shaken. At that time, the sign of the Son of Man will appear in the sky, and all the nations of the earth will mourn. They will see the Son of Man coming on the clouds of the sky, with power and great glory."

CHRIST WILL COME AGAIN PURPOSEFULLY

Not only is the Second Coming of Christ a visible, personal return, it is a purposeful return. His work was not completed in His first advent. He came on a mission of redemption and reconciliation. That part of His mission was completed in the cross-resurrection event. However, as the last Adam, the author of a new creation, something remains to be completed at His Second Coming.

God's plan required a redeemer who would provide an acceptable sacrifice for sin and who would break the power of sin by defeating death (the penalty for sin). Christ accomplished this in His first Advent. There remains, then, the completion of God's plan when Jesus presents the trophies of His grace to the Father, which requires the Second Coming of Jesus Christ at the end of the age (Ephesians 5:27; Jude 24).

The Second Coming of Jesus Christ is the culminating event in God's great plan of world redemption. It is a necessary corollary to the incarnation, cross, resurrection and ascension. Reason requires it, as Dr. R.O. White says, "The hope of Christ's return is not indulging in an emotional binge; it is the logical conviction that Christ's Lordship over history requires it. Without an advent goal, the course of history seems a dreary vista of endless cycles of sin, suffering and sorrow, eternally repeated in a meaningless dance of phantoms."

At the Second Coming of Jesus Christ, dramatic developments take place that alter the course of human history and usher in the eternal Kingdom of God.

THERE WILL BE A RESURRECTION OF THE DEAD

One major development that occurs at the Second Coming of Christ is the resurrection of the dead. Resurrection is a prominent teaching of the Bible. Without resurrection, no person who has ever lived can live again. Death is an enemy that prevents a person from ever experiencing the fulfillment of God's eternal purpose of living forever in the Paradise of God. Death is not the continuation of life in a different form and place. Death is the absence of life. The terms "death" and "life" are contradictory. They do not mean the same thing.

Scripture is clear about the need for resurrection, the fact of resurrection and the time of resurrection:

THE NEED FOR RESURRECTION

The Apostle Paul wrote to the church at Corinth and clearly established the need for a personal resurrection. In 1 Corinthians 15:12-19, he said, "But if it is preached that Christ has been raised from the dead, how can some of you say that there is no resurrection of the dead? If there is no resurrection of the dead, then not even Christ has been raised. And if Christ has not been raised, our preaching is useless and so is your faith. More than that, we are then found to be false witnesses about God, for we have testified about God that He raised Christ from the dead. But He did not raise Him if in fact the dead are not raised. For if the dead are not raised, then Christ has not been raised either. And if Christ has not been raised, your faith is futile; you are still in your sins. Then those also who have fallen asleep in Christ are lost. If only for this life we have hope in Christ, we are to be pitied more than all men."

THE FACT OF RESURRECTION

In this same passage, he stated the fact of resurrection. "But Christ has indeed been raised from the dead, the first fruits of those who have fallen asleep. For since death came through a man, the resurrection of the dead comes also through a man. For as in Adam all die, so in Christ all will be made alive" (1 Corinthians 15:20-22).

He went on to mark the time of the resurrection with the Second Coming of Christ. "But each in his own turn: Christ, the first fruits;

then, when he comes, those who belong to him" (1 Corinthians 15:23).

Several other scriptures make a clear reference to the fact of resurrection:

"Do not be amazed at this, for a time is coming when all who are in their graves will hear his voice and come out – those who have done good will rise to live, and those who have done evil will rise to be condemned" (John 5:28-29).

"For my Father's will is that everyone who looks to the Son and believes in him shall have eternal life, and I will raise him up at the last day" (John 6:40).

"For the Lord himself will come down from heaven, with a loud command, with the voice of the archangel and with the trumpet call of God, and the dead in Christ will rise first. After that, we who are still alive and are left will be caught up together with them in the clouds to meet the Lord in the air. And so we will be with the Lord forever" (1 Thessalonians 4:16-17).

Jesus is coming again to raise the dead. He alone has the power and the authority to destroy this enemy of man. "Since the children have flesh and blood, he too shared in their humanity so that by his death he might destroy him who holds the power of death – that is, the devil – and free those who all their lives were held in slavery by their fear of death" (Hebrews 2:14-15).

When Jesus arose victorious over death and the grave, He declared to His followers that all power and authority had been given to Him. He is the supreme Lord, who holds in His hand the keys of death and the grave. "I am the Living One; I was dead, and behold I am alive forever and ever! And I hold the keys of death and Hades" (Revelation 1:18).

He alone can and will raise the dead. Because He lives, we too shall live.

THERE WILL BE A UNIVERSAL JUDGMENT

The Second Coming of Jesus Christ leads to judgment for mankind. "For he has set a day when he will judge the world with justice by the man he has appointed" (Acts 17:31). "I charge thee therefore before God, and the Lord Jesus Christ, who shall judge the quick and the dead at His appearing and his kingdom" (2 Timothy 4:1).

For many people, the idea of a divine judgment never crosses their mind. They live from day to day, respecting the laws of the state, but they are oblivious to the moral law of God.

The Bible clearly states that everyone who has ever lived will be summoned to stand before the Judge of the universe when Jesus comes again. "For we must all appear before the judgment seat of Christ, that each one may receive what is due him for the things done while in the body, whether good or bad" (2 Corinthians 5:10).

Every person is accountable to the sovereign God who created him. Divine accountability has always been a factor in man's relationship to God.

This accountability can be seen in the very beginning of time, when God created man and placed him in His garden paradise. God gave man dominion so that he was free to go wherever he chose to go and to do whatever he chose to do. Man was God's caretaker as king of the earth.

God set a boundary for man to remind him that he was subservient to his Creator. There would be a penalty to pay if man transgressed the boundary that God had clearly established. God built accountability into His relationship with man from the beginning of time.

Another classic illustration of divine accountability and judgment occurred at the time of Noah. The massive flood that destroyed all living things except those who were sheltered in the Ark was an act of divine judgment.

Jesus referred to this event when He was talking with His disciples about His Second Coming and the judgment that was to come. "As it was in the days of Noah, so it will be at the coming of the Son of Man. For in the days before the flood, people were eating and drinking, marrying and giving in marriage, up to the day Noah entered the ark; and they knew nothing about what would happen until the flood came and took them all away. That is how it will be at the coming of the Son of Man" (Matthew 24:37-39).

Peter also spoke of the flood in Noah's day as a reminder that divine judgment is a certainty at the end of the present age. "First of all, you must understand that in the last days scoffers will come, scoffing and following their own evil desires. They will say, 'Where is this "coming" He promised? Ever since our fathers died, everything goes on as it has since the beginning of creation.' But they deliberately forget that long ago by God's word the heavens existed and the earth was formed out of water and by water. By these waters also the world of that time was deluged and destroyed. By the same word the present heavens and earth are reserved for fire, being kept for the day of judgment and destruction of ungodly men" (2 Peter 3:3-7).

The final judgment, which takes place at the Second Coming of Jesus Christ, is two- dimensional. The first dimension of the final judgment is that of personal salvation. Jesus came into the world on a mission of salvation. People needed to be saved from the wrath of God, and Jesus was the only one who could bring salvation. Everything associated with His first Advent had to do with personal salvation. "For the Son of Man came to seek and to save what was lost" (Luke 19:10).

God went to extraordinary lengths to save man from the guilt, power and consequence of his sin. Salvation is an act of divine grace and love. The only reason why Jesus laid aside the glory that He had with the Father and entered the realm of humanity as the last Adam was to make possible our salvation.

Sin disqualifies one from ever entering God's Kingdom paradise, and there isn't any one of us who could do anything to change that reality. The Bible says that we have all sinned and stand under the condemnation of God. "For all have sinned and fall short of the glory of God" (Romans 3:23). Furthermore, "Whoever believes in him is not condemned, but whoever does not believe stands condemned already because he has not believed in the name of God's one and only Son" (John 3:18).

The primary issue on the day of divine judgment is one's personal salvation. On that day, God will not be interested in how nice a person you are. He won't be primarily interested in your philanthropy, your achievements or your recognitions. He won't be deciding your ultimate destiny on the basis of your religious practices or denominational affiliation. On the day of divine judgment, the primary issue will be one's personal salvation.

The only question that will matter is, "What has been your response to God's gracious offer of salvation? Have you accepted Jesus Christ as your personal Lord and Savior? Have you been born again?" That's the issue. Jesus declared, "I tell you the truth, no one can see the kingdom of God unless he is born again" (John 3:3).

The day of divine judgment is a day of demarcation, of separation and differentiation. Neither the color of one's skin nor his nationality, religious orientation or social pedigree will have any bearing on his case. On that day, there will only be two classes of people – the saved and the lost.

Revelation 20 pictures the final judgment as a legal setting in which the Judge is seated on His throne and before Him are gathered the defendants who must make a convincing case to be set free. "Then I saw a great white throne and Him who was seated on it. Earth and sky fled from His presence, and there was no place for them. And I saw the dead, great and small, standing before the throne, and books were opened. Another book was opened, which is the book of life. The dead were judged according to what they had done as recorded in the books" (Revelation 20:11-13).

This is an awesome scene. The Judge sits on his throne with all the evidence against the defendants who stand before Him written in the books of heaven. When one considers that the record of his life is recorded in heaven, he realizes that he cannot possibly make a case for himself that will convince the Judge to overlook his wrongs and extend mercy.

Added to this sobering thought is the idea that the "accuser" stands nearby ready to remind the Judge that all these so-called believers are nothing more than guilty sinners deserving of death – just read the books! It appears that Satan exercises the role of accuser before the throne of God. "Then I heard a loud voice in heaven say: 'Now have come the salvation and the power and the kingdom of our God, and the authority of his Christ. For the accuser of our brothers, who accuses them before our God day and night, has been hurled down.'" (Revelation 12:10). If Satan is still around when the final judgment takes place, I suspect that he will be there to do all in his power to thwart the redemptive program of our Lord, but it will be to no avail.

When the books are opened to reveal the record of my life, the accuser will have plenty to bring up to make a case why I shouldn't enter the Kingdom of God. However, when God opens the books, he will see written in blood across the pages of my life story the word "forgiven" – initialed, "JC!"

That's what it means to be saved. Sins are forgiven – blotted out by the blood of Christ – never to be remembered against us anymore! The password to the Kingdom of God is "Jesus."

The primary issue in divine judgment is one's personal salvation, but beyond that is the question of the believer's stewardship of life. The question is, "What have you done as a believer with the gift(s) that God has given you to be used in His Kingdom service?"

We have all been given some gift to use in service to Christ. "The end of all things is near. Therefore be clear-minded and self-controlled so that you can pray. Above all, love each other deeply, because love covers over a multitude of sins. Offer hospitality to one another without grumbling. Each one should use whatever gift he has received to serve others, faithfully administering God's grace in its various forms. If anyone speaks, he should do it as one speaking the very words of God. If anyone serves, he should do it with the strength God provides, so that in all things God may be praised through Jesus Christ. To him be the glory and the power forever and ever. Amen" (1 Peter 4:7-11).

There are a variety of gifts, and it would appear from Scripture that every believer has been given one or more gifts. Some gifts are more prominent than others, but all are necessary and are of equal value. Unfortunately, the flesh sometimes enters into our use of these gifts, and their purpose and usefulness is distorted. If a person does anything in the name of Jesus for any other reason than to serve the body of Christ and bring honor and glory to Christ, he is doing it for the wrong reason.

There is a popular acronym that has been around for a long time: WWJD. It stands for the words, "What Would Jesus Do?" That's an important question, which – if applied properly to life's decision-making process – should prove helpful. Another acronym that I created for my personal use is DIGG – "Does It Glorify God?" If a person considers the outcome of his thoughts or actions in the light of his life purpose – to glorify God – it should make a real difference.

Everything about one's life, speech, actions and service should be directed toward the service of one another, the well-being of the Body of Christ, and for the praise and glory of Jesus Christ our Lord. At the glorious Second Coming of Jesus Christ, divine judgment will take place when the sovereign God of the universe brings man to complete accountability.

THERE WILL BE REWARDS AND PUNISHMENT

All of life moves toward destiny. According to the Bible, there are two destinies that will be determined in the judgment. Everyone will be either saved or lost – will live forever or experience eternal death in the fires of hell.

The judgment determines rewards and punishment for every person who has ever lived. Following the judgment sinners will be punished. "Then He will say to those on His left, 'Depart from me, you who are cursed, into the eternal fire prepared for the devil and his angels. For I was hungry and you gave me nothing to eat, I was thirsty and you gave me nothing to drink, I was a stranger and you did not invite me in, I needed clothes and you did not clothe me, I was sick and in prison and you did not look after me.' They also will answer, 'Lord, when did we see you hungry or thirsty or a stranger or needing clothes or sick or in prison, and did not help you?' He will reply, 'I tell you the truth, whatever you did not do for one of the least of these, you did not do for me.' Then they will go away to eternal punishment, but the righteous to eternal life" (Matthew 25:41-46).

"God is just: He will pay back trouble to those who trouble you and give relief to you who are troubled, and to us as well. This will happen when the Lord Jesus is revealed from heaven in blazing fire with his powerful angels. He will punish those who do not know God and do not obey the gospel of our Lord Jesus. They will be punished with everlasting destruction and shut out from the presence of the Lord and from the majesty of His power on the day He comes to be glorified in His holy people and to be marveled at among all those who have believed. This includes you, because you believed our testimony to you" (2 Thessalonians 1:6-10).

"Enoch, the seventh from Adam, prophesied about these men: 'See, the Lord is coming with thousands upon thousands of his holy ones to judge everyone, and to convict all the ungodly of all the ungodly acts they have done in the ungodly way, and of all the harsh words ungodly sinners have spoken against him.'" (Jude 14-16).

"The Son of Man is going to come in his Father's glory with his angels, and then he will reward each person according to what he has done" (Matthew 16:27).

THE SECOND DEATH AS PUNISHMENT FOR SIN

The second death is death from which there is no prospect of ever being resurrected. "Blessed and holy are those who have part in the first resurrection. The second death has no power over them" (Revelation 20:6).

"Then death and Hades were thrown into the lake of fire. The lake of fire is the second death. If anyone's name was not found written in the book of life, he was thrown into the lake of fire" (Revelation 20:14-15).

"But the cowardly, the unbelieving, the vile, the murderers, the sexually immoral, those who practice magic arts, the idolaters and all liars – their place will be in the fiery lake of burning sulfur. This is the second death" (Revelation 21:8).

The punishment of the second death, about which the Bible speaks, is final and complete. I'm not sure that people understand the finality of divine punishment for sin. God will not have anything remaining in His creation that offends His nature, defeats His purpose or pollutes His Paradise.

The idea that a fire could be burning forever – with the stench of human refuse that is discarded there – is unbiblical and contrary to the nature of God. God will cleanse the universe of all things that are contrary to His purpose and plan.

THE REALITY OF HELL

The fire of hell is real, powerful and eternal in respect to its effect – so much so that those who are cast into the lake of fire are consumed by the fire to the extent that nothing remains of them, whatsoever. The language of Scripture regarding the destruction of the wicked leaves nothing to one's imagination. "I will sing to the Lord all my life; I will sing praise to my God as long as I live. May my meditation be pleasing to him, as I rejoice in the Lord. But may sinners vanish from the earth and the wicked be no more" (Psalm 104:33-35).

"For as ye have drunk upon my holy mountain, so shall all the heathen drink continually, yea, they shall drink, and they shall swallow down, and they shall be as though they had not been" (Obadiah 16).

The idea of the final, complete destruction of the wicked is the most severe fate that one could possibly experience. To be is what makes life meaningful. God is the ground of all being and in His self- revelation to Moses, He told Moses His name was "I am". "I am" is a statement of being. I am somebody. I live; I know; I am known. In the destruction of the wicked in the last day, one's fate is tantamount to non-being – as if one never existed. Jesus spoke of the judgment of the ungodly when he said, "Not everyone who says to Me, 'Lord, Lord,' shall enter into the kingdom of heaven; but he that does the will of my Father which is in heaven. Many will say to Me in that day, 'Lord, Lord, have we not prophesied in thy name? and in thy name have cast out devils? and in thy name done many wonderful works?' And then will I profess unto them, I never knew you: depart from Me, ye that work iniquity" (Matthew 7:21-23).

To be looked upon by the Creator as one whom He never knew has to be the most devastating sentence ever imposed. Who I am never existed. If Jesus never knew you, you are nothing – non-being.

William Shakespeare – in his famous play, *Hamlet* – made a profound statement at the outset of Act Three, Scene One, in which Hamlet asks the question, "To be, or not to be, that is the question." The context of this opening line of the soliloquy seems to indicate that Shakespeare may have had a much better understanding of human destiny than most people think. This question is one of the most profound in all of human literature. There is a discussion in the context of the question concerning all of the ills that are associated with life and the sense that death would relieve one of these adversities. The question is more than just a question of life and death. It is a question of being verses non-being. The question is profound.

Interestingly, the Bible uses the figure of highly combustible material to illustrate what happens to a person in hell fire. Terms associated with the end of all things are highly combustible terms like "weeds" and "chaff," which are said to be burned up, destroyed and perish. "As the weeds are pulled up and burned in the fire, so it will be at the end of the age. The Son of Man will send out His angels, and they will weed out of His kingdom everything that causes sin and all who do evil. They will throw them into the fiery furnace, where there will be weeping and gnashing of teeth" (Matthew 13:40-43). "They will be entangled among thorns and drunk from their wine; they will be consumed like dry stubble" (Nahum 1:10). "Surely the day is coming; it will burn like a furnace. All the arrogant and every evildoer will be stubble, and that day that is coming will set them on fire, says the Lord Almighty. Not a root or a branch will be left to them" (Malachi 4:1-2). "But the wicked will perish: the Lord's enemies will be like the beauty of the fields, they will vanish – vanish like smoke" (Psalm 37:20).

The second death – as punishment for sin – is total, complete and final, resulting in the eternal destruction of the sinner. They will be no more – as if they never existed –non-being.

Sinners will suffer eternal punishment, and the righteous will be rewarded with unending life – not because of any goodness or merit they possess, but because of the righteousness of Christ, which is imputed to them.

ETERNAL LIFE IS REAL

Eternal death is death forever. Eternal life is life forever. "Then they will go away to eternal punishment, but the righteous to eternal life" (Matthew 25:46).

"Behold, I am coming soon! My reward is with Me, and I will give to everyone according to what he has done" (Revelation 22:12).

"But because of your stubbornness and your unrepentant heart, you are storing up wrath against yourself for the day of God's wrath, when his righteous judgment will be revealed. God will give to each person according to what he has done. To those who by persistence in doing good seek glory, honor and immortality, He will give eternal life. But for those who are self-seeking and who reject the truth and follow evil, there will be wrath and anger. There will be trouble and distress for every human being who does evil: first for the Jew, then for the Gentile; but glory, honor and peace for everyone who does good: first for the Jew, then for the Gentile. For God does not show favoritism" (Romans 2:5-11).

"And when the Chief Shepherd appears, you will receive the crown of glory that will never fade away" (1 Peter 5:4).

When Christ returns at the end of the age, He will be glorified in His saints – the trophies of His grace – the new creation. "When Christ, who is your life, appears, then you also will appear with him in glory" (Colossians 3:4).

"God is just: He will pay back trouble to those who trouble you and give relief to you who are troubled, and to us as well. This will happen when the Lord Jesus is revealed from heaven in blazing fire with His powerful angels. He will punish those who do not know God and do not obey the gospel of our Lord Jesus. They will be punished with everlasting destruction and shut out from the presence of the Lord and from the majesty of his power on the day He comes to be glorified in His holy people and to be marveled at among all those who have believed. This includes you, because you believed our testimony to you" (2 Thessalonians 1:6-10).

THERE WILL BE A NEW HEAVEN AND A NEW EARTH

One of the things that will happen at the time of His appearing is the passing away of the old order of things, including the present heaven and earth. He will make everything new. "Behold, I will create new heavens and a new earth. The former things will not be remembered, nor will they come to mind. But be glad and rejoice forever in what I will create" (Isaiah 65:17-18).

"As the new heavens and the new earth that I make will endure before me, declares the Lord, so will your name and descendants endure" (Isaiah 66:22).

"But in keeping with his promise we are looking forward to a new heaven and a new earth, the home of righteousness" (2 Peter 3:13).

"Then I saw a new heaven and a new earth, for the first heaven and the first earth had passed away, and there was no longer any sea. I saw the Holy City, the new Jerusalem, coming down out of heaven from God, prepared as a bride beautifully dressed for her husband. And I heard a loud voice from the throne saying, 'Now the dwelling of God is with men, and He will live with them. They will be His people, and God Himself will be with them and be their God. He will wipe every tear from their eyes. There will be no more death or mourning or crying or pain, for the old order of things has passed away.' He who was seated on the throne said, 'I am making everything new!' Then he said, 'Write this down, for these words are trustworthy and true'" (Revelation 21:1-5).

The eternal Kingdom of our Lord will be established, and He will reign. "In the time of those kings, the God of heaven will set up a kingdom that will never be destroyed, nor will it be left to another people. It will crush all those kingdoms and bring them to an end, but it will itself endure forever" (Daniel 2:44).

"He was given authority, glory and sovereign power; all peoples, nations and men of every language worshiped him. His dominion is an everlasting dominion that will not pass away, and his kingdom is one that will never be destroyed" (Daniel 7:14).

"When the Son of Man comes in his glory, and all the angels with him, he will sit on his throne in heavenly glory" (Matthew 25:31).

"The Lord will be king over the whole earth. On that day there will be one Lord, and his name the only name" (Zechariah 14:9).

"For to us a child is born, to us a son is given, and the government will be on His shoulders. And He will be called Wonderful Counselor, Mighty God, Everlasting Father, Prince of Peace. Of the increase of His government and peace there will be no end. He will reign on David's throne and over his kingdom, establishing and upholding it with justice and righteousness from that time on and forever. The zeal of the Lord Almighty will accomplish this" (Isaiah 9:6-7).

"The seventh angel sounded his trumpet, and there were loud voices in heaven, which said: 'The kingdom of the world has become the kingdom of our Lord and of His Christ, and He will reign forever and ever'" (Revelation 11:15). Jesus is coming again, and He will reign forever in the paradise of God.

CHAPTER 6

FORECASTING THE FUTURE – CONTINUED

I n the New Testament, the fact of the Second Coming of Jesus Christ is a clearly established doctrine. It is the one event to which all Biblical prophecy points as the climactic event of human history. The second coming of Jesus Christ inaugurates the Kingdom age as a transitional moment between time and eternity.

THE QUESTION OF TIME

The question that most people have is not whether or not Jesus will return – or even what will happen when He returns – but rather, "When will He return?" The subject of "when" is difficult to answer. Some have thought that they had it figured out, and they set a date when they expected it to occur. Date setting is a bad hobby to get into. The Bible clearly states that no one knows the time of this stupendous development – only God the Father.

Acts 1:6-8 speaks of an encounter that Jesus had with His disciples following His resurrection. "So when they met together, they asked him, 'Lord, are you at this time going to restore the kingdom to Israel?' He said to them: 'It is not for you to know the times or dates the Father has set by his own authority.'"

"No one knows about that day or hour, not even the angels in heaven, nor the Son, but only the Father. Be on guard! Be alert! You do not know when that time will come" (Mark 13:32-33). No one knows when that time will come.

GOD AND TIME

The word "time" is an interesting word. What is time to God? God is timeless – infinite. He doesn't look at a clock or a calendar. He created time for man. We are creatures of time. Everything we do is measured in some way by time. We measure our life by years of time; we measure our years by months; we measure our months by days; and we measure our days by hours. We watch the calendar, and we pay attention to the clock. Time is important to us, but not to God. So, if you ask the question, "What time is it, prophetically?" the answer is only relevant to man. God is always on time. That is, when time reaches its fulfillment – everything it was created to hold – God will step into history, and time will be no more. That's the way it has always been. Galatians 4:4 says, "But when the time had fully come ('in the fullness of time,' KJV), God sent his Son, born of a woman, born under law, to redeem those under law, that we might receive the full rights of sons."

In the human dispensation of time, God has certain developments that must take place to accomplish His purposes; and, when time has reached its fulfillment – when everything that God created time to hold is realized – it will usher in eternity.

TIME AND ETERNITY

In eternity past, there wasn't any time; and, in eternity future, there won't be any time. This world – the existence of man – is an interruption in eternity in the sense that God had a purpose to accomplish, and that purpose had a time limit (from our perspective). The rebellion of Satan at some point in eternity past prompted God to create a world – and a world of human beings – to complement the realm of spirit beings, in order to rid his creation of all things that offend so that He would possess a people who would live in unbroken fellowship with Him in His paradise, for His glory, forever.

WHEN IS SOON?

The general sense is that He is coming "soon." That, too, is an interesting word. "Soon" doesn't necessarily mean, "right away" (as we normally use the term). "Soon" is a word of anticipation and expectation. It is a word that is defined by the context in which it is used. It may mean "in a few minutes," or "in a few hours" or "any day now." It may simply mean "shortly" or "sooner rather than later." Almost everyone has had the experience of taking a trip with some children in the car who have no idea of distance or time. They just know that they are going somewhere. After traveling a short distance, one of them questions, "Are we there yet?" Another asks, "How much longer?" The standard reply in these situations is, "Pretty soon! Take a nap; and, when you wake up, we will be there." Sure! "Soon" can't be tied to an hour or a date. All that we know is that it anticipates something that is coming in the future. It is relative and anticipatory.

When the Bible uses the word "soon" in the context of the Second Coming of Christ, it is anticipatory; it suggests that the Second Coming could occur at any time – consequently, we must be always ready. It speaks to the fact that the Second Coming is always viewed as imminent – something that has the possibility of occurring at any time. In that sense, it is understood as "soon."

At any rate, the timing of His coming was of utmost interest to His disciples, even though they didn't have the body of Scripture that we have today to enlighten them. When Jesus met with them on the Mount of Olives, they wanted to know when he would return. "As Jesus was sitting on the Mount of Olives, the disciples came to him privately. 'Tell us,' they said, 'when will this happen, and what will be the sign of your coming and of the end of the age?'" (Matthew 24:3).

DISCERNING THE TIMES

While we can't know the actual time of His coming, I believe that we can know the season of the end. There are numerous clues in Scripture. On one occasion, Jesus told the Pharisees, "When evening comes, you say, 'It will be fair weather, for the sky is red,' and in the morning, 'Today it will be stormy, for the sky is red and overcast.' You know how to interpret the appearance of the sky, but you cannot interpret the signs of the times" (Matthew 16:2-3). From this statement, it would appear that Jesus was telling the Pharisees and Sadducees that if they paid attention to what God was doing in the world, they would have a better understanding of the times.

People who believe in the Second Coming of Jesus as their future hope have always tried to ascertain when His return would take place. The problem that we face in calculating the "when" is the difficulty that we have in reading the signs. N.T. Wright, in his book, *Surprised by Hope*, makes this observation, "All language about the future, as any economist or politician will tell you, is simply a set of signposts pointing into a fog." In other words, no one really knows what next month will be like, what next year will be like or what the next decade will be like. This uncertainty about the future is distressing. We want to know what tomorrow might bring.

In the first century, Jesus' followers lived in daily expectation of His return. His disciples were familiar with this pattern of His coming and going. In the three years during which they walked with Him, He would often leave them – sometimes unannounced – but he always came back. Why should it be any different this time? They expected His return at any time. Following his resurrection and ascension – and as days stretched into months and years – questions arose about if and when He would return and what His absence might mean to those who fell asleep in death. This consternation prompted Paul to write to the church at Thessalonica to reassure them that His apparent delay didn't change anything.

Throughout the history of the Christian Church, men of God have studied the Scriptures and considered times when they felt that the Bible predicted His return. World conditions influenced how people thought about the Second Coming. When things are going well, people have a tendency to ignore spiritual things. When times are difficult, people often are drawn to consider what it may mean in the light of Biblical prophecy.

THE TWENTY-FIRST CENTURY

At the outset of the twenty-first century, life is both hopeful and fearful. Charles Dickens once said, "It was the best of times, it was the worst of times, it was the age of wisdom, it was the age of foolishness, it was the season of light, it was the season of darkness, it was the spring of hope, it was the winter of despair." His description of life in the mid-nineteenth century seems to fit this generation very well. On the one hand, we are the most advanced generation to have ever lived; and, on the other hand, we are confronted on a daily basis by global crises that leave us fearful and distressed. People everywhere are worried about the future. There is a universal sense that we may be living in the last days. The apostle Paul wrote, "But mark this: there will be terrible times in the last days. People will be lovers of themselves, lovers of money, boastful, proud, abusive, disobedient, unforgiving, slanderous, without self-control, rash, conceited, lovers of pleasure rather than lovers of God – having a form of godliness but denying its power" (2 Timothy 3:1-5).

In an age like this, there is one message that speaks eloquently to the fears of mankind, and it is this: "Jesus is alive and well, reigning as Lord at the Father's right hand. Soon, He will leave His mediatorial throne and return in power and glory to complete God's eternal plan of redemption." The message of the Second Coming of Jesus Christ is the hope of the world. It is the message that the angels gave to His followers when He ascended to the Father. It is the message that motivated the early Church to faithfully take the Gospel around the world. It is the message that sustains believers in these last days of time. Jesus will come again, just like he said he would – personally, purposefully and powerfully – and that day may be closer than any of us realize.

There is a universal sense that we are living in the last days and that the crises that we are dealing with in this generation are pregnant with prophetic implications. There has never been a time in the history of the world quite like the present.

Ed Dobson, writing in his book, *The End*, said, "At no other time since Jesus ascended into heaven have so many remarkable events and trends come together – events and trends predicted in the Bible to be features of the end times." There has never been a time in the history of the world quite like the present.

Herbert Lockyer, in his book about the Second Coming, *The Drama of the Ages*, said, "The human race is moving toward the most stupendous events in the world's history. National and international events and crises are heavy with prophetic significance."

Numerous events are taking place in our world, all of which give us cause for concern. Our global society is still a world at war, a world at odds politically, a world economically distraught, a world socially redefined, a world morally bankrupt and a world where hope is fading.

We are living in a time of unprecedented violence, terror, instability and fear. People want to know the meaning of these developments. Do they have any Biblical significance? What can we expect to happen next? Are we living in the last days? Where are we in the course of time? Is it possible to know when we are approaching the end of the age?

Jesus addressed the subject of the end of the age on the occasion of His teaching His disciples about the destruction of the temple (recorded in Matthew 24). Jesus had just pointed out that there was coming a day when the massive stones of the temple, with which they were so familiar, would be toppled so that not one of these stones would be left standing on another.

The disciples were filled with questions, and they began to inquire, "Tell us, when will this happen?" In other words, "When will this temple be destroyed?" That was question number one. And then they asked, "What will be the sign of your coming and of the end of the age?" Somehow, in their minds, they viewed the destruction of the temple and the end of the age as concurrent events.

JESUS' RESPONSE

Matthew 24 contains Jesus' response to these questions. He actually said very little about the destruction of the temple, which occurred in AD 70, choosing rather to concentrate on the bigger question, "What shall be the sign of your coming and of the end of the age?" In that respect, He taught his disciples that there would be one period of time – a season of the end, a generation – when world developments would occur in a radically different manner, distinguishing that period of time from any previous generation of human history.

DISTINGUISHING FEATURES OF THE LAST GENERATION

It is fair to say that ever since Jesus ascended to the Father with the promise of returning, believers in every generation have looked for His reappearing, interpreting developments in their day as evidence of His impending return. However, according to Scripture, one generation will stand out from all previous generations as the last (or terminal) generation.

Christians have always been fascinated by the prophetic signs in the Bible. If you read church history, you will discover that hardly a generation passed but what some student of the Bible was reading the prophetic signs and applying them to developments and situations in his day and making projections as to when Jesus would be coming. Our age really isn't any different. We are doing basically the same kind of thing when we refer to our generation as the terminal generation. Much literature being written suggests that we are the last generation to live before Jesus comes. That may be true, or it may not be true, but the fact of the matter is that we are all interested in knowing when that day will come and what may be the meaning of developments that are taking place all around us. We need to be careful as we study this subject, as we read our Bibles and examine the different prophetic signs that are given there (that point to the end), that we do not rush to hasty conclusions. One important principle to keep in mind is that we do not make major projections out of minor developments. In other words, we do not assign some special significance to something that is just a common occurrence or development in every generation of time.

THE NATURE OF PROPHETIC SIGNS

As you read through the Bible, you'll discover that the prophetic signs have both a general character and a specific character. This is one of the remarkable things about the Bible – part of the genius and the wisdom of God. He wrote the message of this Book in such a way that if you were living in the first century – even if you were one of those followers of Jesus who heard the very teachings of Jesus from His own lips verbally – you'd be living the next day, the next week and the next month with the expectation that Jesus is coming and that it may be today. And if you only knew the first century, and you read these early primitive Christian documents that had been formed into what we call the Bible, and you read these statements of Jesus and of the apostle Paul and others, you would get the idea from the way the Bible speaks and the character of life that you observed, that this could be the time of His return. You could live with that expectancy, and it would have a profound effect upon the quality of your spiritual life because you really believed that Jesus could come that very day. Or, you could be living in the fifth century, or the tenth century, or the fifteenth century, and you could read the same Bible, look at the same situations around you and come to the same conclusions, because there is a general character about the prophetic signs of the Bible. I believe that God intended it to be that way so that believers could read the Bible and could live with the hope and the expectancy of seeing Jesus in their own lifetime.

That does something for a person. What a difference it makes in a person's life if he really believes that he might see Jesus return to this earth in his own lifetime! It affects the way he does his business; it affects his relationships; and it affects the dedication and sincerity of his faith – how he practices and works out his Christian experiences. This is the genius of the Bible – that God would write these things in such a way that there would be an application of the prophetic message in every generation of time. We can fault those who have made a specific application; we can tell those who have stood up that they never should have said, "Jesus is coming today," or "Jesus may come this year," because the Bible says that no man knows the day or the hour when Jesus will come. We tend to render a harsh criticism of these people. I say, "Let them sleep!" The Scripture is written in such a way that it is not at all unusual for a person to make an application of this word to the generation in which he is living. And I don't believe that there is any disservice to God in doing that if there is a sincere understanding that this may be the time. It is one thing to live with a sense that His return is imminent and another thing to set a specific time or date.

There is a general character about the signs that I think is productive spiritually for the Church of Jesus Christ, and as you read Matthew 24, Jesus seems to be saying, "Watch out, now, what you do with these signs that I am going to give you! Don't overplay them, and don't make more of them than what I mean them to be for you!" For instance, He says, "Many shall come in my name, saying, 'I am Christ,' and shall deceive many. You shall hear of wars and rumors of wars. See that you be not troubled, for all of these things must come to pass, but the end is not yet." Notice how He takes them down through a series of developments that will be common to every generation of time, and He's careful to say to them, "Don't make more of these things than you ought to make! Live every day in that expectation and hope that the word that I have given you may come to pass in your own time!" There is definitely a general character to the signs.

While that is true, there is also a specific character or nature to the signs. That is, those things that are common to every generation of time will have a very dramatic or radical and unusual display in one generation of time (as contrasted with previous generations), which will be the generation in which Jesus returns. There are two phrases that often are used in Scripture that help us distinguish the general from the specific. The first is used in Matthew 24:6, when Jesus says – in respect to some of the "signs" that He is giving – "All these things must come to pass, but the end is not yet." In other words, these are general in nature. The other phrase is used in Matthew 24:21 – "unequaled from the beginning of the world until now – and never to be equaled again." This phrase sets the sign apart in a rather specific sense.

Jesus told a parable about a fig tree that demonstrates a way to determine when the seasons of time change: "Now learn this lesson from the fig tree: as soon as its twigs get tender and its leaves come out, you know that summer is near. Even so, when you see all these things, you know that it is near, right at the door. I tell you the truth: this generation will certainly not pass away until all these things have happened. Heaven and earth will pass away, but my words will never pass away" (Matthew 24:32-35).

In this parable, Jesus was saying that we can learn from nature about a change in seasons. When a branch is tender and puts forth leaves, you know that summer is near. So, nature has a certain law built into it, and it doesn't reverse itself. Obviously, there are some freak developments in nature as you go along, such as life in the

Northeast. Spring will come, and it may be April or so, and the grass begins to turn a little bit green, and you start to see some crocuses appearing, and bright flowers line the front of the house or walkway, and then you see the buds coming out on the trees and leaves, and then all of a sudden you get hit with a six-inch snowstorm. Now, what does that mean? Does it mean that nature has decided to revert to winter? Not at all! It's a freak development. You know, when you see those buds and leaves on the trees, that you are moving into a new season of time, regardless of some freak snowstorm that suddenly appears. The snow doesn't mean a thing. It is the obvious law of nature that when the branch is tender, the sap begins to flow. The bud appears, then come the leaves, and it tells you something about the time or season of the year. What Jesus was saying is that just as nature indicates a change in seasons, so God will demonstrate by His actions when the world moves into the season of the end. "When you see all these things, know that it is near, even at the doors. Verily I say unto you, this generation shall not pass 'til all these things be fulfilled."

I don't agree with Hal Lindsey's prophetic system at all, but I like the phrase that he uses about the "terminal generation." I'm not sure that the application that he makes is necessarily and totally accurate, but I tend to believe that there is a generation that God has marked prophetically that will be a generation in which the signs that Jesus has given to us concerning His second coming will be demonstrated in that period of time – that generation of time. A generation can be anywhere from 30, 40, 70, or possibly 100 years, depending on who you read.

What we need to understand is that when Jesus speaks of the signs – when He describes the general character of them – and then refers to a generation that will have a certain significance in that there will be a fleshing out of certain signs in that particular period of time that will give birth to the dawning of that day, He says, it's a certain and sure thing. "Heaven and earth shall pass away but my words shall not pass away." I think we need to ask ourselves the question, "How do we know when we have moved from this age of general application to the generation or the period of time that Jesus had in mind when He said, 'this generation shall not pass away until all these things be fulfilled'?" It seems to me that the signs, if they are going to have any significance in respect to this specific period of time – or this generation that is alive when Jesus comes – must have a certain character or quality about them. It's not just that the things that Jesus talks about will suddenly appear, because I challenge you to read anything in Matthew 24 that you cannot give application to previously in history.

You may take some question with me on the word "tribulation," but everything that Jesus talks about here has already been and has repeated itself historically in every generation in greater or lesser degrees, so that it becomes somewhat difficult for us to determine or understand when we move from the period of general application to that specific application unless there is something radical – something distinctive and unique – about the signs in one generation as opposed to all the other periods of history. That's what I'd like to think. I'm of the opinion, as I read my Bible, that there will be one generation that is the terminal generation – the last generation of time – which will stand apart from every other generation, when these same signs will be present, but will be present in a dramatic, radical, unique demonstration – something totally unique to that generation.

There are three words to keep in mind that may help one understand what I mean when I talk about a unique, radical development of the signs. The three words are, concurrence, clarity, and cosmic quality. The first word is "concurrence." That is, the fact that the major prophetic signs would all be present in one generation at the same time. As you go back through history, you read your Bible and you read history, you can find certain signs; you can find one here in this time period and find one there in that one, and you can find one somewhere else – that's how people have arrived at these conclusions that Jesus was about to return because they could see a particular sign. The terminal generation will not be identified because a particular prophetic sign is evident, but rather by virtue of the fact that all the things Jesus talked about concerning the end of the age are evident in a demonstrable manner. It doesn't seem, as I read history, that there has ever been a generation in which all the pieces of the prophetic puzzle fit together on the desk at the same time as they do now. There is something radically different about our generation. Personally, I'm convinced that all the pieces of the prophetic puzzle are there in front of us on the desk. They may not all have been fitted together exactly the way they need to go, but none of them seem to be missing.

Another distinctive characteristic of this generation in respect to the signs is the clarity of the signs. There was a time in which Bible scholars would debate the signs with great vigor. One prophetic student would say, "This is what it means," and someone else would say, "No, this is what it means." If you can cull out of prophetic literature today the extraneous thoughts that have been added by men and get down to the core understandings that are displayed in much of this literature, you will discover there is a general agreement in the Christian community about the meaning of the signs. That is, there is an unusually remarkable, radical clarity to the signs in our day, so that even the unbelieving world is picking up its ears and wondering what world developments might mean. It is not unusual to have a neighbor or acquaintance question if world conditions point to the end of the world. There is a clarity about the signs that is unusual to our generation.

The third word has to do with a certain cosmic quality about the signs that is unusual and unique to our generation. By that I mean that it doesn't really matter where you live on the face of the earth today, it all reads the same way; it all looks the same way. Imagine that you could go back in history just a short period of time – a generation (however many years you want to ascribe to that period of time) – and start thinking about the kind of world that existed one generation ago. You lived in one part of the world and you got a message from another part of the world that things were happening and Jesus was coming because of these developments that were taking place, and you would shake your head and say, "I can't see that, I can't understand that," because the world in which you're living is nothing like the world over there. A generation ago, the world was disconnected, and there was very little similarity between one nation and one section of the world and another, but in our generation – in our time – we have become a global village. What is unique about our day and our age is that it doesn't really matter where you live;

conditions are basically the same. People in one part of the world are aware of the same developments, the same needs, have the same anxieties and fears and the same distresses that someone else has in a different part of the world. There is a cosmic quality to the signs that is unique to this generation, so that as I look at these teachings of Jesus, and as I think of the prophetic signs that are given, I am leaning strongly toward the point of view that we are living in the very last of the last days, and this may indeed be the generation to which Jesus was referring when He said, "This generation shall not pass away until all these things be fulfilled."

Many people believe that our generation fulfills the Biblical conditions for the end of the age. This is certainly a unique age. The conditions that have been common in all previous generations have occurred in this generation in a much more extreme, radical and universal manner. Consider the number of earthquakes and the magnitude of them. From 1900 to 1910, there were three earthquakes somewhere in the world that measured 6.0 or more on the Richter scale. In the decade from 1930 to 1940, there were five. From 1950 to 1960, there were nine. From 1960 to 1970, there were 13. Between 1970 and 1980, there were 46. Between 1980 and 1990, there were 53. Between 1990 and 2000, there were 1,661. Seismic developments are getting more frequent and more serious every year. It is not unusual to hear of an earthquake at 7.0 or greater on the Richter scale with much loss of life and material destruction. As I am writing this section, the news media are reporting a massive earthquake in Japan, measuring 8.9 on the Richter scale and producing a destructive tsunami stretching across the Pacific Ocean. According to reports, this quake is one of the most severe ever recorded in human history.

In Romans 8:19-22, the apostle Paul spoke of nature as "groaning" while anticipating deliverance from the effects of the curse. "The creation waits in eager expectation for the sons of God to be revealed. For the creation was subjected to frustration, not by its own choice, but by the will of the one who subjected it, in hope that the creation itself will be liberated from its bondage to decay and brought into the glorious freedom of the children of God. We know that the whole creation has been groaning as in the pains of childbirth right up to the present time." The situation extends beyond the massive earthquakes that are common in our age. We have witnessed volcanic eruptions, tsunamis and other dramatic demonstrations of the power of nature. Nature's "groanings" have become louder and more frequent in recent months. The scene is apocalyptic. All of society is troubled, breeding a state of universal unrest that is characteristic of the last days.

Added to what is going on in nature, consider the number of wars and the massive destructive force of our weaponry. Ever since sin entered the world, warring has been a part of man's nature. Historically, there have been 13 years of war for every year of peace. Since 1950 (since the end of World War II), there have been nearly 70 conflicts in which 10,000 or more people have been killed. Many of these wars have been going on at the same time. The spirit of warring (enmity) is part of man's sinful nature. Consider the moral decadence and the culture of violence that we live in today. Consider the severity of Christian persecution that is rampant today.

This may be the midnight hour of human history. This may be the terminal generation.

THE SIGN OF THE TIMES

Reading the 'signs of the times' can be a little tricky especially if all we are interested in is interpreting developments around us as indicators of the end of the age. We would be better served to restrict our query to how Jesus dealt with the issue in His teaching. The signs of the times (addressed by Jesus in Matthew 24) can best be grouped under three major headings. The first is a reference to an end-times global witness to the gospel; the second deals with the subject of Satan's massive cosmic counter-offensive of evil – a period of great distress and tribulation – and the third speaks to issues related to the Middle East and the nation of Israel.

GOD'S LAST-DAYS KINGDOM OFFENSIVE

According to Jesus' teaching in Matthew 24, the last days will be characterized by a dramatic global evangelistic thrust, unparalleled in the history of the church – what we might call "God's Last-Days Kingdom Offensive." Jesus said, "The gospel of the kingdom will be preached in all the world for a witness to all nations, and then the end will come" (Matthew 24:14). This is one distinguishing mark of the last days.

Jesus links an explosive missionary activity to the end of the age, which is what his disciples were asking about. The last generation, the end of the age, is to be a period of intense gospel witness spanning the face of the globe – a massive mobilization of all segments of the Church in an attempt to fulfill the Great Commission in one generation.

With the resources and technology available to this generation, many Christian leaders believe that the Great Commission can be achieved in our lifetime. I personally believe that it will be achieved in our lifetime.

Missions have always been the primary business of the Church, but what we are seeing take place today is different in scope and intensity from anything ever seen in the history of the Church. The surge in global evangelization that characterizes this age is unparalleled in human history. It is one of the things that make this generation so unique.

The greatest spiritual conquests today are being made in some of the world's most densely populated areas, such as South America, Asia and Africa, where great revivals have been reported over the past few decades. I have read that as many as 1,000 new churches are planted every week in this part of the world.

A report that I saw a few years ago, in an issue of *Current Thoughts and Trends*, indicated that, in 1960, there were 50,000,000 Christians in Africa. I am told that, today, there are more than 360,000,000, an increase of about 700% in less than a generation. That number continues to increase dramatically in this area of the world.

A program on the Trinity Broadcasting Network told of an evangelistic event in Lagos, Nigeria, where – on November 12, 2000

– an estimated 2,000,000 people came together in one place for an open-air meeting. This type of evangelistic campaign is fairly common in Africa. Loudspeaker towers, capable of being heard two miles away, carried the message to the huge crowd. When the invitation was given, 1,300,000 people accepted Jesus Christ as their Savior. They were prayed with, by 200,000 trained counselors, scattered throughout the crowd. 1,300,000 conversions in one place, at one event, in one moment of time! That's more people than live in the state of Rhode Island, or Maine, or Alaska, or Montana, or Wyoming, or Vermont, or North or South Dakota. These are truly days of harvest for the kingdom of God.

The massive global evangelistic effort that is being carried out by a number of denominations and a host of para-church groups is having a profound impact on the world for Christ. According to the Lausanne statistics task force, the growth of the Church in this generation is far greater than previously thought or reported.

The historically verifiable records of this special task force conclude that the number of born-again Christians has grown three times faster than the world's population in the past few decades. That's an astounding development when you realize that 240,000 more people are born into the world every day than die.

Even more startling is the fact that, since the mid-1960s (a significant prophetic date, in my opinion), the number of Christians throughout the world has grown by an astonishing 1,000%. God is on the move today, all around the world.

Larry Buckman, of Apoyo Ministries, has stated that, according to his research, more than 150,000 people accept Christ worldwide every day. Walter Kaiser, former president of Gordon-Conwell Theological Seminary, has made the statement that, "According to one estimate, if our Lord tarries in his second coming, another 1,000,000,000 believers will be added by our Lord to the Church in this decade." The Center for Global Christianity regularly tracks the success the gospel is having in 239 countries, 9,000 denominations and 5,000 major cities around the world, and has determined that two new believers somewhere in the world are coming to know Jesus Christ as Savior every second of every day, every week, every year.

Dr. Pat Robertson, president of the Christian Broadcasting Network, has reported that, according to his research, there are currently 2,200,000,000 professing Christians in the world. Talk about kingdom harvest! There has never been anything like it ever before in the history of the Church.

What is making this all possible are the developments that the prophet Daniel spoke about as a sign of the end in Daniel 12:1-4. In that passage of Scripture, Daniel prophesied about a time of great distress – an age of confusion and chaos – and a time when knowledge would increase. Each of these factors has contributed in some way to the great Kingdom harvest of these last days.

While we are surrounded by distress, confusion, and chaos, the one thing that sets this generation apart from all other generations is the increase in knowledge to which Daniel referred.

This is certainly not a reference to business as usual. The idea of knowledge increasing from generation to generation is not radical in any sense of the word. It is obvious that Daniel was foretelling something about the increase in knowledge in the last days that would distinguish that period of time from any previous generation in a remarkably demonstrative manner. A strong case could be made that our generation fits that profile very well.

This is the information age. Communication lies at the heart of life for people everywhere, who are now able to talk to other people anytime they please, from anywhere they please, using a variety of communication devices. And it's so easy. Everywhere you look, somebody is texting someone else or talking on a cellular telephone.

This is the generation of the cell phone, beepers, e-mail, I-pods, I-pads, e-books and wireless devices. In 2009, 1,200,000,000 cell phones were sold.

Many people don't realize it, but the first cell phone didn't appear until 1973, and didn't go public until 1977. The first e-mail was sent in 1971. That's in our lifetime – in this generation. E-mail is now thought of as being passé. I'm told that only old people use e-mail.

We are experiencing a communications revolution. In this generation, we have gone from radio (which took 38 years to reach 50,000,000 users) to television (which took 13 years to reach 50,000,000 users) to the internet (which took only four years to reach 50,000,000 users) to the I-pod (which took only three years to reach 50,000,000 users). I am told that it took Facebook less than nine months to attract 100,000,000 users. In the six or seven years since Facebook entered the social media arena, it grew to more than 500,000,000 active users. During any given day, 50% of the active users log on to Facebook. The average user is connected with 130 friends. People spend over 700,000,000,000 minutes per month on Facebook. About 70% of Facebook users are outside the United States.

We are living in a different age. Consequently, this generation communicates the gospel differently than previous generations.

100 years ago, the primary means of communicating the gospel was through print media. In the twenty-first century, print media are growing obsolete. I was sitting next to a lady on a recent flight who was reading a book electronically on an I-pad. I noticed that a man in the seat in front of me was also reading something on his Kindle or I-pad – an electronic device capable of storing more than 300 books. The device is about six by nine inches and is less than half an inch thick. Justin Nash, the director of communications for the Advent Christian General Conference, recently told me that according to his research, more books were sold in the electronic format in 2010 than in print.

This generation has witnessed a communications revolution. Computers have revolutionized life in the twenty-first century. IBM has a new computer (named "Watson") that is capable of processing 500 gigabytes of information per second – the equivalent of 1,000,000 books.

The gospel is being communicated globally in ways that only this generation could achieve. One development that is unique to this generation is the use of video and DVDs. The story of the Bible is being told in hundreds of languages in video format. One of these developments is the creation of the *Jesus* film in 1979. The film depicts the life of Christ (based primarily on the Gospel of Luke). It was filmed on location in Israel. According to the *New York Times*, the *Jesus* film is "likely the most watched motion picture of all time." The *Jesus* Film Project estimates that the film has been viewed more than 5,000,000,000 times in numerous languages and countries of the world, resulting in more than 225,000,000 decisions to accept Christ as Savior.

Another remarkable project of this generation is known as God's Story Project, which is an 80-minute video titled *God's Story: from Creation to Eternity*. This compelling evangelistic tool is now available in more than 250 languages and is being used around the world to bring the story of God's love and saving grace to unreached people groups.

Another remarkable development of this generation is the rise of Christian television networks. One of these networks is the worldwide television ministry of the Trinity Broadcasting Network, which has celebrated more than 36 years of televising the gospel. As of this writing, this network is on the air 24 hours a day around the world, beaming their signal from 33 satellites to more than 5,000 television stations, the internet and thousands of cable systems around the world.

CBN, the oldest Christian broadcasting network, is currently reaching into 200 countries of the world and broadcasting in 70 different languages. There are very few places in the world where the gospel is not being preached. In many of the third-world countries, where people live in abject poverty, you are likely to see a television antenna or satellite dish on their hut. In one generation, Christian television programming is reaching virtually every continent in our global village.

Another remarkable development is something called streaming. Streaming video is content sent in compressed form over the internet and displayed by the viewer in real time. With streaming video or streaming media, a web user does not have to wait to download a file to play it. Instead, the media is sent in a continuous stream of data and is played as it arrives. The user needs a player, which is a special program that decompresses and sends video data to the display and audio data to speakers. A player can be either an integral part of a browser or downloaded from the software maker's website.

Streaming video is usually sent from prerecorded video files, but can be distributed as part of a live broadcast feed. In a live broadcast, the video signal is converted into a compressed digital signal and transmitted from a special web server that is able to do multicast

– sending the same file to multiple users at the same time. With this technology, Biblical teaching can be sent to people all over the globe simultaneously at little cost. The potential for communicating the gospel is virtually unlimited.

None of this was possible a generation ago. Daniel didn't have the slightest idea what he was talking about when, under the inspiration of the Holy Spirit, he said (speaking of the last days), "knowledge shall increase."

This generation has seen an explosive increase in knowledge that is unparalleled in human history. Billy Graham has stated that 90% of all the engineers who have ever lived are alive today. According to experts on this subject, it is estimated that 98% of everything that we know today has been learned in this generation (or since the mid 1960s). That's a phenomenal statistic when you consider that we have been around for a few millennia.

The rate of increase in knowledge in this generation is unparalleled in any previous generation. Knowledge is estimated to have doubled between the time of Christ and the year 1900. It is thought to have doubled again between 1900 and 1950. After that, knowledge doubled in seven-year intervals until about 1990, when it was thought to double every two to three years. Today, I am told that knowledge doubles every 18-24 months. If you were to assign an arbitrary value of 10 to knowledge in AD 1, it would register a value of more than 200,000 today, most of which will have been gained in the last few decades.

The gospel is being preached in the whole world, aided by this massive increase in knowledge and technology. This generation is unique in that respect. What is happening today isn't just a repetition of what has occurred in previous generations. No previous generation has ever seen anything even close to this. This generation fits the Biblical profile for the terminal generation.

This is the generation that is called to evangelize the world. Consider, if you will, the amazing career of evangelist Billy Graham, called and commissioned by God as his end-times spokesman. For 60 years, Billy Graham took the gospel around the world, preaching to more people in a live-audience format than anyone in history. Records show that he has preached in 185 countries and to more than 210,000,000 people. In addition to the hundreds of thousands who have been added to the Kingdom of God, his ministry over the years has been a potent social and political force as he has counseled presidents and world leaders on every continent.

At 86 years of age, and in poor health, he concluded what was thought to be his last evangelistic crusade in the city of New York, where 90,000 people jammed the stadium on Sunday afternoon, June 26, 2005, in sweltering heat, to hear this man of God. I don't think it is coincidental that this man, God's end-times global spokesman, finished his anointed preaching career at this point in time. I have an eerie feeling that it may be one more sign that the end is very near.

God's Kingdom Offensive continues to sweep across the face of our world, reaping the final harvest, just as Jesus indicated that it would, when – speaking of the last days – He said, "This gospel of the kingdom will be preached in the whole world as a testimony to all nations, and then the end will come."

SATAN'S MASSIVE COUNTER-OFFENSIVE OF EVIL

It should also be noted, according to the teaching of Jesus in Matthew 24, that another sign of the season of the end – the terminal generation – will be Satan's massive counter-offensive of evil: a time of tribulation, terror, trouble and distress, unparalleled in human history.

This is how Jesus put it: "For then there will be great distress, unequaled from the beginning of the world until now, and never to be equaled again" (Matthew 24:21).

Interestingly enough, Daniel spoke about a similar condition as a characteristic of the last days. "At that time, Michael, the great prince who protects your people, will arise. There will be a time of distress such as has not happened from the beginning of nations until then. But at that time your people – everyone whose name is found written in the book – will be delivered" (Daniel 12:1). In other words, the last days will be uniquely distressful, violent and troublesome – a conflict of cosmic proportions engaging the forces of good and evil.

In Matthew 13:24-30, Jesus told an interesting parable about wheat and weeds. It is a story of how a farmer went out and sowed good seed in his field, but when it began to grow it was noticed that weeds appeared to be growing alongside of the wheat. The workers thought that they should go and pull up the weeds, but the farmer said, "No. Let them both grow together until the harvest, at which time the weeds will be pulled up and burned." The point of this parable is the presence of both good and evil in society. We all know the character of weeds. Weeds grow faster than the good seed, and they tend to overwhelm the good. Such is the nature of evil in the last days. Paul said that there will be terrible times in the last days (2 Timothy 3:1). We can expect an increasingly aggressive campaign of evil as we near the end of the age. The devil knows that his time is short.

Satan, the adversary of both God and man, is the author, source and director of all the evil and violence that we are witnessing today. He has declared war on the Church and on all things that are associated with God's redemptive activity in the world. Satan will not let God's Kingdom offensive move forward without a major counter-offensive of evil.

Revelation 12:17 describes the origin of Satan's conflict with God and his subsequent attack on the Church. "Then the dragon (that's Satan) was enraged at the woman (the woman is a prophetic symbol for the Church), and he went off to make war against the rest of her offspring – those who obey God's commandments and hold to the testimony of Jesus (Christian believers)."

The last days are days of intense spiritual warfare. That's what the Book of Revelation is all about: the launching of God's kingdom offensive head to head with Satan's counter-offensive of evil, which has been unleashed on the masses of humanity throughout the world. God's kingdom offensive is empowered by the Holy Spirit, and Satan's massive counter-offensive of evil is empowered by all the demonic forces at his command.

A.W. Tozer has said, "There are two spirits in the world – the Spirit of God and the spirit of Satan, and these are at eternal enmity." Three words sum up Satan's activity in the last days: Tribulation, Antichrist and Armageddon.

The foundation for this distress is a moral revolution. This end-times spiritual warfare is being waged on two fronts. First of all, it is an attack on biblical morals; and, secondly, it is an all-out evil insurgency designed to create a state of unrest, fear, violence and terror among the masses. It is set in the context of a major cultural shift from a strong Judeo-Christian moral influence that has characterized society for generations to a basic amoral society, devoid of any Biblically-based values.

The days of moral absolutes are passed. This generation doesn't know the difference between right and wrong. In fact, in respect to moral values, the terms "right" and "wrong" are not used.

Researcher George Barna reported in 2002 that 83% of teens in America believed that moral truth depends on the circumstances. We know that as "situation ethics." He went on to say that only 9% of teens raised in the church believe in moral absolutes. However, it isn't just the young people who have lost their bearings. Many adults have abandoned the strict moral code of Scripture for a more accommodating position on social issues.

In another survey conducted by the Barna group among a representative sample of American adults, it was discovered that most Americans consider themselves to be Christians, despite the fact that very few adults base their moral decisions on the Bible, and surprisingly few believe that absolute moral truth exists. As I stated earlier, an even more startling fact is that only 30% of people who claim to make moral decisions based on specific principles named the Bible as the source of those principles. Part of the problem is that many Christians in this generation are soft on the Bible. We give it respect, but we don't really know (or heed) what it says. There are many nominal Christians today who are Biblically illiterate. If they were asked to name the first five books of the Bible or the four Gospels, they might struggle with the question.

This is a different era. A generation ago, people knew the difference between right and wrong, even though they often made poor decisions. They knew the difference. This is a generation in which the distinction between right and wrong has been blurred. Things have changed.

One of the first signs of the last days is a moral revolution replacing the Biblical standards of right and wrong with an attitude of permissive personal indulgence. Jesus spoke of a last-days apostasy in Matthew 24:10 and following; He indicated that many would turn away from the faith. This deadening of spiritual sensitivities – this moral and spiritual deterioration of society – opens the door for Satan to carry out his campaign of evil.

The late Dr. Edwin K. Gedney, speaking of Matthew 24:29 (which reads, "The sun will be darkened and the moon will not give Its light"), says, "The appearance of these celestial signs – sun, moon and stars – is evidence of a great world disorder and panic caused by the withdrawal of moral force." A radical moral shift has taken place in our culture in one generation, creating a crisis of hope. We don't know the difference between right and wrong, which leaves us perplexed about the great issues of life that confront us on a daily basis. The pervasiveness of evil has rotted away the moral foundations of our culture. This is a generation that has lost its way in respect to moral values. The compass doesn't know which way is north.

One distinguishing feature of this generation is a drug culture characterized by violence. Drug addiction has expressed itself in a number of criminal acts. Anyone under the age of 40 probably thinks that this is the way it has always been. Such is not the case. Things have changed dramatically in this generation. 100 years ago, there were fewer than 10 murders a year in the United States. Statistics show that today there are (on average) 45 murders a day somewhere in the United States. People feel unsafe walking alone on the streets of our cities. Added to this, home invasions have become commonplace. Many schools are experiencing random acts of violence – and something new, called "bullying." There is a rash of brazen bank robberies, muggings and rapes. The home, which was the bedrock of society a generation ago, is more like a war zone today.

The moral breakdown of society is reflected in the same-sex marriage movement, which has taken center stage in our culture. It all started with a ruling made by the Supreme Court of the United States on Thursday, June 26, 2003. A supposedly conservative court struck down a sodomy law that had been in place for the previous 18 years. The ruling divorces biblical morals from the fabric of American life, further blurring the distinctions between right and wrong. The implications for the future are revolutionary in respect to this issue of the marriage of same-sex partners and the redefinition of what constitutes a family. The road we are on as a nation is leading us into a societal wilderness. No one knows with any certainty where it is going, but it isn't good.

In this short time, the issue has gained national prominence. We are in the midst of a sexual revolution. I'm not talking about cheating on a spouse or an incident of adultery – things that have been around as long as we have – or even a more modern development that we refer to as cohabitation. I'm talking about a sexual revolution.

This is an age when a top item on the political and social agenda is a redefinition of marriage. The issue is same-sex marriage, and we're not just talking about it, but we are acting through the judicial and legislative branches of government to legalize it.

At this writing, five states have legalized same-sex marriage. The legalization of same-sex marriage is a natural outgrowth of the secularization of society, which began in earnest in the decade of the 1960s. Secularization is the move to base moral decisions on human values as opposed to religious values. Secularization has crept into all levels of government, and it has shaped the political climate of this generation.

New England is the least religious (and most secular) region of the country. At this writing, four of the five states nationwide to have legalized same-sex marriage are in New England – New Hampshire becoming the latest on January 1, 2010, joining Massachusetts, Connecticut and Vermont (California has been back and forth on the issue, which may not be resolved until the Supreme court rules on the matter).

The issue of same-sex marriage has been passed by several legislatures, but when the issue has been placed on the ballot for the general public to decide, the legislation has generally been overturned. This battle for the moral fabric of our country will continue to occupy center stage in the months and years ahead. Same-sex marriage is one of the top social issues facing America today.

We are in the midst of a sexual revolution. Talk about the last days! The apostle Paul wrote about this kind of lifestyle as a sign of the last days in Romans 1:18-27. In this passage of Scripture, Paul spoke of how, in the last days, men and women will ignore the plain teaching of God's Word and engage in immoral acts with one another.

We are living in the nighttime of human history. The prince of darkness reigns, and the blackness of this world's night is deepening by the hour. This is an age of unparalleled intellectual and technological progress, which is offset by a radical regression of moral and spiritual values.

Satan is spoken of in Scripture as a master deceiver, and he has certainly done an effective job of duping modern man into thinking that what we once called "sin" is really something to be embraced and enjoyed. Satan's greatest deception in this generation is what I call the sophistication of sin.

Lawmakers are writing new standards of morality into law, legalizing our sins, so that we are deceived into thinking that we are OK. We wonder, "What's so bad about us?" The prevailing attitude is that there is no such thing as sin. We have stooped so low as to popularize, glamorize and institutionalize evil to the point that it has become an acceptable way of life. The idea of personal sin is antiquated. This is what I mean when I say that the greatest deception of our age is the sophistication of sin. Satan is at work, undermining the values that have guided us as a nation, substituting his perverted agenda in the name of personal choice.

The moral and spiritual shift that characterizes this generation – the darkness of our cultural night – is an unmistakable sign that we are living in the last days. In a moral sense, we are living in a different era. We are living in the nighttime of human history. The prince of darkness reigns.

First John 5:19 reads, "We know that we are children of God and that the whole world is under the control of the evil one." Notice what this says – "the whole world is under the control of the evil one!" The prince of darkness reigns. Our adversary, the Devil, is in control of principalities, strongholds, powers and dominions that were surrendered to him by the first Adam, which explains our predicament.

The breakdown of our moral foundation has contributed to a state of lawlessness, crime and violence. There are no longer any moral restraints.

One by-product of this moral decline is the global nuclear threat. World leaders are understandably concerned about the proliferation of weapons of mass destruction. President Barack Obama hosted a world nuclear summit in 2010, in which leaders of 47 countries came together to discuss the potential of global terror created by nuclear bombs in the hands of terrorists. The problem is exacerbated by the fact that the global stockpile of nuclear bomb-making material is now large enough to make 120,000 suitcase bombs, one of which could reduce an entire city to ashes. Much of this material is unsecured in countries like India, Pakistan and North Korea, which continue to build their nuclear arsenals. World leaders know that terrorist groups like al-Qaeda have been actively working to secure bomb-making material. The situation is very frightening.

One development that reflects this global state of distress is the War on Terror, which was launched following the tragic events of September 11, 2001 – an event which dramatically altered the perspective on life for millions of Americans. For many, hope vanished in a thunderous crash and a cloud of smoke and ash that rained death and destruction. Life took on a new meaning. It will never be the same. A new age – the age of terror – was born, and with it universal heartache, bloodshed, distress and fear.

Iraq was the focal point of this global conflict initially. The United States and its coalition partners battled a heavily armed, resilient and passionately committed insurgency. Saddam Hussein warned about this even before the invasion of Iraq took place.

In a video aired on al-Jazeera television, Ayman al-Zawahiri (Osama bin-Laden's second in command) said, "If you don't leave today (speaking of the U.S. presence in Iraq), you will leave tomorrow, with tens of thousands of dead, and double that figure in disabled and wounded."

The conflict in Iraq has been costly, with more than 4,300 United States casualties reported by the end of the year 2009. Afghanistan has cost the United States over 1,000 deaths by June 1, 2010, and the total is rising steadily. July of 2010 was the worst month to that point in time in the Afghan war, with more than 66 U.S. servicemen killed.

This is a strange situation. It isn't Iraq or Afghanistan against the coalition forces (as we are prone to think). Iraq is divided politically and religiously; different factions are fighting each other. Iraqis killed thousands more of their own countrymen than they did U.S. forces. This civil unrest is a war within a war.

Iraq is (and will continue to be) a dangerous place. In August of 2010, the last U.S. combat brigade was withdrawn from Iraq, leaving Iraqi security forces to fend on their own. The President of the United States held a news conference in which he announced that the war with Iraq was over. Supposedly, with this development, the Iraqi problem is fixed, and now the world is a safer place. Iraq is not the final battlefield – just the most recent one. Many people don't understand it, but this isn't about politics, terrorist groups or weapons of mass destruction. This is a religious war, despite what the politicians say. Radical Islam views the United States and its allies as tools of Satan. This is Jihad (holy war). Iraq and Afghanistan just happen to be where our attention is focused (and for good reason). What is happening in these countries is religiously inspired violence. Islamic states are driven by their religious convictions, and they have a passionate hatred for America. In this generation, terrorism has become a fact of everyday life.

The source of this terror is radical Islam, specifically al-Qaeda. Al-Qaeda became a terrorist force in the late 1990s, when Osama bin-Laden brought together a group of like-minded passionate followers in Pakistan, just at the end of the war against the Soviets in Afghanistan.

During this war, bin-Laden and al-Qaeda helped finance, recruit and train thousands of fighters from different countries to be part of an Afghan resistance to defeat the Soviet Union. What al-Qaeda learned in this conflict is that military might won't necessarily win the day.

From statements made by al-Qaeda – and various documents that have been discovered – it appears that al-Qaeda's global objectives revolve around the idea of Islamic control of the world through working with Islamic terrorist groups around the world to overthrow regimes that it deems as non-Islamic or anti-Islamic. In February of 1988, al-Qaeda (under the banner, "The World Islamic front for

Jihad against the Jews and Crusaders") issued a statement saying that it was the duty of all Muslims to kill U.S. citizens – civilian or military – and their allies everywhere.

Over the years, al-Qaeda has networked with other Islamic terrorist groups that share the same passionate hatred for Christians and Jews to form a formidable enemy force. In the early 1990s, al-Qaeda produced an Operations Manual referred to as, "The Encyclopedia of the Afghan Jihad." The "manual" is a detailed how-to guide for using handguns, explosives and biological and chemical weapons. Materials belonging to a captured al-Qaeda operative in England detailed techniques for forgery, surveillance and espionage.

Al-Qaeda is a global terrorist organization at war with everyone and everything non-Muslim. There are terrorist cells in every country of the world, but their location and existence is secretive.

Alexandra Marks, a staff writer for the *Christian Science Monitor*, has stated, "Anyone who can tell you how many terror cells are operating in the United States can also tell you how many angels can dance on the head of a pin." We may not know how many cells exist, but we know that they are there. We hear of terrorist activities like the Fort Hood, Texas, rampage of a United States military officer, Major Nidal Malik Hasan, who was a Muslim. He opened fire on his fellow soldiers, killing 13 of them and wounding scores of innocent bystanders. After the fact, we learned that he had contact with the radical arm of Islam, which orchestrated the attack. The same can be said about the avowed terrorist attempt to blow up a plane in flight on Christmas Day, 2009, as it flew from Europe to Detroit.

In the spring of 2010, another terrorist, whose linkage with al-Qaeda was substantiated, made an attempt to blow up a vehicle in Times Square, New York. There have been more than 32 foiled terrorist plots against United States targets since September 11, 2001.

Al-Qaeda and its operatives will continue to aggressively target civilians, Christians and military installations in the years ahead as we approach the end of the age. The attacks, which will likely escalate, may shift focus depending on developments among the nations. One thing of which we can be certain is the fact that Israel will be the focus of Muslim Jihad. This is a development that has the potential to trigger Armageddon.

PERSECUTION OF CHRISTIANS A FORM OF TERRORISM

However, terrorism is not limited to political institutions or declared battlefields. Tribulation and terror have many faces.

Christians today are under intense persecution in some parts of the world from the same source, and this anti-Christian sentiment is growing into a global predicament. In a Christian news service to which I subscribe, there are reported incidents of severe persecution suffered by Christians in various parts of the world on a daily basis.

Many people view these developments as the early stages of the time of tribulation spoken of in the Bible as a sign of the end of the age. Scripture seems to indicate that the violence, terror and distress associated with the tribulation is universal in extent and intensifies as we approach the climax of human history. We need to understand that the tribulation or "time of trouble" spoken of in Scripture is not something that will come to pass at some future date after the Church has been taken out of the world, but something that we all (even believers) experience as a part of life.

Jesus told his disciples, "In the world you will have tribulation; but be of good cheer, I have overcome the world" (John 16:33). Persecution of Christians has been with us since Jesus first appeared on the scene of human history. Speaking of conditions in the last days, as they affect believers, He said, "Then you will be handed over to be persecuted and put to death, and you will be hated by all nations because of me. At that time, many will turn away from the faith and will betray and hate each other, and many false prophets will appear and deceive many people. Because of the increase of wickedness, the love of most will grow cold" (Matthew 24:9ff). It surely sounds like believers will experience a state of great distress and tribulation.

Furthermore, what would be the meaning of the verses that follow in Matthew 24 (about the days being shortened for the sake of the elect) if believers were never intended to experience any tribulation? "For then there will be great distress, unequaled from the beginning of the world until now – and never to be equaled again. If those days had not been cut short, no one would survive; but, for the sake of the elect, those days will be shortened" (Matthew 24:21-22). The days are shortened for the sake of the elect, who are obviously suffering great distress and persecution – so much so that their survival is questioned.

We are now living in the nighttime of human history. The prince of darkness reigns. Tribulation is a part of life now. Trouble is a part of life now. We suffer pain – physically and emotionally – now. We cry a lot. Jesus warned that his followers would experience tribulation in this life and in this world. Everyone goes through it – even the so-called Great Tribulation.

Our society is besieged with violent acts, a reflection of the moral bankruptcy of our culture. The violence that characterizes society today is global in nature, and it is totally unpredictable – Madrid, London, Cairo, Paris, New York, Boston or Fort Hood. It can happen anytime, anywhere, to anyone. We are living in a new age – the age of terror, violence and distress.

Satan and his demonic forces are behind all that is going on preparing the way for the intervention of God in human history just as Jesus said would be the case at the end of the age. Society is becoming more and more secular, more and more materialistic, more and more godless, and more and more violent. At times, it seems that this deterioration is irreversible. The violence, terror and persecution that characterize this generation are clear indicators that we are living in a new era of human history – a time of global distress – as predicted by Jesus, when He said, "There will be signs in the sun, moon and stars. On the earth, nations will be in anguish and perplexity at the roaring and tossing of the sea. Men will faint from terror, apprehensive of what is coming on the world, for the heavenly bodies will be shaken" (Luke 21:25-26).

Another striking reference to this distress among the nations is recorded in Revelation 16:13ff. Notice what is stated here: "Then I saw three evil spirits that looked like frogs; they came out of the mouth of the dragon, out of the mouth of the beast and out of the mouth of the false prophet. They are spirits of demons performing miraculous signs, and they go out to the kings of the whole world, to gather them for the battle on the great day of God Almighty. Then they gathered the kings together to the place that in Hebrew is called Armageddon." The mention of Armageddon here is in the context of Satan's powerful last-days counter-offensive of evil. What is described here is a diabolical scene of terror, flooding the face of the whole earth and directly affecting the governments of men. The source of the great terror is the dragon (Satan), accompanied by the beast (which represents human governments) and the false prophet (obviously an anti-Christian religious system). Satan is the perpetrator. The beast and the false prophet are his allies, forming an unholy trinity. It is all demonic in nature (spirits of demons) and supernatural in character (performing miraculous signs). The agencies affected seem to be governments, because these agents of evil go out to the kings (political leaders) of the whole earth to gather them for the battle of Armageddon on the great day of God Almighty. The nations of the world are players in that Satan works through world governments to foster terror and create destabilization. All of this evil being perpetrated is setting the stage for the wrap-up of human history.

Make no mistake about it: John was speaking here of a last-days development – a time of great evil, brought on by satanic activity! This onslaught of evil is characterized by deception, destabilization, confusion, unrest, fear and terror.

Satan and his demonic forces are behind all that is going on, preparing the way for the intervention of God in human history, just as Jesus said would be the case at the end of the age. The moral bankruptcy of this generation, coupled with the dramatic global increase in violence and terror, are clear indicators that we are indeed living in the last days.

THE SIGN OF ISRAEL AND THE MIDDLE EAST

When we talk about Israel, the more important question regards our understanding as to who constitute the people of God Biblically. There isn't any question about the fact that Israel is called the people of God in the Bible. The question is, "Are they exclusively understood to be the people of God?" or, more importantly, "In what sense are they the people of God?"

My understanding is that in a Biblical sense, the people of God are those who are in fellowship with God and through whom His purposes are achieved for His glory. If you keep this definition in mind, it will alleviate any confusion that might otherwise arise on this subject. It is difficult to understand how any people can be considered the people of God who are not in fellowship with God.

Adam is a case in point. Adam was created in the image of God for fellowship with God and through whom the purposes of God could be achieved for His glory. He was given dominion over the entire created order. The Lord said to him, "Be fruitful and multiply and fill the earth and subdue it and have dominion." He went on to say, that He had given Adam everything that he would ever need to fulfill God's purposes. Genesis 1 and 2 reveal God's purpose in creation and the role that Adam was intended to have in forming the people of God. God's plan is clearly seen in these opening chapters of the Bible.

However, that purpose was never realized through Adam, whose fellowship with God was broken by his disobedience and sin. Everything that follows in the history of mankind leads to a second Adam through whom the purposes of God will ultimately be achieved. God's plan of a people who will live in fellowship with Him in His Kingdom paradise, for His glory, is achieved through the person and work of Jesus Christ.

There is only one people of God. Galatians 6:11-16 reads, "See what large letters I use as I write to you with my own hand! Those who want to make a good impression outwardly are trying to compel you to be circumcised. The only reason they do this is to avoid being persecuted for the cross of Christ. Not even those who are circumcised obey the law, yet they want you to be circumcised so that they may boast about your flesh. May I never boast except in the cross of our Lord Jesus Christ, through which the world has been crucified to me, and I to the world! Neither circumcision nor uncircumcision means anything; what counts is a new creation. Peace and mercy to all who follow this rule, even to the Israel of God!" Notice the reference to "what counts is the new creation" and the reference to the Israel of God! A.E. Hatch wrote, "There is, after all, one 'Israel of God' – the Church for all ages – one hope for all time. It had its expression, of old, in the Jewish nation; it has its expression, now, in the Church; and it will continue to have an eternal expression in the 'kingdom of God', which shall be established."

The Bible speaks of two creations – the old creation and the new creation. The old creation was a material creation, in which the people of God were created biologically. In the new creation, the people of God are created spiritually. The new creation takes precedence over the old creation as the means by which God's purposes are realized. In the new creation, the biological distinctions are gone. Paul wrote, "Therefore, if anyone is in Christ, he is a new creation; the old has gone, the new has come" (2 Corinthians 5:17). In Christ, there are no more ethnic distinctions. The people of God are formed by the Spirit and not by the flesh. Galatians 3:23-29 says, "Before this faith came, we were held prisoners by the law, locked up until faith should be revealed. So the law was put in charge to lead us to Christ so that we might be justified by faith. Now that faith has come, we are no longer under the supervision of the law. You are all sons of God through faith in Christ Jesus, for all of you who were baptized into Christ have clothed yourselves with Christ. There is neither Jew nor Greek, slave nor free, male nor female, for you are all one in Christ Jesus. If you belong to Christ, then you are Abraham's seed, and heirs according to the promise."

There is only one people of God, whatever name is given to them. There have never been more than one people of God.

Some will raise the question about national Israel being the true people of God. It should be noted that Israel failed every opportunity that God gave them to become the people of God in practice. Even when God sent His Son, the Messiah, about whom their prophets had spoken, they rejected Him. John the Evangelist wrote, "There came a man who was sent from God; his name was John. He came as a witness to testify concerning that light, so that through him all men might believe. He himself was not the light; he came only as a witness to the light. The true light that gives light to every man was coming into the world. He was in the world, and though the world was made through him, the world did not recognize him. He came to that which was his own, but his own did not receive him. Yet to all who received him, to those who believed in his name, he gave the right to become children of God – children born not of natural descent, nor of human decision or a husband's will, but born of God" (John 1:6ff).

The true people of God are born not of the flesh (Israel) but of God (spiritually). There is only one people of God. "Then Paul and Barnabas answered them boldly: 'We had to speak the word of God to you first. Since you reject it and do not consider yourselves worthy of eternal life, we now turn to the Gentiles. For this is what the Lord has commanded us: "I have made you a light for the Gentiles, that you may bring salvation to the ends of the earth"'" (Acts 13:46-47).

So, what are we to think about the place of national Israel as the people of God? After all, God called Abraham and made a covenant relationship with him regarding the land of Palestine, which God promised to his posterity forever and seemingly unconditionally.

It should be noted that the nation of Israel didn't become a nation in the true sense until the law was given under Moses and the constitution of the nation (the 10 commandments) was given. Leviticus 26 sets forth God's expectations for His people and sets forth the consequences of their disobedience. A.E. Hatch said, "This nation of Israel, so lately come out of Egypt, had been a land of slaves, a company of bondmen. In the seclusion of the wilderness, God had transformed a chaotic mass into an organized nation."

The question arises about this unconditional promise regarding land made to Abraham (Genesis 12:7; 15:5-6, 18-21). The issue regarding the land promise is, "To whom is the promise made?" The promise is made to Abraham's offspring, which is the "seed of the woman." If you trace the "seed of the woman" throughout the Old Testament, it leads to the birth of the Messiah, Jesus Christ. Consequently, the unconditional promise of the land to Abraham and his posterity is fulfilled in the new creation in Christ, and it refers not to this world and this time, but to the land that the redeemed shall inherit in the new earth at the Second Coming of Jesus Christ. Abraham was told to look in all directions as far as he could see; this is the land promised to his "seed." Palestine is certainly an important part of that; but, in the true sense, to look in all directions as far as he could see is tantamount to saying that the whole earth would be the inheritance of his "seed." This is consistent with what Scripture says about the new heaven and new earth, the home of the redeemed in Christ Jesus. The message of the Bible about God's eternal purpose is consistent.

The nation of Israel is part of end-time Biblical prophecy, not because they have unconditional title to the land of Palestine, but because God raised them up for a purpose – that purpose being, in part, to be the vehicle through whom the Messiah would come into the world. Additionally, they demonstrate the workings of God with His creation, and they are a testimony to the nations. They are where they are in these end times because God's purposes are still being fulfilled through them.

Charles Krauthammer wrote, "Israel is the very embodiment of Jewish continuity: it is the only nation on earth that inhabits the same land, bears the same name, speaks the same language and worships the same God that it did 3,000 years ago. You dig the soil and you find pottery from Davidic times, coins from bar-Kokhba and 2,000-year-old scrolls written in a script remarkably like the one that today advertises ice cream at the corner candy store."

Israel is the most important, most talked about and most hated of all the nations in the world. One cannot talk about the last days and the end of the age without bringing Israel into the discussion.

More books have been written about Israel and its role in end-time Biblical prophecy than on any other prophetic subject. For many, Israel is the focal point of last-days Biblical prophecy.

There is little agreement, however, on the future of Israel. The key to understanding the place of Israel in end-times Biblical prophecy is the Old Testament prophecies regarding the nation of Israel.

One prophecy that has general agreement respects the re-gathering of the Jews in the Promised Land and the re-establishment of the nation of Israel. The nation of Israel had its beginning in the time of Abraham, and Jews have lived in the land continuously from the time of the conquest by Joshua 3,200 years ago until the present time. The history of the nation of Israel is characterized by captivities, attempted exterminations, and the scattering of its people around the world. However, God promised to bring them back to their homeland in the last days – an action that has happened in our lifetime. The nation of Israel was officially recognized as a sovereign state by the world community of nations in 1948, and Jews continue to immigrate to Israel in large numbers. There are 5,000,000 Jews in Israel today, about one-third of the world's Jewish population. The re-establishment of the nation of Israel is a critical piece of end-times Biblical prophecy; otherwise, the prophecy of Jesus regarding the ending of the times of the Gentiles would have no credence. A second prophecy concerning the nation of Israel is that Jerusalem would come under the control of the Jews, a situation that hasn't existed since 586 BC.

Another prophetic idea embraced by a significant number of Christians has to do with the rebuilding of the temple and the resumption of animal sacrifices. Jesus spoke of the temple in His response to his disciples' questions about His coming and the end of the age.

Temples have always held great prominence in the religious life and rituals of the Jewish people, but Jesus changed all that. He replaced the temple and temple worship. The temple is not needed in the messianic era.

In Matthew 24, Jesus told his disciples that there was coming a day when the temple would be destroyed. This was difficult for them to imagine, but (more importantly) it was hard for them to understand. No temple! What would they do for worship? The temple was the center of their lives as Jews. It was where they met God.

What Jesus was saying to them was that He represented a new way to the Father. The temple would not be needed in this last dispensation of human history, because Jesus Himself would be the means by which people would come to the Father. In other words, from this point on, salvation for mankind would depend on a personal faith in Jesus Christ, as opposed to one's nationality or social pedigree. Jesus said, "I am the way, the truth, and the life. No one comes to the Father except through me" (John 14:6).

The temple was destroyed by the Romans in AD 70, just as Jesus had predicted. Since that day, the Jewish religion and ceremonial practices have struggled without a temple in which to worship.

In his snapshot of Israel's place in end-times prophecy, Jesus said nothing about a rebuilding of the temple. This seems a little strange if indeed the temple was going to be rebuilt at some future date. Jesus certainly knew how confused and distraught His followers were on hearing Him say that the temple would be destroyed. It would have been comforting and reassuring to His followers to simply tell them not to be upset about the news that He shared because the temple would be rebuilt in the last days. But He never even hinted at that.

My sense is that a temple may be rebuilt – but, if it is, it will have no prophetic significance. It would be a natural thing for Orthodox Judaism to want to rebuild the temple. A recent poll shows that two-thirds of Israelis back the idea of a third temple. Blueprints for rebuilding the temple have been in place for a long time, and a group known as the Temple Institute has already created many of the most significant priestly utensils and pieces of furniture necessary for the temple once it is rebuilt.

I would not be surprised to see an attempt made to rebuild the temple at some future point in time – an action that would provoke a conflict of unimaginable magnitude. The location of a rebuilt temple would be on a site currently occupied and administered by Islamic militants. Such an action would rally the Islamic states, led by Iran, which has repeatedly vowed to blow Israel off the map. In November of 2006, Iranian president Mahmoud Ahmadinejad lashed out at Israel, saying that it was "headed toward annihilation." Iran is the most powerful enemy of Israel, and it is in collaboration with other military powers (such as Russia).

Israel and its neighbors are prominent players in end-time Biblical prophecy. Ezekiel, writing more than 2,500 years ago, had quite a bit to say about the coalition of nations that would be arrayed against Israel in the last days. Interestingly enough, the overwhelming majority of the nations mentioned by Ezekiel are modern-day Islamic powers. Eddie Smith, of the U.S. Prayer Center, has made the observation that "every war fought in the future will be a Muslim war."

This is in keeping with what John had to say in Revelation 16 in respect to Armageddon. He spoke of evil spirits spreading out over the whole earth from the unholy trinity. He spoke of the dragon (Satan), the beast (human government) and the false prophet (a hostile religious system). There are several religions that could conceivable fit the profile of an aberrant religious system, but there is only one that is built upon a prophet who is identified historically as a false prophet. The Middle East is where this end-times drama unfolds.

The nations that Ezekiel mentioned in chapter 38 of his prophecy are lined up today in the exact coalition that he described. It's hard to know which of the Arab states will be the dominant nation in the end-time scenario, but don't count Iran out. Iran has the military capacity to inflict serious damage on Israel if they choose to strike first. They have missiles that are capable of reaching Israel, and they may soon have nuclear capability (if, indeed, it is not already in their possession). Iran was the subject of greatest concern at a nuclear summit hosted by the United States in the spring of 2010.

It is difficult to describe the state of Israel and the Middle East today because it is a dynamic situation, subject to change at any moment. Assassinations, suicide bombings or political rhetoric and unrest could set off a chain of events that would trigger Armageddon. The Arab states are united in their hatred for Israel, but they are otherwise politically unstable. The first few months of 2011 demonstrated this instability with a series of political uprisings among Muslim nations, toppling governments and creating international distress. As I write, uncertainty marks the moment and the ramifications in respect to the oil markets are causing global fears.

Perhaps the most prominent sign spoken of in Scripture regarding the place of Israel in end-time Biblical prophecy is what I refer to as the ending of the times of the Gentiles. This is one of the few prophetic benchmarks in the entire Bible that clearly establishes where we are in God's great plan for the ages. According to Jesus' teaching, the last days will be marked by a dramatic historical development affecting the nation of Israel, giving birth to the season of the end, or what the Bible calls the last (or terminal) generation. In other words, something will happen in the Middle East that will clearly mark the beginning of the final chapter of human history.

You get that sense from the parable of the fig tree that Jesus told in Matthew 24, beginning at verse 32. There are two things about this parable that we should consider. One has to do with a change of seasons, and the other has to do with the idea that one generation will witness the wrap-up of human history.

First of all, there is a change of seasons. Something happens specifically to the fig tree to indicate the change. First there are buds; then there are leaves. Nature has a way of letting us know when the seasons change. In the same way, something will happen on the world scene that will mark the birth of the generation that will be alive when the seasons of time change, ushering in the season of the end.

When you study the teaching of Jesus on this subject, it is difficult to find any particular sign of the end that is not already present in some form in every earlier generation. But what does stand out as really unique is what Jesus mentions in Luke 21:24, a parallel passage to Matthew 24. "They (referring to the nation of Israel) will fall by the sword and will be taken as prisoners to all nations. Jerusalem will be trampled on by the Gentiles until the times of the Gentiles are fulfilled (or, come to an end)."

It is my sense that this reference to the ending of the times of the Gentiles is the one mark that God has given us prophetically to help us discern the times. It is a clear indicator on the timeline of human history. I believe the fig tree that Jesus referred to in this same discourse may very well have been a reference to the nation of Israel; and, consequently, it may be the key to understanding the meaning of the last generation.

If you understand the fig tree to be a symbol of the nation of Israel, you must look at Israel to see what (if anything) happens to that nation that might unmistakably fit this prophecy. When you do, you are driven immediately to this phrase in Luke 21:24, "The times of the Gentiles." This phrase, "The times of the Gentiles," is a key phrase in Biblical prophecy. What it refers to is a period of time when the nation of Israel (and, in particular, the city of Jerusalem) would be under the political control of foreigners, or Gentiles.

Most Bible scholars believe that the times of the Gentiles began with King Nebuchadnezzar in 586 BC, when he overran Jerusalem, destroyed the temple and brought the city under his control – the first time such a development had taken place since David had become king about 700 years earlier.

Interestingly enough, Jerusalem stayed under the political control of Gentile powers right up until this present era, with few exceptions – a period of some 2,500 years. In other words, Jerusalem has been trampled on by the Gentiles (as Jesus said would be the case) throughout this entire period of human history.

But something happened in 1948, when the nation of Israel (having been re-gathered in its homeland) was granted recognition by the world community as a sovereign state. Once again, Israel looked at Jerusalem as its holy city. The only problem was that the old city of Jerusalem, East Jerusalem, was still under the control of Gentile powers. In 1967, however, in the Six-Day War, Israel regained territorial and political control over the old city of Jerusalem, the Holy City, and they declared that never again would it be lost to their control. With this decisive development, the times of the Gentiles may have come to an end. The key piece of the prophetic puzzle may have been put into place, inaugurating the final chapter of human history. Jerusalem belonged to the Jews.

The Six-Day War did not end hostilities and tensions in the Middle East. The Middle East remains a time bomb waiting to explode. What we need to understand is that the tiny nation of Israel is surrounded by enemy states. They countries have vowed to push it into the sea. The nation of Israel is a tiny speck of land amidst large landmasses occupied by enemy states. The Arab countries surrounding Israel occupy 640 times the landmass of Israel and outnumber the Jews of Israel 50 to one.

The issue is land entitlement. The Palestinians don't really recognize the legitimacy of the state of Israel. They contend that the land of Palestine is their land going back to the time of Abraham and Ishmael. The Palestinians want the world community of nations to recognize their claims and to create a sovereign Palestinian state. It seems like an easy thing to do, especially since most of the world community of nations supports the idea under certain conditions. It is the subject of international debate. Israel has been generally opposed to the idea, and its government has officially voted against the creation of a separate Palestinian state. More recently Israeli leadership is hinting at possible concessions in regard to a future Palestinian state, but Israel's great fear in all of this is control of Jerusalem. If they agree to support the creation of a sovereign Palestinian state, they may not be able to keep control of Jerusalem.

In the midst of all this conflict and tension, attempts at peace are ongoing. Perhaps the most ardent effort at peace was made in 2003, when world leaders developed a road map for peace in the Middle East, which – if successful – would have resulted in the creation of a sovereign Palestinian state in 2005 along with Palestinian recognition of Israel's right to exist. These rather intense and elaborate efforts collapsed, and violence has continued to mark relations between the two sides.

World leaders understand the strategic nature of Middle East relations, and they are constantly discussing ways to reduce the level of hostility, including ideas about the best way to create a sovereign Palestinian state, which is the sticky wicket. However, what we have discovered, over the years, is that attempts at peace are an exercise in futility, because the bottom-line issues can never be settled at a bargaining table. Peace in the Middle East is basically a matter of rhetoric as opposed to reality, and for one good reason – Jerusalem! Jerusalem, the city of peace, is more like a war zone filled with acts of violence.

In the past, Israel has agreed to negotiate any number of issues with the Palestinians, but they have repeatedly stated that Jerusalem is non-negotiable. Jerusalem is the battle cry of the Middle East, and it may very well be the trigger that launches the battle of Armageddon someday. The Middle East remains a place of intense hostility.

This hostility between Arabs and Jews will not go away. In fact, look for it to intensify! The Middle East is an extremely volatile area of the world. Violence is a way of life. Clashes between Israeli riot police and Palestinian protestors are everyday occurrences. Any one of these clashes is capable of escalating into a major conflict, especially when the trouble centers on the Temple Mount area – a site considered holy by both Muslims and Jews. This is what I mean when I say that Jerusalem may be the trigger for Armageddon someday.

Zechariah spoke of Jerusalem becoming a "cup of trembling" in the twelfth chapter of his prophecy, in speaking of the last days, and the language that he used fits the profile of Armageddon in Revelation 16.

Jerusalem is the reason why many world leaders are nervous about the future. Israel knows that it is still the ultimate target of Islam and that the Arab states will not give up their fight until they have a piece of Jerusalem as well.

The ending of the times of the Gentiles may have moved the world into a new season of time – the season of the end, the last days, the terminal generation. It is my understanding that when Jesus used the phrase "this generation" in the parable of the fig tree, He was referring to a generation that would be alive when the ending of the times of the Gentiles came about and would also be alive when the end of the age comes about. The times of the Gentiles may very well have come to an end in 1967, marking that period of time as the beginning of the terminal generation. Consequently, if you accept the idea that the times of the Gentiles came to an end in 1967, we may expect to see the return of the Lord at any time now.

What is going on in the world today may very well be related to these key prophecies of the Bible (set forth by Jesus Himself in Matthew 24) and may include the developments that lead to the intervention of God in human history. We may be closer to the end of the age than anyone realizes. This generation may be the last generation to exist before His return.

MORE TO THE STORY

But, praise God, there's another chapter to the story! God will write that final chapter. Our hope for the future doesn't rest on the circumstances of life that surround us, but on the sovereignty of God that transcends us. Our hope is not limited to what we can do for ourselves, but rather rests on what God has already done for us in the person of His Son, Jesus Christ. History is His-story, and it will culminate in glorious victory for the people of God. This is the great good news of the gospel. Jesus lives. Jesus reigns. And, Jesus is coming again.

God is sovereign. He is in control. He reigns over all. He has a plan that He is working out in history, which will culminate in the Second Coming of Jesus Christ to establish His eternal kingdom of righteousness and peace on the earth made new, and no person or power – political or military – can prevent it from coming to pass. He has a plan for the future that is not dependent on man or on any circumstances man can create. Even Satan and all his demonic forces are helpless before the sovereign God of the universe when the time comes for Him to act. No power in the universe can hold him back.

We have this certainty based on the authority of God's holy word. First Thessalonians 4:16 reads, "The Lord himself will come down from heaven, with a loud command, with the voice of the archangel, and with the trumpet call of God." Make no mistake about it: Jesus is coming again – personally, purposefully and powerfully – just as He said that He would! It is a certain event and an imminent event.

Jesus is coming in triumph over the forces of darkness. Satan may be the prince of darkness now, and he may be in control of dominions and powers that were surrendered to him by the first Adam. We may be subject to all the consequences of his reign now; but, Praise God, Satan is doomed! His reign is coming to an end. He is going to be destroyed, vanquished, obliterated and vaporized by the brightness of the coming of the King of Kings and Lord of Lords. Satan and all his demonic forces will be destroyed. Darkness will flee away when the light of the world shines on the darkness of this world's night. H. Ernest Nichol, in his great hymn, "We've a Story to Tell to the Nations," expresses our hope in these words: "For the darkness shall turn to dawning, and the dawning to noon-day bright; and Christ's great kingdom shall come to earth, the kingdom of love and light."

The Second Coming of Jesus Christ marks the dawn of God's eternal day, forever dispelling the darkness. Jesus Christ is Victor. No more night! No more violence! No more sinning! No more failure! No more disappointment! No more crying! No more pain! No more disease! No more death! Everything will end where it all began – in Eden, Paradise restored!

QUESTIONS FOR DISCUSSION
1. Why are people, today, more interested in forecasting the future than ever before?

2. What is the most important event that the Bible predicts concerning the future?
3. Discuss some of the popular theories about the Second Coming of Christ.
4. How will we be able to recognize Jesus when He comes?
5. What are some of the things that will happen when Jesus comes?
6. What are some Biblical evidences that the Second Coming may occur in the twenty-first century?

CHAPTER 7

EARTH'S FINAL DAWN

There is coming a time when God's eternal day will dawn and there will never again be any night or darkness. The night of life will be eclipsed by an everlasting sunrise, forever dispelling the darkness. When a day dawns, we recognize it as a particular 24-hour day of the week. But, when earth's final dawn rises on the horizon of eternity, it will not be a 24-hour day – a Sunday, a Monday, a Thursday or a Friday – but a totally new day. Let's call it "Oneday," because it will be the last day ever to dawn, and it will be the one day that will last forever. Earth's final dawn will break on the darkness of this world's night, illuminating the future that God has planned for His people – a future free from the ravages of sin, sickness, pain and death, and filled with blessedness, harmony, peace, joy and life. This is the 'New Age' for which man yearns.

The dawning of this day will be a welcome development, since every man who has ever lived has an inherent longing for this new world – something better than anything that he has ever experienced in this life. God has planted this longing in the hearts of men. Ecclesiastes 3:11 reads, "He has made everything beautiful in its time. Also, he has put eternity into man's heart." What this text says to me is that the innate restless longing for a better life – a more perfect life, without end – is something that man is born with. He searches intently, but he never finds it. Nothing that this world has to offer can ever satisfy that inner longing.

For centuries now, people have sensed a serious problem with life as we know it, and they have sought ways to change the order of things, hoping to create a better world. Man plans ingeniously, and works tirelessly; but, at the end of the day, he questions (in the words of that popular song of the 1950s, by Peggy Lee), "Is This All There Is?"

"I remember when I was a very little girl, our house caught on fire. I'll never forget the look on my father's face as he gathered me up in his arms and raced through the burning building out to the pavement.
I stood there shivering in my pajamas and watched the whole world go up in flames.
And when it was all over I said to myself, 'Is that all there is to a fire?'

"And when I was 12 years old, my father took me to a circus, the greatest show on earth.
There were clowns and elephants and dancing bears.
And a beautiful lady in pink tights flew high above our heads.
And so I sat there watching the marvelous spectacle.
I had the feeling that something was missing.
I don't know what, but when it was over,
I said to myself, 'Is that all there is to a circus?'

"Then I fell in love, head over heels in love, with the most wonderful boy in the world.
We would take long walks by the river or just sit for hours gazing into each other's eyes.
We were so very much in love.
Then one day he went away and I thought I'd die, but I didn't, and when I didn't I said to myself, 'Is that all there is to love?'

"I know what you must be saying to yourselves:
'If that's the way she feels about it, why doesn't she just end it all?'

Oh, no, not me. I'm in no hurry for that final disappointment,
for I know just as well as I'm standing here talking to you,
when that final moment comes and I'm breathing my last breath, I'll
be saying to myself

Is that all there is, is that all there is
If that's all there is, my friends, then let's keep dancing
Let's break out the booze and have a ball
If that's all there is."

THE SEARCH FOR A BETTER LIFE

Disillusionment haunts our existence despite our efforts to change the order of life for the better. One of the most notable efforts was made a few decades ago when President Lyndon B. Johnson announced plans to build what he called, "The Great Society." This was stated to be the most elaborate effort ever made by man to alter the course of human history. President Johnson talked about committing all the resources of the federal government in an effort to eradicate injustice, fear, suffering, disease and crime. He would launch a war on drugs, sickness, injustice, poverty and inferior education. It was mostly political rhetoric, with few tangible results. In more recent years, we heard about another idea of man in what President George H. W. Bush called "The New World Order." The thought was planted in his State of the Union address in 1991. Not much mention was made of it at the time, but it began to gain ascendancy in the years that followed. This "New World Order" would replace the systems of independent national governments with a global community of nations managed by an elite central government. The goal of this New World order was to create a better world. Over the years, it made limited progress, feeding on the emptiness, frustration and hopelessness of mankind.

The concept was an idealistic expression. Realistically, there exist groupings of nations such as the United Nations, the European Union, the Arab League, the Muslim Brotherhood, etc. When these groupings are examined, it is obvious the idea of a New World Order created by man is totally unrealistic. Politically, philosophically and religiously, these groupings are very different. As Daniel prophesied, they "will not cleave one to the other."

Those who advocated a New World Order were simply acting out a plan to address the inner emptiness of man and create a better world. The so-called New World Order was nothing new, and it will not be the last attempt by man to change the order of life. Noticeably absent from all these efforts is where God fits in.

Man's attempts to take control of life and change the order of things for the better are futile. They go all the way back to the Tower of Babel (Genesis 11:1-9). In this passage of Scripture, we read that the whole earth had one language and one understanding. Genesis 10 speaks of Noah and his sons (and their offspring) settling over the face of the earth. This repopulating of the earth after the great flood apparently took a few hundred years. No mention is made of Noah in respect to Babel, even though he lived 350 years after the flood. One would think that the sons of Noah would have rehearsed the history of the flood to their children and grandchildren so as not to forget God, but it appears that by this time man had become so impressed with himself and his exploits that he felt that he didn't need God.

With this exaggerated sense of personal worth, the sons of Ham, who had settled in the region of Shinar, set out to build the perfect society. The goal of their efforts was to make a name for themselves by constructing a city with a tower made of brick and mortar that would reach into the heavens, as if to say, "We don't need you, God; we can do this by ourselves." The inspiration for all of this was Satan, who is always at work deceiving man into thinking that he doesn't need God. He even tried to deceive Jesus into thinking that He didn't need God.

Matthew 4 relates the experience of Jesus at the outset of his public ministry, when he was led by the Spirit into the wilderness to be tempted by the Devil. Interestingly enough, God set this whole thing up. Today, we might call it a sting operation. The point was that Jesus came into the world as the second Adam to rescue man from the devastation brought on by the first Adam. The first Adam plunged the world into sin – with its horrible consequence of death – by believing the lie of the Devil and disobeying God. If the second

Adam was going to undo the effects brought on by the first Adam, He must be subjected to the same temptations and resist the Devil. The three temptations that Satan confronted Jesus with were styled after his temptation to Adam and Eve in the garden. He catches man at his point of need, and he offers a shortcut to achievement. He makes man think that he can do anything for himself and by himself.

In the case of Jesus, Jesus knew why He had come into the world. He knew Who He was. He knew what the outcome of His mission would be. He would be the King of the earth. Satan took Him to an exceedingly high mountain and showed Him all the kingdoms of the world and their glory. Then Satan said to Him, "All these I will give you, if you will fall down and worship me."

This was a powerful deception. Christ knew that He was destined to rule over the kingdoms of men in the kingdom of God that would be established at the end of the age. He also knew that getting to that point would require the rejection of men, suffering and death. It was not a pleasant path that He would need to travel.

Satan was saying to Christ, "You don't need God; I can give it all to you. Why go through all this suffering and anguish when I can hand the dominion to you here and now?"

Satan's greatest lie is simply that man doesn't need God. Every attempt of man to build the perfect world without God will end in utter misery and failure. I call these well-intentioned efforts "Satan's Counterfeit Kingdom." It feeds on the inner emptiness, restlessness, meaninglessness and hopelessness of man. Even today, in the twenty-first century, he's still trying to convince people that he can do it for them (or, at least, through them). His whole strategy seems to be to elevate man to a plane of personal invincibility so as to become a part of God Himself (sound familiar?). What is so tragic is that good people – well-meaning people – out of their deepest yearnings embrace Satan's lie, which only leads to bitter disillusionment. History testifies that man is a rather helpless creature in the face of suffering, sorrow and death. No matter how hard we try, the life for which we yearn never seems to materialize.

The world is on a collision course with destiny, and all the dreams of man for a new and better world – free from sickness, injustice, violence, poverty, fear and war – only lead to bitter disillusionment and failure. Haunting doubts continue to plague our planning for the future. We have become very skeptical. There must be something more than what we know and experience in life – something more than heartache, pain, disease and death. Certainly, this is not the way that God created the world to be. It can't be what He intended, and it isn't. Reading Genesis, we learn that life didn't start out the way it is today; and, reading Revelation, we learn that life won't end this way. God will not leave man to live forever in a world that falls far short of His glory and purpose.

God has acted in Jesus Christ to reverse the pattern of life as we know it. God has acted in Jesus Christ to create a new humanity – a new people of God – to share His glories forever in his kingdom paradise.

Jesus Christ is the central figure in God's great plan of redemption and restitution. What man cannot do by himself, God has already planned to do for him. The life for which we were originally created – the life for which we so desperately long – the life of peace, joy, harmony, blessedness and unending life will come to reality at this crisis point in time, when the kingdoms of this world become the kingdoms of our Lord and Savior, Jesus Christ.

Until then, the search goes on. Every religion is engaged in the search for satisfaction – but to no avail. All the strivings of man are futile in this regard, because man lacks the capacity to alter his existence and ultimate destiny through any of his strivings and by his own means.

However, as believers, the longing will be fully satisfied when Jesus returns to establish his eternal Kingdom on the earth made new. There is a kingdom of God that is distinct from the kingdoms of men.

Daniel made that distinction. When he was interpreting the dream of King Nebuchadnezzar, he outlined the course of human history as a succession of earthly kingdoms. These were real kingdoms that were ruled over by real kings. Miles Grant, writing more than 100 years ago, said (in respect to the identification of a kingdom), "A kingdom is a country ruled by a king, and implies subjects, laws, and a capital." In Daniel 2:44, mention is made of how "in the days of these kings (earthly kingdoms), the God of heaven will set up a kingdom," but it will be distinct from the kingdoms of men in that it will be ruled by God himself. In each case, there is a literal kingdom.

In conversion, a person becomes a citizen of the Kingdom of God. Philippians 3:20 reads, "But our citizenship is in heaven, and from it we await a Savior, the Lord Jesus Christ, who will transform our lowly body to be like his glorious body, by the power that enables him to subject all things to himself." As believers in the Lord Jesus Christ, we have become citizens of His Kingdom. Colossians 1:13 reads, "He has delivered us from the domain of darkness and transferred us to the Kingdom of his beloved Son, in whom we have redemption, the forgiveness of sins."

There is a sense in which believers have dual citizenship. We are citizens of a particular country here and now – subject to the powers that be in governing that country and entitled to certain rights and privileges of that citizenship – but this is a temporary arrangement. As we sometimes sing, "This world is not my home." In conversion, we become citizens of another kingdom. We bow before another Sovereign, even though we have not entered fully into what it means to be subjects of this King.

This world may be our current residence (with a particular street address), but it is not our final destiny. We are pilgrims and strangers here, subject to the effects of the curse that was pronounced when Adam sinned against God. We live in a world that is far beneath the plan and original intention that God had when He created it all.

In the beginning, everything that God created was good (Genesis 1:31). Man was created in an environment of peace and harmony, and he was given dominion over the whole created order (Genesis 1:26; Psalm 8). The great paradox of life is that man was created as the ruler of the world – King of the earth, exercising dominion over it all – but, as it turned out (due to sin), he has spent his years dominated by his environment. D.H. Woodard reflected on this when he said, "That existence, which might have culminated in glorious immortality, shriveled to a few miserable years of time; and the earth, over which he was to preside in glory, has opened her bosom to engulf a hundred generations of his sons." Irony of ironies!

But life as we know it and experience it will someday change. The old order of things will come to an end when God makes all things new. Revelation 21:4-5 gives us this word of hope: "He will wipe all tears from their eyes, and death shall be no more, neither shall there be mourning, nor crying, nor pain anymore, for the former things (the old order of things), have passed away. And he who was seated on the throne said, 'Behold, I am making all things new.'" Earth's final dawn will usher in the eternal Kingdom of our Lord in all its glory. The Kingdom of God will one day exist on the earth and will fill the whole earth (Daniel 7:27; Revelation 5:9-10; Matthew 5:5). God created the world as an exhibition of His glory. The material creation (among other things) is a manifestation of God's glory. Psalm 19:1 states, "The heavens declare the glory of God." Revelation 4:11 points out that the Lord alone is worthy to receive glory, honor and power, "for you created all things, and by your will they existed and were created." Furthermore, God created the world to be inhabited (Isaiah 45:18). With this in mind, it stands to reason that when the Kingdom of God is established on the earth made new, it will manifest His glory in a way never before seen by mortals (Psalm 18; Psalm 72:18-20; Numbers 14:21). The kingdom becomes a glorified world, filled with glorified people and ruled over by the King of glory. The kingdom of God will be established on the earth made new.

THE STAGES OF THE KINGDOM

The Kingdom of God, which has existed before the foundations of the world, is as real as any kingdom of man that has ever existed on the face of the earth. It hasn't been visible to man, but it has existed in stages.

The first stage of the Kingdom of God was the visionary stage. Before the creation of the world, God envisioned a Kingdom that He would create, populated with a people that He would create, who would live in fellowship with him in his Kingdom Paradise, for his glory, forever. Proverbs 3:19 reads, "By wisdom, the Lord laid the earth's foundations; by understanding, He set the heavens in place." This text implies that God had a plan in creation, which is consistent with subsequent Scriptural revelation. The Bible also suggests that no man knows the mind of the Lord or can know the mind of the Lord. Romans 11:33-36 reads, "Oh, the depth of the riches of the wisdom and knowledge of God! How unsearchable his judgments, and his paths beyond tracing out! Who has known the mind of the Lord? Or who has been his counselor? Who has ever given to God, that God should repay him? For from him and through him and to him are all things. To him be the glory forever! Amen." We can only surmise what God was thinking by studying His actions.

The second stage of the Kingdom is what I call the inaugural stage. It became clear what God was thinking when He created the world and everything in it as described in Genesis 1 and 2. The Kingdom involved a real world, with real people, in a real environment that was suited to their needs. The Eden Paradise was a prototype of the Kingdom of God. One can only imagine that if (and "if" is a big word in this context) man had remained faithful to God and had lived by the constitution of Eden, we would still be there today – free from all the misery, strife, disease and death that characterizes our present condition. But God knew that that wouldn't happen; consequently, this stage is called a prototype of the Kingdom. God created man with a free will – an ability to love and make decisions. This was not a flaw in the created order or a failure on God's part to know what would happen. It was a necessary act if God's creative purpose was ever to be fulfilled. God didn't create man as a robot, but as a being who could make a choice to love God and serve Him.

In the original creation, man was created with a will capable of obeying or disobeying the will of the Creator. If His goal in creation was a people who would live in fellowship with Him, He knew that mans will must be tested and a choice made (to serve Him or not). "In fellowship with him" means that a choice has been made: the will has been exercised to be subservient to the Creator.

This was true of the angelic realm of creation as well. In fact, the problem was first encountered in the angelic realm, with the rebellion of Satan, who led other angelic beings to join him in rebellion against God. With this fractured relationship – and with Satan's presence in the inaugural stage of God's kingdom – it was inevitable, given man's free will, that man would rebel. God demanded man's allegiance, but He did not control it.

One could question what might happen in the manifest stage of the Kingdom at the end of the age given the free will of man.

We can be confident that in the manifest stage of God's Kingdom, this problem will never occur again. The Kingdom will be inhabited only by those who have chosen (willed) to follow Christ and to live forever in fellowship with Him. This decision seals one's relationship with God for time and eternity. The fellowship between God and the inhabitants of his Kingdom will never be broken. We will have been changed – immortalized – and made like Him.

In the inaugural stage of God's Kingdom, we are given a glimpse of what might have been and what will be when He makes all things new and establishes his eternal kingdom on the earth made new.

The third stage of God's Kingdom is what I call the hidden stage. The prototype in Eden has disappeared, nowhere to be found on earth. The rule of the King has been subjugated to the rule of the enemy, Satan (1 John 5:19). God has not abandoned his kingdom goal. He is working in history to institute a plan of recovery. Several significant developments take place that remind us of this even though it appears that things have gotten out of control. The enemy has so polluted the mind of man and instilled a divine hostility in man that in the time of Noah, God has had enough of man's sin and rebellion to the degree that he regrets that He ever made man (Genesis 6:5-6). God demonstrates His sovereignty by sending His judgment in the form of a flood that destroys all life on the earth except for those who found grace and safety in the ark. It is important to note that in this judgment the earth itself is not destroyed.

The outline of God's redemptive plan begins to emerge with the call of Abraham and the promises made to him to be the father of many nations. Genesis 12 delineates the call and what it entails. Throughout the history of Abraham's descendants, God has been at work in manifest actions to ultimately achieve His purpose.

The primary role of the nation of Israel (contrary to popular opinion) is to be the human vehicle from which the Messiah would be born. The selection of the nation of Israel and the calling of them to be the people of God was not to choose a particular nation, eliminating all other peoples from the prospect of salvation, but rather to provide a biological line – a seed – from which the Messiah would ultimately come. The nation of Israel was a type or symbol of the people of God, putting in place His expectations and requirements, establishing a pattern of atonement for sin and providing the means by which He would become one of us. Robert McConnell, in a pamphlet titled *The Jew in Prophecy*, says, "It would appear from Scripture that God created the nation of Israel for three purposes: first, as a repository for truth (Romans 3:2); second, as a witness for Himself before the other nations of the world; and, third, as the human channel through which the Messiah would come (Micah 5:2)." If God was going to send his Son on a mission of recovery and redemption, He must be born of human flesh and partake of the human condition to demonstrate victory over the tendencies of the flesh. God could have decreed salvation for whomever He chose; but, instead, He sent the second Adam to be one of us and to live a sinless life so that he might die in our place (as our substitute) in order that we might live. That required a nation (or a race) of human beings, out of which the Messiah would be born. Most of what prophetic scholars ascribe to Israel as a nation is incidental to their primary purpose. This hidden stage of the Kingdom lasted about 2,000 years.

This brings us to the next stage of the Kingdom, the announced stage, which consists of the ministry and message of Jesus. With the arrival of the King, the world was told that the Kingdom of God had come. This did not mean that the manifest stage of the Kingdom had dawned, but that it was no longer hidden. Jesus was presented as the King who was appointed to reign.

The prophets had spoken of this day when Isaiah said, "For to us a Child is born, to us a Son is given, and the government will be on His shoulders. And he will be called Wonderful Counselor, Mighty God, Everlasting Father, Prince of Peace. Of the increase of His government and peace there will be no end. He will reign on David's throne and over his kingdom, establishing and upholding it with justice and righteousness from that time on and forever. The zeal of the Lord Almighty will accomplish this" (Isaiah 9:6-7).

An angel appeared to Mary with the news that she had been chosen by God to be the one through whom the Messiah would come. Luke 1:26-33 reads, "In the sixth month, God sent the angel Gabriel to Nazareth, a town in Galilee, to a virgin pledged to be married to a man named Joseph, a descendant of David. The virgin's name was Mary. The angel went to her and said, 'Greetings, you who are highly favored! The Lord is with you.' Mary was greatly troubled at his words and wondered what kind of greeting this might be. But the angel said to her, 'Do not be afraid, Mary, you have found favor with God. You will be with child and give birth to a son, and you are to give him the name Jesus. He will be great and will be called the Son of the Most High. The Lord God will give him the throne of his father David, and he will reign over the house of Jacob forever; his kingdom will never end.'" The angel linked the birth of this child to Isaiah's prophecy in that this Child would reign and of His Kingdom there would be no end.

John the Baptist was raised up to prepare the way for Christ, and John's message in that regard was, "Repent, for the kingdom of heaven is at hand!" The message of Jesus was all about the Kingdom of heaven. Nelson, in his *Illustrated Bible Dictionary*, copyright 1986, Thomas Nelson Publishers, shows how intertwined the message and deeds of Jesus were to His kingship. He writes, "The entire ministry of Jesus is understood in relation to this important declaration of the presence of the kingdom. His ethical teachings, for example, cannot be understood apart from the announcement of the kingdom. They are ethics of the kingdom; the perfection to which they point makes no sense apart from the present experience of the kingdom. Participation in the new reality of the kingdom involves a follower of Jesus in a call to the highest righteousness" (Matthew 5:20).

The acts and deeds of Jesus likewise make sense only in the larger context of proclaiming the kingdom. When John the Baptist asked whether Jesus was "the Coming One" (the Messiah), Jesus answered by recounting some of His deeds of healing (Matthew 11:5). The reference in these words to the expectation of a Messiah, especially of the prophet Isaiah, (Isaiah 29:18-19; 35:5-6; 61:1), could not have been missed by John. At the synagogue in Nazareth, Jesus read a passage from Isaiah 61 about the coming messianic age, and then He made the astonishing announcement, "Today this Scripture is fulfilled in your hearing" (Luke 4:21).

Everything that Jesus did was related to this claim that the kingdom of God had dawned through His ministry. His healings were manifestations of the presence of the kingdom. In these deeds, there was a direct confrontation between God and the forces of evil (Satan and his demons). Summarizing His ministry, Jesus declared, "I saw Satan fall like lightning from heaven" (Luke 10:18). Satan and evil have been put on notice now that the kingdom has made its entrance into human history. This is an anticipation of the final age of perfection that will be realized at Christ's return. With the coming of the King, the Kingdom of God was no longer hidden.

Following the announcement stage, the formative stage (or building stage) of the Kingdom was set in motion. Jesus told His followers that He was going away to prepare a place for them. The traditional understanding of this text is that Jesus was a construction manager and (when He went back to the Father) He would spend his time building a literal place for His followers to inhabit when He returned. It is my understanding that when Jesus ascended following His resurrection, His going to prepare a place was intended to convey the idea that His followers would live forever with Him an a real place and that He was going to pave the way for His followers to subsequently be with Him for eternity. He would not be engaged in a literal building of something, but instead would sit at the Father's right hand as Savior, Redeemer and Lord. He was the Door through whom one might enter in and be saved.

After Jesus had finished His mission on earth with signs and wonders, He ascended to the Father to preside over the work of the gospel through His Church, the formative or building stage of the Kingdom. John the Revelator was given a glorious picture of this phase of God's Kingdom in Revelation 4 and 5. The vision that John was given was God's way of assuring him that His purpose of forming a people who would live with Him in His kingdom paradise, for His glory, forever, would be accomplished despite what might appear on the surface to be a defeat.

John was transported by the Spirit to the throne room of God. The setting is the ascension of Christ following His ministry on earth culminating with His crucifixion and resurrection. This could have been a time of questioning and doubt for the followers of Jesus. The events of the last days of our Lord's life on earth must have left them wondering what it all meant. They had followed Jesus with the idea that He was the Messiah and had come to establish the Kingdom of God. After all, this was the message that they heard Jesus preach everywhere that He went. Now, He was gone, and the Kingdom hadn't come. In one of their last conversations with Jesus, recorded in Acts 1, they had inquired if this was the time when He would establish the Kingdom of God, but He told them that it wasn't for them to know the when. So, what did these developments mean?

John stands in awe before the throne of God, surrounded by heavenly luminaries. What was he to make of this majestic scene – the appearance of the rainbow, flashes of lightning, rumblings and peals of thunder, and lamps blazing?

One thing that caught his attention was a large scroll in the hand of God, with writing on it. It was sealed with seven seals. He noticed an angel who was calling attention to the scroll and crying out for someone who was worthy to break the seals and open the scroll. To his great dismay, no one in heaven or on earth was identified as being worthy to open the scroll. Somehow, John understood the centrality of this scroll to the success of God's purpose of creating a people who would live in fellowship with Him in His kingdom paradise, for His glory, forever. John was devastated by this development. To think that it's over – there won't be a future Kingdom! He began to weep profusely – how could this be?

It was at this point that one of the elders around the throne spoke to him and told him that he didn't need to weep. It wasn't over. Satan may have locked the Messiah in his place of captivity, but He was no longer dead; He was alive forevermore, right there among the heavenly luminaries. The Lamb that was slain is worthy, and He will open the scroll and break its seals.

This is a scene of victory for the program of God and for the people of God. Notice the celebration: "And they sang a new song: 'You are worthy to take the scroll and to open its seals, because you were slain, and with your blood you purchased men for God from every tribe and language and people and nation. You have made them to be a kingdom and priests to serve our God, and they will reign on the earth.' Then I looked and heard the voice of many angels, numbering thousands upon thousands, and 10,000 times 10,000. They encircled the throne and the living creatures and the elders. In a loud voice, they sang: 'Worthy is the Lamb, who was slain, to receive power and wealth and wisdom and strength and honor and glory and praise!' Then I heard every creature in heaven and on earth and under the earth and on the sea, and all that is in them, singing: 'To him who sits on the throne, and to the Lamb, be praise and honor and glory and power, forever and ever!' The four living creatures said, 'Amen,' and the elders fell down and worshiped."

Christ completed His mission of redemption and ascended in triumph to the right hand of the Father, where he reigns as Lord over the Church. This is the gospel age (or church age) when – through the ministry of the Word and Spirit – people are repenting of their sins, accepting Jesus Christ as Savior and Lord. The Kingdom is being populated daily through the ministry of the Church. God's creative purpose of forming a people who will live in fellowship with Him in His Kingdom paradise, for his glory, is being accomplished. This is the formation stage of the Kingdom – the church age. What remains is the manifest stage of the Kingdom, which will be accomplished at the second coming of Jesus.

The future of our world may be summed up by two developments: the Second Coming of Christ and the restitution of all things. Acts 3:19-21 reads, "Repent, then, and turn to God, so that your sins may be wiped out, that times of refreshing may come from the Lord, and that he may send the Christ, who has been appointed for you — even Jesus. He must remain in heaven until the time comes for God to restore everything, as he promised long ago through his holy prophets."

The question is, "Where is the heaven that He will descend from?" Most people have a warped sense of "heaven," thinking that it is some celestial abode to be inhabited when a person dies. Heaven is used in different ways in Scripture. In the May, 2007, issue of the *Signs of the Times*, the question is asked about the third heaven that Paul is said to have been caught up to in 2 Corinthians 12:2. The answer that is given is as follows: "In the Bible, the first heaven is the atmosphere. When the Bible says that 'God created the heavens and the earth' (Genesis 1:1), it's talking about the atmosphere. Genesis 1:20 speaks of God creating the birds that 'fly above the earth across the face of the firmament (air) of the heavens'. The second heaven is the place where the sun, moon and stars are located. Psalm 19:4 says, 'In the heavens He (God) has pitched a tent for the sun.' Psalm 8:3 speaks of 'your (God's) heavens, the work of your fingers, the moon and the stars, which you have set in place.' The third heaven is Paradise, the dwelling place of God (Revelation 2:7; 22:1-2). In 1 Kings 8:30, Solomon prayed to God, asking Him to, 'hear from heaven, your dwelling place.' In 2 Corinthians 12:3-4, Paul says that the heaven that he was caught up to was Paradise."

Heaven is not a particular 'place' somewhere up there in the sky. It appears from Scripture that heaven is referenced as distinct from the earth. The place that Jesus went away to prepare, according to Scripture, is a new heaven and a new earth where we will live forever with the Lord. God's Kingdom plan will be realized when Jesus comes again and the redeemed in Christ Jesus will live forever in the paradise of God for His glory. 'The Place', isn't up there; it is right here. The terms "Kingdom of Heaven" and "Kingdom of God" are used interchangeably in the Gospels, and they speak of the future home of the redeemed – the earth made new.

In order for this to happen, revolutionary developments need to take place. For one thing, this world in which we live is under a curse (because of man's sin), which results in blight, decay, disease and death. Furthermore, sin must be eradicated and the effects of sin removed. Also, the enemy of God and man (Satan) must be destroyed – along with the demons that he controls – and the dominion that he wrested from man must be recovered.

All of this will happen at the Second Coming of Jesus Christ in power and glory. Jesus has overcome sin and the grave, having dealt Satan a mortal defeat in the cross/resurrection event. All that remains, is for Satan to be destroyed; and, by "destroyed," is meant obliterated from the universe, consumed by the power of God, never to exist in any form in any place ever again.

There are several key words in Scripture on which, hang the fulfillment of God's creative purpose. One of these words is "change." Things are going to change when Jesus comes. Life as we know it – the world as we know it – everything that we know and experience will change. "Change" is a key word in the Bible. Everything will end where it all began – in Paradise restored. Everything will change to what it was in the manner it originally came about – by the word of the Lord.

THE UNIVERSE WILL CHANGE

For one thing, the universe will change and be made totally new. To imagine the universe being made totally new is beyond human comprehension. We know very little about the universe in terms of how it functions and its magnitude, but what we do know is mind-boggling.

No one really knows how expansive our universe is, or if (in fact) our universe is all that there is. In every generation, scientists have explored the universe using a variety of techniques and methods in an attempt to discover how vast the universe is. Furthermore, there is a great deal of confusion (or disagreement) about the age of our universe and its size.

Some conjecture that our universe is between 10,000,000,000 and 13,000,000,000 years old, based on the speed of light and the fact that light reaching the earth from distant stars would take more than 10,000,000,000 years to reach us if you accept all of the scientific calculations as fact. A light-year is the distance that light travels in one year – almost 6,000,000,000,000 miles.

Creationists contend that the earth is roughly 6,000 years old based on the history of man as outlined in Genesis. The age of the universe and the age of the earth may not be the same. Genesis 1:1 simply says, "In the beginning God created the heavens and the earth." However, as you read further about the process of creation, the actual earth as we know it today – with land separated from water – didn't take place until the second or third day.

We are told that new galaxies are forming all the time as the universe is rapidly expanding. As we learn more about the universe, some discoveries have disturbed and perplexed scientists. In an article published a few years ago – under the title, *New-Found Old Galaxies Upsetting Astronomers' Long-Held Theories on the Big Bang* – Kenneth Chang reports, "Gazing deep into space and far into the past, astronomers have found that the early universe, a couple of billion years after the Big Bang, looks remarkably like the present-day universe." He went on to say that recent discoveries "could challenge a widely accepted picture of the evolution of the universe." It sounds to me as if these scientists are saying the same thing that the Bible says about creation but struggling to acknowledge it. It happened all at once, when God called it into being.

An astronomer named Williams made a presentation at a meeting of the American Astronomical Society in San Antonio, Texas, several years ago, in which he calculated that the universe is stuffed with 50,000,000,000 galaxies, not the 10,000,000,000 that astronomers previously thought. The size of the universe, although unknown, is staggering to the mind of man. The more we learn about the vastness and complexity of the universe, the more majestic and powerful we see our God to be.

Seth Borenstein, reporting for the Associated Press in February of 2011, said, "Scientists have estimated the first cosmic census of planets in our galaxy, and the numbers are astronomical: at least 50,000,000,000 planets in the Milky Way. At least 500,000,000 of those planets are in the not-too-hot, not-too-cold zone where life could exist. The numbers were extrapolated from the early results of NASA's planet-hunting Kepler telescope. Kepler science chief William Borucki says that the scientists took the number of planets that they found in the first year of searching a small part of the night sky and then made an estimate on how likely stars are to have planets. Kepler spots planets as they pass between Earth and the stars that they orbit. So far, Kepler has found 1,235 candidate planets, with 54 in the Goldilocks zone, where life could possibly exist. Kepler's main mission is not to examine individual worlds, but to give astronomers a sense of how many planets – especially potentially habitable ones – there are likely to be in our galaxy. They would use the one-four-hundredth of the night sky that Kepler is looking at and extrapolate from there. Borucki and colleagues figured that one of two stars has planets and one of 200 stars has planets in the habitable zone, announcing these ratios at the American Association for the Advancement of Science annual conference in Washington. And that's a minimum, because these stars can have more than one planet and Kepler has yet to get a long enough glimpse to see planets that are further out from the star, like Earth, Borucki said. For example, if Kepler were 1,000 light-years from Earth and looking at our sun and noticed Venus passing by, there's only a one-in-eight chance that Earth would also be seen, astronomers said. To get the estimate for the total number of planets, scientists then took the frequency observed already and applied it to the number of stars in the Milky Way. For many years, scientists figured that there were 100,000,000,000 stars in the Milky Way, but last year a Yale scientist figured that the number was closer to 300,000,000,000 stars. Either way, it shows that Carl Sagan was right when he spoke of billions and billions of worlds, said retired NASA astronomer Steve Maran, who praised the research, but wasn't part of it. And that's just our galaxy. Scientists figure that there are 100,000,000,000 galaxies. Borucki said that the new calculations lead to worlds of questions about life elsewhere in the cosmos. 'The next question is, "Why haven't they visited us?" And the answer? "I don't know," Borucki said.'

The universe is immense, and no one knows with any certainty how immense it all is. The mind of man ponders, "Does the universe have an edge? And, if so, how far out is that edge? And, is there anything beyond the edge?"

It is difficult for us to think in terms of infinity. We live in a time/space existence, in which everything that we deal with can be measured or has a beginning and an ending. We know where it came from, what it does and where it goes. How do we understand the infinite?

When we talk about the universe changing at the end of time, we need to understand what changes – and what the universe is – in Biblical terms. The Bible is not written as a scientific textbook, but what it describes is verified by what science has discovered.

The universe is defined in the Bible as the heavens and the earth. For man, the universe is what we can see – the canopy of the heavens above us. It is an infinitely large universe.

John the Revelator was given a vision of the change that the universe will undergo, but what he saw was unexplained and limited. Revelation 21:1 simply says, "I saw a new heaven and a new earth, for the first heaven and the first earth had passed away, and there was no longer any sea." It would seem that the change that John observed was what he could see without defining the scientific implications of it. There is one major change that he observed that differentiates the new heaven and earth from the first heaven and earth – that is, there was no longer any sea. Structurally, water has been a fundamental aspect of the old order of things from the time of creation. Genesis 1 tells us, "In the beginning, when God created the heavens and the earth, darkness was over the face of the deep, and the Spirit of God hovered over the face of the waters." What is even more interesting is what is said in Genesis 1:6-8 – "Let there be an expanse between the waters to separate water from water. So God made the expanse and separated the water under the expanse from the water above it. And it was so. God called the expanse 'sky.' And there was evening, and there was morning – the second day."

It would appear from John's vision of the new heaven and the new earth that water may not be present in the same sense in which it was in the first heaven and earth. There is still the presence of water in the river of life, which we will discuss later, but one significant change is the absence of the sea. One could argue that the reference to "no longer any sea" is a reference to the oneness of those who inhabit the new heavens and the new earth, since (in prophecy) the sea symbolically references the masses of people who populate our planet. However, the reference to "sea" in this context is not a symbolic reference, since we are talking about a literal new heavens and new earth. If "sea" is symbolic, then we must be consistent and understand heaven and earth in the same manner. I know of no reputable exegete who takes this passage symbolically.

In the original creation, we are led to believe that it never had rained (Genesis 2:5-6). There went up a mist from the earth, and watered the face of the earth. It may very well be that in the palingenesis of all things, the new heaven and new earth will be the same as the original, and there won't be any need for a sea or rain. It worked then, and it could work when God re-creates the heaven and the earth.

The vision that John received challenges our imagination in a variety of ways. Is it conceivable that the solar system – of which planet earth is a part, and on which we are dependent for light, warmth, seasons and the rainfall necessary for the sustenance of life – will no longer be a part of the new heaven and new earth?

I, for one, could do without seasons. I've shoveled enough snow in my lifetime. Having been clothed with immortality in the resurrection of the last day, we won't be dependent on anything for life. Revelation 22:5 says, "There will be no more night. They will not need the light of a lamp or the light of the sun, for the Lord God will give them light. And they will reign forever and ever." I suspect that there are fundamental changes ahead in the structure of the universe as we know it.

One other conjecture has to do with how much of what God created for our well-being – that is, our heaven and earth – will actually change. Is it possible that there are heavens beyond our universe that will not change or need to change? Genesis 1 speaks of God creating the heavens and the earth. John said that he saw a new heaven (singular) and new earth, for the first heaven and the first earth were passed away. I take this to mean that what we recognize as our environment of life – heaven and earth – will no longer exist as it is presently. In order for there to be a new heaven and a new earth, the old one needs to be removed.

THE COSMOS WILL BE DESTROYED

John did not describe what happened to the cosmos in this passage; he simply told us what happened. Other scriptures speak specifically to the destruction of the physical universe (Matthew 24:35; 1 Corinthians 7:31; Hebrews 1:10-12).

Peter, writing in the first century, said, "First of all, you must understand that in the last days scoffers will come, scoffing and following their own evil desires. They will say, 'Where is this "coming" he promised? Ever since our fathers died, everything goes on as it has since the beginning of creation.' But they deliberately forget that long ago by God's word the heavens existed and the earth was formed out of water and by water. By these waters also the world of that time was deluged and destroyed. By the same word the present heavens and earth are reserved for fire, being kept for the day of judgment and destruction of ungodly men. But do not forget this one thing, dear friends: with the Lord a day is like 1,000 years, and 1,000 years are like a day. The Lord is not slow in keeping His promise, as some understand slowness. He is patient with you, not wanting anyone to perish, but everyone to come to repentance. But the day of the Lord will come like a thief. The heavens will disappear with a roar; the elements will be destroyed by fire, and the earth and everything in it will be laid bare. Since everything will be destroyed in this way, what kind of people ought you to be? You ought to live holy and godly lives as you look forward to the day of God and speed its coming. That day will bring about the destruction of the heavens by fire, and the elements will melt in the heat. But in keeping with his promise we are looking forward to a new heaven and a new earth, the home of righteousness."

Peter told us what happens to the present heaven and earth – it will be destroyed, discarded, dismantled, as if it never existed. The picture given by Peter is one of being totally consumed.

One may wonder how this can be. For a Bible-believer, it isn't a matter beyond comprehension. God created it in the beginning by the word of His mouth, and He can destroy it in the same way by the word of His mouth. The word that God speaks is all-powerful.

Furthermore, there are significant elements in the created order that can bring about this destruction if He so chooses. One interesting understanding has to do with the structure of the earth. Beneath the ground we walk on is a molten core – an infinitely hot molten core. We live on top of a firebox. We don't think about it, but every so often we are reminded of it when a volcano erupts. An erupting volcano is a pressure valve for the firebox beneath the earth's surface. In respect to this, the earth is surrounded by water in oceans, seas, lakes and rivers. When this burning lava hits an ocean of water, a great explosion takes place. Can you imagine the destruction that could be released by the natural reaction of the molten core of the earth and the waters under the earth and around the earth being brought together?

We are told of the destruction of life in the days of Noah, when there was the great flood that God brought in judgment on the people of Noah's day. Interestingly enough, in all the Biblical accounts of this great flood, mention is made of the part that water played in the destruction.

In Peter's reference to the final destruction, he cites the flood of Noah's day as an example. He says about it, "They will say, 'Where is this "coming" he promised? Ever since our fathers died, everything goes on as it has since the beginning of creation.' But they deliberately forget that long ago by God's word the heavens existed and the earth was formed out of water and by water. By these waters also the world of that time was deluged and destroyed. By the same word the present heavens and earth are reserved for fire, being kept for the day of judgment and destruction of ungodly men" (2 Peter 3:4-7).

There is reference to fire and water, but no explanation as to the interplay of these devouring elements in the final destruction. It's as if to say that the elements are all there in nature, in the structure of the earth, to bring about total destruction at the word of the Lord.

If you go back to the original description of what took place in Noah's day, recorded in Genesis 7, this is what you read: "In the six hundredth year of Noah's life, on the seventeenth day of the second month – on that day all the springs of the great deep burst forth, and the floodgates of the heavens were opened. And rain fell on the earth 40 days and 40 nights." Most of the time, when we talk about the flood of Noah's day, we focus on the rain that fell for 40 days and 40 nights. Notice, in this reference, that the flood came about not exclusively (or even primarily) from the rain that fell, but more importantly from the waters under the earth gushing up out of the earth with the water that fell as rain. The Lord had told Noah earlier that He was going to send this flood to destroy man and all living things on the earth. "The Lord was grieved that He had made man on the earth, and His heart was filled with pain. So the Lord said, 'I will wipe mankind, whom I have created, from the face of the earth – men and animals, and creatures that move along the ground, and birds of the air – for I am grieved that I have made them.' But Noah found favor in the eyes of the Lord" (Gen 6:6-8). "So, God said to Noah, 'I am going to put an end to all people, for the earth is filled with violence because of them. I am surely going to destroy both them and the earth'" (Gen 6:13-14). According to this original account of the flood, everything was destroyed, and water was the destroying element. But, notice, it wasn't just rain that fell for 40 days and 40 nights, but "the springs of the great deep burst forth." In the structure of the earth, water is present in abundance; and, even though no indication is given that water will play a destructive role at the end of the age, the presence of the fire and water are both destroying elements – especially when the fire meets the water, as in a volcanic eruption. In Noah's day, water was the destroying element because God's purpose was to destroy everything that lived on the earth but not to destroy the earth or the universe. In the final consummation at the end of the age, both the heavens and the earth will be destroyed.

No one knows the "how" of the final consummation, but we do know that the earth and everything in it will be destroyed, so that even the elements will melt with fervent heat. Scripture teaches that this conflagration at the end of the age will consume not only the heavens and the earth, but also Satan, his demon spirits, evil and evildoers. It will be all-consuming. All things that offend will be destroyed.

This is the language of annihilation. Some people have a problem with the idea of a total consummation, choosing rather to believe in the continuation of Satan, his demon spirits and evildoers in the unending fires of hell. The idea of annihilation (destruction of being, resulting in non-being) is a controversial subject among Bible-believing Christians, and it raises some interesting questions. However, the Bible uses specific and clear terms when speaking of the final punishment of unrepentant sinners, Satan and demonic spirits.

One such term – "perish" – is used repeatedly in this regard (Romans 2:12; 1 Corinthians 1:18; 1 Corinthians 15:13-19; 2 Thessalonians 2:9-10; John 3:14-16; Luke 13:3; and 2 Peter 3:9 – to name a few). Another term that is used to describe the ultimate destiny of the unrepentant is the term "destroy" or "destruction" (Philippians 1:27-28; 2 Thessalonians 1:5-10).

One rule of Biblical interpretation is that the Bible should be understood in the common meaning of the words as they were used and understood in the time in which they were written. They should be understood literally (at face value) unless otherwise indicated.

Webster defines the word "destroy" as, "to put out of existence; to subject to a crushing defeat: annihilate." D.A. Clark comments,

"Whatever sin may promise of pleasure or advantage, the end to which it necessarily tends is the destruction of body and soul."

James Moffatt, translator of the Bible into contemporary speech and professor at Union Theological Seminary, wrote in an article on hell, published in the Literary Digest, on April 5, 1930, "But hell may not be a soul's damnation in that terrible torment which an elder generation was wont to picture, or another chance for purification and redemption, or the acute agony of a remorseful soul. It may be annihilation." This thinking is consistent with Matthew 10:28, which reads, "Do not be afraid of those who kill the body but cannot kill the soul. Rather, be afraid of the One who can destroy both soul and body in hell" (NIV).

Other Scriptures speak to the same condition of being destroyed or cut off (Psalm 37:20, 28; Psalm 145:20; Job 21:30; Isaiah 1:28; Matthew 7:13-14). To "perish" (or "be destroyed") is to be consumed as if one never existed, like "becoming extinct."

The manner in which the destruction comes is depicted Biblically as a consuming fire. According to Scripture, God will send a great conflagration in judgment at the end of the age, so that Satan, demonic spirits and unrepentant sinners will be destroyed (or consumed), never to exist in any form ever again. The destroying element is fire from heaven.

At the time of God's judgment in the great flood of Noah's day, the destroying element was water, but in the final act of divine judgment, the destroying element is fire (2 Peter 3:1-7, 10). This is not such an astounding thought. God has visited our world in the past with fire from heaven, possibly to demonstrate to us that all things are possible with God. One demonstration was the incredible experience of Elijah on Mount Carmel with the prophets of Baal (1 Kings 17:20ff). Another classic judgment by fire from heaven is the destruction of Sodom and Gomorrah, recorded in Genesis 19:23-25. One passage of Scripture, which speaks to the matter of God's final judgment by fire that will engulf the whole cosmos, is Malachi 4:1. Matthew 25 paints a picture of the final judgment and depicts Jesus speaking to those who fail their final exam. Matthew 25:41 reads, "Then he will say to those on his left, 'Depart from me, you who are cursed, into the eternal fire prepared for the devil and his angels'" (NIV).

The conflagration at the end of the age – this all-consuming fire – includes not only unrepentant sinners, but also "the devil and his angels." The sentence is for those in the human realm of being who have not accepted God's gracious offer of salvation combined with Satan and his agents, all of whom belong to the spirit realm of being. This raises some interesting questions about the nature of man and the nature of created spirit beings. There are some who have a problem with the idea of total consummation of man although the Bible is very clear at this point. The problem is their belief in the immortality of the soul.

H.L. Hastings, in his classic work, *Pauline Theology*, originally published in 1853 and reprinted by Dr. David Dean as *After the Verdict*, says of Paul's teaching regarding the nature of man: "Let me remind you of a few facts.

"First, The Apostle Paul is the only writer in the whole Bible who makes use of the word immortal or immortality.

"Second, He never applies it to sinners.

"Third, He never applies it to righteous or wicked in this world.

"Fourth, He never applies it to man's soul at all, either before or after death.

"Fifth, He speaks of it as an attribute of the King Eternal (1 Timothy 1:17).

"Sixth, He declares that He is the only possessor of it (1Timothy 6:16).

"Seventh, He presents it as an object which men are to seek after by patient continuance in well-doing (Romans 2:7).

"Eighth, He speaks of it as revealed or brought to light (not in heathen philosophy, but) in the Gospel of the Son of God (2 Timothy 1:10).

"Ninth, He defines the period when it shall be "put on" by the saints of God, and fixes it at the resurrection, when Christ, who is our life, shall appear (1Corinthians 15:52-54).

"Tenth, Therefore, he never taught the immortality of the soul as it is now taught; and, hence, when he declared that sinners should be destroyed, or perish, or die, or be burned or devoured by fire, he did so without any 'mental reservations' or 'theological definitions.' In other words, that he said what he meant, and meant what he said."

But the question is raised, "What about Satan and other spirit beings?" Satan was created by God as a member of the spirit realm of being, which is distinct from the human realm of being and the realm of other living things. Everything about the human realm is associated with death. As far as we know, the spirit realm doesn't experience death. The death sentence was pronounced on the human realm of being as a consequence of sin. The human realm was not the only realm that rebelled against God and sinned. How is it that the spirit realm – which also rebelled against God – doesn't experience death? What is the nature of this realm that doesn't appear to die?

While their continued existence isn't explained in Scripture, their end is. They will not escape the final consummation of all things that offend. Scripture tells us clearly that their destruction in the fires of hell is as certain as hell itself. The difference in respect to their punishment for rebellion appears to be that it has been deferred to the end of the age at the final consummation (2 Peter 2:1-4). The spirit realm is a created realm, and anything that God created, God can destroy. Timothy Dwight, president of Yale University, wrote, in 1897, "Whatever has been created can certainly be annihilated by the power that created it."

THE FUTURE HOME OF THE REDEEMED

Out of the ashes of destruction, God will create a new heaven and a new earth – the final dwelling-place of the redeemed in Christ. His original Kingdom goal of a people who will live in fellowship with Him in His Kingdom paradise, for His glory, forever, will be realized. We will have a new home (Isaiah 65:17). We will not be flying away to some celestial abode; rather, God will give us back our home in a renewed, restored Paradise. Myles Monroe, in his book, *Rediscovering the Kingdom*, says, "Believers often talk about going to heaven when they die. Although that is true," (so Monroe thinks), "God has made arrangements to make sure that we don't stay there. God's Word would fail, because He has plainly stated that He created us to have dominion over the earth. God's Word can never fail." Monroe argues that God's original intention in creation was for man to be king of the earth. The earth is where we will spend eternity with Jesus and all the saints of the ages. It is our home by creation (Genesis 2:8), it is our home by inheritance (Matthew 5:5), it is our home by promise (Acts 7:5 – we are Abraham's seed according to Galatians 3:29) and it is our home as the redeemed in Christ Jesus (Revelation 21:1-3). God made the earth to be inhabited: "For thus saith the Lord that created the heavens; God himself that formed the earth and made it; he hath established it, he created it not in vain, he formed it to be inhabited: I am the Lord; and there is none else" (Isaiah 45:18, KJV).

It is interesting to note the connection between God's plan of redemption and the future home of the saints and how the earth figures prominently in both. The earth is the stage where man plays out his life from birth until death, where he awaits resurrection out of the earth to inhabit the new earth as his eternal home. God sent Christ to the earth to be born as a babe, to live among us and subsequently die on a cross and be buried in a tomb of the earth. God could have done anything that He chose to do to reverse the order of things and redeem His creation. He could have provided any sacrifice to satisfy His justice. The fact that Christ came to earth demonstrates the importance that God places on the earth and His purposes for the earth. It links the earth with God's ultimate purpose in creation. The earth was the scene of man's disobedience and sin. The earth is the place of Satan's dominion (wrested from man), as is evidenced by the cemeteries that dot the landscape. The earth is also the place of Christ's triumph over death and the grave and the place where God will inhabit eternity with His children (Revelation 21:3).

Everything changes on that day when Jesus comes again and the kingdoms of this world become the kingdom of our Lord Jesus Christ (Revelation 11:15). We are given some clues as to what this new home will look like, although the images are symbolic. Revelation 21 and 22, describes the future home of the redeemed in spectacular terms.

John uses the illustration of a bride who has been adorned for her husband to describe the New Jerusalem. No better imagery could have been chosen. The ugliest woman is beautiful in the eyes of her beloved when she walks down the aisle to meet him. The beauty is not in the dress or apparel, but in the person. So it is with the future home of the redeemed. The beauty of that city is the glory that it radiates as our home.

The city shines with the glory of God and is described by precious jewels and pure gold. The imagery is beyond comprehension. As one reads what John describes in Revelation 21:9–22:6, one can only imagine the glory and wonder of it all. Paul reminds us in 1 Corinthians 2:9, "No eye has seen, no ear has heard, no mind has conceived what God has prepared for those who love Him."

In his book, *We're the 'sons of God'. . . So What?*, author David Alves describes the new earth experience: "The opulent, glorious majesty of that beautiful kingdom and the manifest presence of the Royal King himself will awe and preoccupy us forever. Our place in paradise will be settled. . . . What more will we want? What more could we desire than to see love reign over the universe? All longings will be fulfilled. All hopes realized. Love will rule in a kingdom of love . . . on a new earth of unspeakable beauty and crystalline perfection."

What more can be said about this city – this future home of the redeemed – other than that it is a place of beauty, joy, blessedness, harmony, peace, happiness and life? No more pain, no more heartache, no more suffering, no more sin, no more violence, no more war, no more sickness, no more death!

GOVERNMENT WILL CHANGE

Not only will be have a new home, but we will live under a new rule. Daniel 2:44-45 tells us that when God intervenes in the affairs of men at the Second Coming of Christ to establish His eternal Kingdom, He will rule this state of life Himself. "In the time of those kings, the God of heaven will set up a kingdom that will never be destroyed, nor will it be left to another people. It will crush all those kingdoms and bring them to an end, but it will itself endure forever." Notice the reference to not leaving it to another people. He did that once, and we didn't handle it very well.

John expresses it in Revelation 21:3 with these words, "I heard a loud voice from the throne saying, 'Now the dwelling of God is with men, and he will live with them. They will be his people, and God himself will be with them and be their God.'" God will dwell in the midst of His people.

In the first Kingdom Paradise, God set man to rule over the creation. This time, He will provide the Ruler to govern the affairs of this eternal Kingdom. He has a King designated to sit upon the throne of government. Jesus will come again to reign in the eternal Kingdom of God, not for a temporary period of time, but for all eternity.

Isaiah prophesied about it. Isaiah 9:6-7 says, "For to us a Child is born, to us a Son is given, and the government will be on His shoulders. And He will be called Wonderful Counselor, Mighty God, Everlasting Father, Prince of Peace. Of the increase of His government and peace there will be no end. He will reign on David's throne and over his kingdom, establishing and upholding it with justice and righteousness from that time on and forever. The zeal of the Lord Almighty will accomplish this."

The government will be upon His shoulders, and the increase of His government will have no end. Jesus is the King, and He will reign forever in that city called glory.

The dominion is His. One thing that man lost in Adam's transgression was the divinely bestowed dominion. When God created man, He placed him in the garden Paradise as the ruler over it all. He was given authority and dominion. He was the king of the earth.

When Jesus comes again in power and glory, He is coming to reign. He will exercise dominion over all creation.

Job spoke to this when he said, "I know that my Redeemer lives, and at the last He will stand upon the earth" (Job 19:25). When Job said, prophetically, speaking of Christ, "He will stand upon the earth," it is a statement of rule, dominion and power. In this context, "to stand" means to exercise authority and dominion. He will take control.

Dominion is a key understanding in Scripture. The problem that we have in life today is that Satan exercises dominion over the creation. In the beginning, when God created the world and everything in it, His purpose was to form a people who would live in fellowship with Him in his kingdom Paradise, for his glory, forever. The Eden Paradise was where this purpose was set forth and initiated.

In the creation of man, God gave him dominion over the whole created order. That is, he was more than the steward (or caretaker), he was king of the earth and ruler. Genesis 1:26-30 tells us that God created man in His own image and made him ruler over the entire creation. To be the ruler over all is to have dominion over all. Rule equates with dominion.

When Satan succeeded in getting man to disobey God and worship Satan by obeying his directives, man forfeited his dominion, so that 1 John 5:19 reads, "We know that we are children of God, and that the whole world is under the control of the evil one." The problem with life is the fact that Satan is ruling the affairs of men from his position as the god of this world.

However, in the cross/resurrection event, Jesus wrested that dominion back to His control. Satan was dealt a crushing defeat. Following His resurrection, Jesus made the statement, "All authority in heaven and on earth has been given to me" (Matthew 28:18). Dominion is restored.

Hebrews 2:14-15 says, "Since the children have flesh and blood, He too shared in their humanity so that by His death He might destroy him who holds the power of death – that is, the Devil – and free those who all their lives were held in slavery by their fear of death." Death is the last stronghold of Satan – the symbol of the dominion that he exercises. However, when Jesus went into that stronghold, He broke the power of Satan and took control of this enemy of God and man, regaining complete dominion. As the scripture says, "Death no longer has dominion" – notice that word "dominion" – death no longer has dominion over Him. Romans 6:9 says, "Knowing that Christ, being raised from the dead, dieth no more; death hath no more dominion over him." Dominion is the issue. Who rules the affairs of men? Who rules over the nations? Who has dominion over all the forces arrayed against God and man? Who is Lord?

Total dominion now rests in Christ. What man lost, Christ recovered. He is the King Who rules and reigns in the Kingdom of our Lord and Savior, Jesus Christ. His is the dominion that endures from generation to generation throughout all eternity. Psalm 145:13 reads, "Your kingdom is an everlasting kingdom, and your dominion endures through all generations." To live forever under the kingship of Christ will be life's great joy.

THE QUALITY OF LIFE WILL CHANGE

Not only will we have a new home and a new government, but we will live forever under a new constitution of life. A fundamental change will be the character or quality of life in God's kingdom Paradise.

This change involves the removal of the curse. The curse is what happened in the original Eden Paradise as a result of man's sin and disobedience. The curse changed life for Adam and Eve and their posterity from peace, harmony, joy and life to suffering, sorrow, heartache, disease and death. Genesis 3:16-19 reads, "To the woman, He said, 'I will greatly increase your pains in childbearing; with pain you will give birth to children. Your desire will be for your husband, and he will rule over you.' To Adam, He said, 'Because you listened to your wife and ate from the tree about which I commanded you, "You must not eat of it," cursed is the ground because of you; through painful toil you will eat of it all the days of your life. It will produce thorns and thistles for you, and you will eat the plants of the field. By the sweat of your brow you will eat your food until you return to the ground, since from it you were taken; for dust you are and to dust you will return.'"

Notice what has changed! Pain is introduced. Also, Eve – who was co-regent with Adam – is now made subject to him. Adam is told that he no longer will be able to stroll through the garden and pick anything that he wants to eat. From this time on, the garden will not be there unless he prepares the soil manually, plants the seed, weeds the garden and harvests the crop. Toil is new to the existence of man. Labor becomes intense as man now deals with thorns and thistles, suggesting the difficulty that will characterize provision for continued living. Also, reference is made to the fact of death, which

Adam didn't understand. God made it clear what He meant when he told Adam that he was created from the dust of the ground and he would subsequently return there.

When sin entered the world in the original garden Paradise, life changed dramatically. Every generation since has experienced the effects of that change, and it isn't good. When God looked on His original creation he said, "It is good." Since the introduction of sin and the pronouncement of the curse, God's assessment of it all is that what He sees isn't good.

But, praise God, things are going to change back to the life of the original Eden Paradise! It is difficult for us to grasp the meaning of it all. Perhaps a walk down the Main Street of life will help us understand how life will be different in that city called Glory. The Lord is here among us to help us see beyond the moment and to comfort and encourage us amidst life's heartaches and trials. We are never alone in this world of woe.

It doesn't really matter where your residence is; Main Street looks the same. As we start our stroll down the Main Street of life, we come upon a scene of utter devastation. People are running in every direction, confused and bewildered, not knowing what to do or where to go. Sirens are screeching as police cars, ambulances and fire trucks arrive on the scene. A terrorist has taken control of a commercial aircraft and flown it into a skyscraper, which is destroyed in the explosions that follow. A cloud of smoke, ashes and debris fill the air. It is a scene of utter devastation. Thousands of people are killed. As you stand at a distance weeping and wondering, the Master comes alongside of you and says, "I'm sorry for what man has done to his fellow man. Sin is a terrible taskmaster. In the new world that I'm going to create for your future habitation, there'll be no more terrorists."

We move on down the Main Street of life, and next we encounter an older man, curled up on the sidewalk, trying to keep warm from the cold of winter. Next to him is a cardboard box, where he sleeps, and a tattered coat, which covers him. His possessions are meager – to say the least – but I noticed that he had a well-worn New Testament beside him. I asked him, "Who are you? Where do you live? What do you eat for food?" He doesn't seem too interested in talking about it, but it's obvious that he is a homeless man, with no family to love and care for him and only scraps of food that he pulls from a nearby dumpster to keep him alive. It's sad – very sad – to see someone like this abandoned by society in a world of plenty. As your heart grieves for this homeless man and the thousands of others like him, the Master comes alongside of you and says, "I share your sorrow for the plight of the homeless, but someday he will have a wonderful home where he will be happy, loved, and never hunger anymore. I'm going away to prepare a home for those who are my children."

We move on down the Main Street of life and we pass the crowded hallway of a local school. The police have arrived and shot a student who had opened fire on a group of students who had gathered outside the cafeteria to pray for their school. There is bloodshed everywhere – and bodies of young people, lying on the floor, having been killed and wounded by this deranged gunman. You remember hearing of other situations just like this, and you wonder, "Why does this have to happen?" Innocent young people with great promise are denied life by a mentally disturbed person. The Master comes alongside of you and speaks of the cruelty of life since sin entered into the world. This isn't the way that God created it to be. The Master shares how in that new world that He is going to prepare, there will be no more crime and no guns, knives or other devices of death, There will be no more deranged people, since – in that new world – all who live there will be made like Jesus Himself.

We continue our walk down the Main Street of life and notice a courtroom where a frightened woman stands before the judge seeking a restraining order on her husband, who has repeatedly beaten her and demeaned her and is now threatening to kill her. She remembers how wonderful things were in the first several years of their life together. He was the man of her dreams. He was a good provider and father to their three children, but ever since he started drinking, things haven't been the same. She had noticed how he came home from work later than usual, but she was unaware of his drinking problem. When she occasionally asked him about it, he would get angry and the abuse started. Your heart aches for this beautiful wife and mother, when the Master comes alongside and reminds you that spousal abuse is a result of sin, which changed the character of life way back in the garden. God created husband and wife to live together in harmony and love. Alcohol is just one of the factors that destroy this relationship, and the Master says, "In that new world that I'm going to prepare, there will be no more abuse. People will live in perfect harmony and love."

A little further down the Main Street of life, we notice a woman standing on her front porch with two beautiful girls with their arms thrown around each other, sobbing profusely. The girls have just come home from school, and their mother was waiting for them with some sad news. You come a little closer and hear the mother telling the girls, "Daddy won't be coming home anymore. He has decided to leave us and live with another woman." No one can speak, being overwhelmed with grief. In their hearts, they wonder how they will ever make it alone, with no husband – no father – to love and care for his family. As you stand there, feeling the pain of the moment, the Master comes alongside of you and whispers, "In that new world that I'm going to prepare, there won't be any more heartache, broken homes or divorce."

Continuing your walk down the Main Street of life, you come upon another similar scene, except that this time the father, mother and three children are standing all together in the kitchen with tears streaming down their cheeks. You wonder what has caused this pain, when you hear the father sharing with the children that he and their mother have just returned from the doctor, who has confirmed that the severe headaches their mother has been having over the past few months have been caused by an inoperable brain tumor, and the doctor has given their mother six months – or possibly less – to live. Life on Main Street is filled with anguish and suffering. As you stand there, trying to make sense of it all, the Master comes alongside of you and whispers, "In that perfect new world that I am going to prepare, there won't be any more crying, suffering or sickness. The old order of things will have passed away."

One more stop on Main Street reminds you of what is all too common as you pass the local hospital, where a woman who appears to be in her early 60s has just been called from work. She has been ushered into a back room of the hospital and is standing beside a table where her husband is lying, having just been pronounced "dead on arrival" from a massive heart attack. This is a total shock, as they hadn't noticed any signs of a possible heart problem. How could this be? They were nearing retirement and had talked about how they might spend the remaining years of their life together, happily serving others and watching their two sons grow up and become successful in their chosen careers. In the midst of this heartache and grief, the Master comes alongside of you and whispers, "In the new world that I am going to prepare, there will be no more death."

Life is a vale of tears. We cry a lot from all the suffering, heartache and pain that we encounter along the way, but praise God, in that new world that He has gone to prepare for us, things are going to change! It is a total, all-encompassing change. Changed from darkness to light; changed from bondage to freedom; changed from sorrow to joy; changed from blight to blessedness; changed from death to life; changed from perishable to imperishable; changed from mortal to immortal!

It is difficult for us – in our finiteness – to grasp the wonder of it all. While we cannot fully grasp the majesty and grandeur of the city called Glory, we can imagine a little of what it will be like based on what has been revealed in God's word.

THE CITY CALLED GLORY

John of old was given a revelation of that blessed state, which we can only imagine. We know that it is a state of blessedness, joy and life. All the things that have made life difficult, burdensome, and painful will have passed away. Life will be totally different in that city called Glory.

I've pondered what it might be like and have visualized how, when we enter the city, the sights and sounds will be awesome. This is a different Main Street in the city called Glory than what we have known. It runs alongside the river of the water of life, which flows from the throne of God. It is an amazing sight. This water is bright as crystal. On the banks of this river is the tree of life, laden with its fruit. Colorful songbirds chirp their melodies and the lion lies down with the lamb. All is peace and tranquility.

As we begin to walk down the street of the city, before long we come to a junction that I call Reunion Square. I expect that we will recognize one another in the Kingdom. The Bible doesn't have a great deal to say about this, but we know that Jesus (in his post-resurrection body) had distinguishing features. His disciples could recognize Him for Who He was. We, too, will be recognizable in some sense, but anything that would detract from the beauty, joy and blessedness of that state will be blotted out. Reunion Square will be a wonderful place to visit. There are saints here that we only heard about in Scripture. Jesus told the centurion who came to Him seeking healing for his servant, "I say to you that many will come from the east and the west, and will take their places at the feast with Abraham, Isaac and Jacob in the kingdom of heaven" (Matthew 8:11-12).

Also, the Apostle Paul spoke of meeting in the Kingdom with some who had come to faith under his ministry. First Thessalonians 2:19-20 reads, "For what is our hope, our joy, or the crown in which we will glory in the presence of our Lord Jesus when he comes? Is it not you? Indeed, you are our glory and joy." We will celebrate ministry, friendships and relationships in that city called Glory. Loved ones who were not saved will not be missed or remembered, since no unhappiness or sorrow will enter in.

Can you imagine what it will be like to visit with some of the great heroes of the faith – men like Moses, Abraham, Isaac, Jacob, David, Daniel, the three Hebrew worthies, Luke, and Paul, to name a few? Besides these noted personalities, there will be some of lesser note, but whom it will be just as wonderful to see. I expect to see the pastors who helped shape my life. They were men of God who faithfully preached the whole counsel of God. I'll never forget J. William Denton, who baptized me in 1941 at Marion-By-The-Sea, and pastor Everett E. Pender, who served as my pastor during my adolescence; then too, my Sunday School teachers (most notably, Bruce Plummer and Lyman Howland), who told me the stories of Jesus; and others, like Carlyle B. Roberts, and Leon Horne who encouraged me and helped direct my way when times were difficult; and my parents, who gave me a solid foundation for life, and my children and grandchildren – many loved ones, colleagues, and friends! These will be exciting times that we'll spend listening to the stories and recounting the experiences of life in which the grace and presence of the Lord was evident. We will have eternity to visit and celebrate the goodness of the Lord. No need to hurry along – we'll be here forever!

When we finally decide to go in a little deeper (there's so much to see and explore!), we will come to a place that I think of as Paradise Park. There are people here that I knew in the old life, but what a difference here in Paradise Park! I'd like to introduce some of them and listen to their story. Everybody here has a story. One of the great blessings in this place is hearing the stories of how Jesus has touched people and made them whole.

Let me introduce you first to a young lady whose name is Margaret. I remember her as a 13-year-old girl living in a rural village in Vermont. I was her pastor. I remember the day that her family called and told me that they needed to see me. I went immediately to the home, and we stood together in the kitchen while her father and mother told me that the doctor had just diagnosed her with leukemia and told her parents that she might only have six months or so to live. I remember you, Margaret, as a sweet young lady who always smiled and gave a simple testimony, "I love Jesus." A few months went by, and you seemed to grow weaker with each passing day. One summer day, I was visiting a campmeeting a few hours away from where you lived when a state trooper came onto the grounds looking for me and said that you were in the hospital and the family had sent for me to come as soon as possible. He told me that he shouldn't do it, but he would give me an escort over those country roads to help expedite my travel back to the hospital. I was grateful for his assistance, and I arrived at the hospital in record time. When I entered the door and went to your room, your parents were standing outside the door waiting for me. Your father said, "Thanks for coming, Pastor, but I'm afraid it's too late. She hasn't spoken or responded to anyone for a few hours now." I said, "I want to go in anyway." I went into your hospital room, where you were lying on a bed, enclosed by an oxygen tent. As I stood by your bed, I spoke to you and said, "Hello, Margaret! This is pastor Taber. I just wanted to come and tell you, 'Jesus loves you'". You smiled and breathed your last breath. I'll never forget that moment. But, look at you now, Margaret – alive and well, with rosy cheeks, the picture of perfect health! What happened? "Jesus touched me and made me well."

Here is another young lady that I recognize. You look so different from the last time that I saw you, Amy. I remember that you were sitting in a wheelchair in a country church in Maine where I was preaching on the Second Coming of Jesus, and you were so excited. I remember that after the service we talked a little; and, as a few of the men helped carry your wheelchair down the front steps of the church, I told you about this day when – in the city called Glory – Jesus would touch you and free you from your infirmity. You're here in that special place now, but where's your wheel chair? "I don't need it anymore. Just like you told me, Jesus touched me, and made me whole. I can walk; I can run for the first time in many years. Thank you, Jesus!"

Follow me over here, if you will! I'd like you to meet Harold. I remember you, Harold, from when I was a boy living in the big city in Massachusetts. Every Saturday, my mother would go downtown to visit the five-and-ten-cent store, and I liked to go with her. You always stood on the sidewalk beside the door, playing your accordion. Passersby would throw pennies and small change into the tin cup that you had attached to your accordion. One day, I asked my mother why you stood there playing the accordion every day, and she told me that you were a beggar. She said that you had no one to love you and care for you. You depended on the small change that people threw in your tin cup to survive. I remember asking her for an extra penny that I could put in your cup. I loved to listen to you play some of the old familiar hymns of the Church. Here you are, Harold, in Paradise Park in the city called Glory, and you are still smiling and playing "Amazing Grace," "What a Friend We Have in Jesus" and, "Jesus Loves Me This I Know." I love it, Harold, but there's something different. Where is your tin cup, Harold? "I don't need it anymore. Here in the city called Glory, I am loved and cared for. I will never want for a home or food ever again. Thank you, Jesus!"

As we move on to the other side of the park, I notice an elderly lady named Dorris. You look wonderful, Dorris, so much better than the last time that I saw you. I remember visiting you in the nursing home and celebrating your ninety-fifth birthday. You were always determined to do things on your own, even at your advanced age. I noticed that you had a large gash over your right eye, which was all black and blue. It was an ugly sight. You told me that you had fallen and struck your head on the commode when getting out of bed on your own to go to the bathroom. Growing old was not a pleasant experience. But, look at you now! You are the picture of perfect health. What changed for you? "Jesus touched me and gave me new health and vitality." So, how long have you been here, and what is your age now? "Aging is no longer a problem. Here in the city called Glory, we don't count time by years anymore. This is a land where we'll never grow old. We'll just live forever in the presence of our Lord and Savior, Jesus Christ."

There's one more person that I want you to meet here in Paradise Park. His name is Michael. Michael was born in a Boston hospital – the first child born to his parents. It was an exciting day, shared by his parents and grandparents, who had gathered to celebrate the birth of this beautiful baby boy. I was present on the occasion; and, as the day wore on, I noticed that Michael never cried like other newborns. He seemed to be quite limp and weak. The next morning, I decided to return to the hospital to see the baby, knowing that, while it wasn't visiting hours, they might let me in, seeing that I was a clergyman. I remember going to the nurse's station and telling them that I was Reverend Taber and had come to see baby Michael. The nurse led me down a corridor and asked me to wait outside the nursery door while she went in to get the baby. She returned with Michael in her arms; and, as I looked into his beautiful face, she said, "What a tragedy!" I had suspected that something might be wrong, but I was unprepared for her comment. I remember saying, "Yes! Thank you!" I walked away with a heavy heart. You see, I was his grandfather. All the joy of the previous day was blown away by her comment, "What a tragedy!" What was I to do now? I couldn't go see my daughter, for I wouldn't know what to say, and she wouldn't understand what I was doing there so early in the morning and why I looked so distraught. I couldn't tell my wife, or anyone, and must live with this knowledge until something else might develop that would identify the problem. Subsequently, tests were done that diagnosed the problem as Prader-Willi Syndrome, a debilitating disorder characterized by overall weakness, an insatiable appetite and likely retardation.

Michael's mother worked with him faithfully, going above and beyond what any parent could do to help control his appetite and strengthen his muscles. In spite of her heroic efforts, Michael struggled greatly, unable to control his appetite. One of the aspects of this syndrome is that a person doesn't know when they are full. They aren't to blame for the problem, which is beyond their ability to control physiologically. Fortunately, he didn't seem to suffer any significant retardation. He graduated from high school with honors, which is a testimony to his mother's love and care. He loved to sing and to go to church.

The syndrome wreaked havoc on his body, causing multiple surgeries for spinal weakness. Michael was never able to run and play like other kids. In fact, he couldn't even ride a bicycle. The tragedy is that he is a beautiful person, with so much to offer, but robbed of the normalcy of life by this debilitating syndrome.

But look at him now, in Paradise Park! Michael is running and jumping, totally healed from his infirmity. Thank you, Jesus!

What a glorious day that will be when we gather with Jesus in that place that He has gone to prepare! "Now the dwelling of God is with men, and he will live with them. They will be his people, and God himself will be with them and be their God. He will wipe every tear from their eyes. There will be no more death or mourning or crying or pain, for the old order of things has passed away. He who was seated on the throne said, 'I am making everything new!' Then he said, 'Write this down, for these words are trustworthy and true'" (Revelation 21:3-5).

God has a wonderful future planned for those who are His children by faith. Everything will end where it all began – in Eden (Paradise restored). God's plan in creation – the formation of a people who will live in fellowship with Him in His Kingdom Paradise, for His glory, forever – will become reality at the end of the age, at the Second Coming of Jesus Christ, when earth's final dawn arises, when the old order of things passes away and He makes all things new. Praise His Holy name!

In times like these, there is one prayer that we should all be praying earnestly: "Even so, come, Lord Jesus" (Revelation 22:20, KJV).

QUESTIONS FOR DISCUSSION
1. Review the various stages through which the Kingdom of God has gone (and will go).
2. What changes will occur in the Universe when Jesus comes?
3. Compare and contrast the flood of Noah with the final judgment.
4. Where will the redeemed live in eternity?
5. Share the stories of some of the people that you are looking forward to seeing in the Kingdom.

EPILOGUE

I was visiting the local Dunkin Donuts shop one morning about 5:30, which is my usual routine. I purchased a plain bagel, toasted well done, with cream cheese on the side and a cup of Dunkin Donuts coffee. That's my breakfast.

Since I am a regular there, I thought that I should tell the manager that I wouldn't be in for a couple of weeks while I was away doing research and writing. If I miss a day or two, she always mentions that they all missed me and wondered if I was all right.

She and a couple of other members of her crew were standing together as I explained my mission. The question arose as to what I was researching and writing. I explained that I was writing a book on eschatology – a layman's introduction to eschatology. The group looked totally bewildered until one of them asked, "Eschatology – what's that?" They had never heard the term, and they didn't have a clue as to what it was all about.

I responded by saying, "Eschatology is a study of end-time events." That prompted a similar query: "End-time events?" It was as if the idea of end-time events was a weird idea. End time of what?

A male customer, who was standing nearby, remarked, "It doesn't look very good, does it?" His comment/question caught me off guard for a minute. I was wondering how involved my answer should be. Finally, I replied, "It all depends on whose side you are on."

That's what this book is all about: introducing you to the end of the story of human civilization and the ultimate triumph of the Lord

Jesus Christ over the forces of evil. If you read the Book, you discover that – at the end of the story – Jesus wins, and everyone who has acknowledged Him as Savior and Lord shares in His conquest and lives forever in the Paradise of God where there is no more heartache, disease or death. So, in the final analysis, it all depends on whose side you are on.

I would encourage everyone who reads this material to open your heart to Jesus, confess your sin to Him and invite Him to come into your life, forgive your sin and lead you into the glorious future that He has planned. In the end, God's plan in creation of a people who will live forever in fellowship with Him in His Kingdom Paradise, for His glory, will become reality. I hope to see you there.

QUESTIONS FOR DISCUSSION
1. How would you define the word "eschatology"?
2. What is strange (to many people) about the idea of "end-time events"?
3. From your point of view, right now, does the future look good?
4. Have you accepted Jesus as your Lord and personal Savior?
6. If not, you can do so right now by simply praying a prayer of confession of sin and asking Jesus to forgive you and become your Savior and Lord. It is important to talk to a Pastor or other Christian about your decision and begin to attend and become active in a Bible believing church.

Some Rules Can Be Established as Guides for the Study of Prophecy

By Edwin K. Gedney *

A. *There are axioms for use in prophetic study.*

I n many areas of knowledge it is possible to set up certain simple propositions that lie basic to more complex problems and that are themselves so obvious that they are accepted without elaborate proof. Such statements are called axioms. Those who have had a course in geometry will recall that in the textbooks, the more elaborate propositions are preceded by a few simple axioms such as, "a straight line is the shortest distance between two points," a statement so evidently true in Euclidean geometry that all accept it as true without questions or attempt at proof. So also there are statements that can be made in prophetic study that are either expressly stated in Scripture or are so obvious from the context as to be accepted without proof or question by any who regard the Scripture as authoritative.

1. All Bible prophecy is from one source – God – and is therefore inherently harmonious. Therefore any system of prophetic

interpretation should reflect this quality by self-consistency or internal harmony.

2. Prophecy has to do basically with the plan of God or some specific aspect or part of that plan. Therefore no prophetic passage can be isolated and given a particularized interpretation apart from logical reference to the total plan. God's plan is the formation of a people who will live in fellowship with Him in His Kingdom Paradise, for His glory, forever.

3. Some prophecies are given in symbol and some are to be taken literally and specifically. Occasionally the blending is such that it may be difficult to be sure which emphasis to place on the passage. While this situation is not at all disturbing to the intuitive Eastern mind to which most of the prophecies were originally given, it is often a stumbling block and a confusion to our logical Western thinkers. In general we may adopt the principle that if a book or larger passage is dominantly symbolic in character, any doubtful passage contained in it should be regarded as also probably symbolic until demonstrated to be literal. Likewise a statement of doubtful nature in a passage dominantly literal in application should first be given a literal interpretation unless good evidence appears for not doing so.

4. Because of its unique authorship and the relation of prophecy to some aspect of the basic plan of God, if a certain type of symbol is observed to signify a definite type of thing or action in one Spirit-inspired passage, it may logically be expected to signify a similar type of thing in another prophecy so inspired.

5. Some prophecies are parallel, giving variant presentations of the same event or sequence of events from different viewpoints (Dan. 2, 7, 8, 11). Others may be consecutive in time of fulfillment (Ezek. 36-39).

6. The Old Testament prophecies are largely concerned with the Jewish people as a nation, but the New Testament is notably deficient in this relation.

7. The high points of prophecy relate to God's direct introjection of Himself into history. They are not the affairs of Israel, the restoration of the Roman Empire, the rise and career of Antichrist despite the emphasis placed upon these events by many interpreters since the Reformation. The focus of the Old Testament and the Gospels, which recount events still essentially Old Testament in character and outlook, is the coming of the Messiah – "God in Christ reconciling the world to Himself" – not a restoration of the throne of David in a literal sense, in a literal Jewish state, among the current nations of the world as the mistaken prophetic interpreters of the Jews indicated. The focus of the Epistles, Acts and Revelation, the beginning of truly New Testament times, is upon the return of this Redeemer at the end of the age to complete His redemptive work. The hope constantly emphasized in the New Testament is not man going to Heaven at death for reward in an inadequate immaterial or bodiless state, but it is Christ coming back to man, physically to raise the dead, to receive His disciples to Himself, to judge and make His awards, and so to transform the earth that it will be a suitable dwelling place for His people forever.

The many lesser aspects of prophecy upon which so much emphasis is often placed are relatively minor affairs revolving around and dependent upon these great foci. Worthy of deep study as these lesser matters are they must never be allowed to obscure or displace the greater in the minds of men. The Church may disagree markedly about the various aspects of the appearing of Antichrist without loss, but the dramatic appearing of Christ in visible bodily form with great glory and power is its only hope and should never be obscured or devitalized by human speculation. Neither should such speculation be permitted to misdirect the Christian mind from this blessed hope to over-involvement with a syndrome of lesser matters, as has often occurred.

Let us strive to retain constantly in mind in a fresh approach to prophetic studies that the Spirit of all prophecy is to relate events in some way to the testimony of Jesus (Rev. 19:10). Let us attempt to avoid the evident natural tendency to be drawn aside into entrancing by-ways, and endeavor to retain in sharpest focus the great high points in our prophetic faith.

8. The Jewish prophets through John the Baptist could not perceive the Gentile Church clearly. Indeed, it took special revelations and drastic experiences in New Testament times to stretch the minds of Peter, Paul and others to grasp the great fact that God desired to extend the blessings of hope to the non-Jewish world.

9. The prophets often did not themselves understand the significance of the revelations that came through them. Sometimes this was interpreted to them (Dan. 7:15, 16) and sometimes they were left in ignorance (Dan. 12:8-9), just as a secretary is sometimes taken into the confidence of the one who dictates her letters and sometimes not.

10. In prophecy there are commonly two elements; the ethical, dealing with sin and righteousness, and the predictive, dealing with events. Very few prophecies are either all one or all the other but usually evince a balance. The predicted event may grow out of ethical behavior (Gen. 2:17), or behavior may be stressed in the light of the certainty of coming events (2 Pet. 3:10:14).

11. Prophecy is inspired by God and requires the Spirit of God for effective understanding (1 Cor. 2:9-16). The supernatural aspects of such things as the mysteries of the cross and the resurrection have been ridiculous to the non-spiritual mind from the time the Greek philosophers broke up the meeting with Paul at Mars Hill in Athens at the mention of the resurrection, to the modern humanist university classroom in America (Acts 17:32). When Paul states that the cross is a stumbling block to the Jew

and foolishness to the Greek he is using terms that may well be extended to modern times (1 Cor. 1:21-24). Like the Jew, the rigid legalistic religionist with his doctrine of salvation by works and penances cannot admit the complete efficacy of the cross. Like the philosophical Greek, the modern materialistic humanist on both sides of the iron curtain in the scientific age can see in Jesus only the son of Joseph, and regards all attempts to identify supernatural aspects in Him as foolishness. This applies also to the liberal Christian thought that retains much of the content and format of Christianity while denying inspiration and other vital supernatural aspects. Trees are they, having shape and form, but twice dead and plucked up by the roots – wandering stars tracing an ephemeral path across the intellectual horizon while the great Sun of Righteousness goes on age after age warming the hearts of men with His life-giving effulgence. It is in this vein that Jude writes and ascribes this devitalized, fruitless condition to the absence of the Holy Spirit (Jude 12-19). It follows logically that if the prophecy came by the moving of the Holy Spirit in holy men of old (2 Pet. 1:21), then we should endeavor to be holy men, filled with the same Spirit, in interpreting the words that they wrote as the Spirit desires it to be done. This axiom will no doubt be completely obtuse to the liberal mind.

12. Time is not always valued in the human sense in prophecy. In dealing with prophetic writings we are dealing with God in an unusually intimate way and hence are often confronted with ideas that seem confusing to us because they relate to the character of God which is markedly different from our own. One of the most obvious of these differences is in regard to the concept of time. We live in the stream of time and recognize all events in three distinct phases; past, present and future, and conceive of all things as having two definite aspects, a beginning and an ending. We have no way of comprehending eternity except by speaking of it as a "time without end," or "time that is everlasting." It is almost impossible for us to get more than the faintest idea of timelessness or the existence of something that has no definite temporal beginning and ending so conditioned

are we to thinking wholly in terms of time. On the other hand, God exists in eternity, a type of duration that we do not understand but of which that type of duration called "time" by us is a small part or aspect. Because He exists in both eternity and time, God can understand time, but because we now exist only in time we cannot comprehend eternity. God can and does speak to us in the verb tenses with which we are familiar – past, present and future. However, because He exists around and beyond as well as within time, He sometimes uses these tenses in ways unfamiliar and even confusing to us. It may be said that God exists in the eternal present and often speaks in this sense. This is, in effect, the meaning of the name Jehovah by which He revealed Himself to Moses. The word signifies "The self-existent one," often appropriately shortened to the simple "I am." This was the sense in which God's Son answered the Jews when He said, "Before Abraham was, I am" (Jn. 8:58). God is at all points in the stream of time; something we cannot be and therefore find hard to comprehend.

God also speaks sometimes of events future to us in the past tense as though they had already happened, He having determined or foreknown them. Occasionally, prophets, being caught up in the Spirit, have acquired some of this divine perception and have used these tenses in the divine sense. Paul, speaking of the unfolding program of God writes, "Whom He did foreknow, them He also did predestinate to be conformed to the image of His son...moreover, whom He did predestinate, them He also called; and whom He called, them He also justified; and whom He justified them He also glorified" (Rom. 8:29-30). From our viewpoint some of this has been accomplished, some is being accomplished, and some is yet to be done, but to God it is all past and finalized because He has decreed it and views the whole sequence of its performance at once from outside of time. Those readers who are familiar with the twentieth century concept of relativity will find a striking similarity here to the application of that concept to the evaluation of time in the scientific sense. Einstein tells us that a single event is observed to occur at different times by observers in different systems with a difference dependent upon the relationships of their systems. We definitely exist in and are presently confined to a system different from that of God, the system that has a beginning and an end for all things including itself. We are conditioned to measure everything in that system in terms of past, present and future, and to think of them all as having finite duration. God exists in this system but has also a larger existence in a totally different system, eternity, which embraces ours as a small unit and from the viewpoint of which He may consider our time, either in a particular event or totally, as past, present or future depending up on the point in eternity from which He views it.

God is essentially timeless. "One day is with the Lord as a thousand years, and a thousand years as a day" (2 Pet. 3:8). This does not mean that He cannot or does not use and measure time, indeed in the organization of the cosmos He has done so with a minuteness and accuracy completely unattained by man at his best. It means that while God has duration just as He has spatial existence, He is not bound by time as we understand it anymore than He is confined by space as we understand that. Some day this will be true of us also to some degree, but not now. When all the "times" shall be fulfilled and all things are made one in Christ (Eph. 1:10), then we who today live through a short fragment of the stream of time will be raised or transmuted into a form capable of existing in and comprehending the region of eternity (1 Cor. 15:50-54). While we will no doubt measure duration in an effective mathematical way, this will not be a limitation upon ourselves as it is today. Now we have the power to measure and use time but cannot escape its limitations; then we shall not longer have to strive desperately to use productively just a few of the years available to us between the temporal end points of birth and death. This peculiar difference between the divine and human attitudes toward time is important to bear in mind in studying prophecy.

B. *Some rules for interpreting prophecy may be established.*

1. The first rule follows naturally from the eleventh axiom. Be in such close communion with God that His Spirit may assist the mind in prophetic study. When Daniel observed by the study of the prophetic books that he was living in times of prophetic significance, he devoted himself to fasting and prayer and confession of sin that he might draw yet closer to God and comprehend the situation in the light of His will more clearly (Dan. 9). In the modern day, unfortunately, most of us turn rather to the library and the commentaries for more light. There is nothing wrong with these devices, indeed they are an excellent source of ideas, but this procedure consists in doing nothing more than any secular scholar would do in studying an area in his field. The prophetic student is dealing with matters that transcend libraries and human philosophies; he needs the presence of the Holy Spirit.

2. The serious prophetic student will do well to prepare an orderly and consistent table of symbols and their basic meaning as a reference for future study. This can often be done as one reads along, or by means of a good concordance by which the various uses of the particular symbol can be located. Strangely enough this seems seldom to have been done by prophetic students.

3. Because of axiom two, it is well to study and interpret prophecy as a whole, resisting the impulse to start with an aspect that may be of particular personal interest such as the millennium, or the Antichrist. It will be well to begin with those prophecies the meaning of which is given directly in Scripture and about which there can be no doubt, and work from them to the less definite areas. A good discussion of this type of approach, more characteristic of the Historical school than any other, is found in the first part of a book by H. Grattan Guinness entitled *Key to the Apocalypse*.

4. It is a good policy not to disassemble or divide a prophecy into separated parts if it is feasible to explain the fulfillment logically without doing so, even if such a separation seems to fit in well with your pet theory unless there is good scriptural reason. The Lord made such a division in the case of Isaiah chapter 61 which was the text for His sermon inn the synagogue at Nazareth (Lk. 4:16-20). He quoted only the portion of the passage that applied to His particular ministry at the time, the remainder awaiting the end of the Church Age, which Isaiah could not see, for its fulfillment. However, this is a very delicate business for human beings to undertake and many have gone far astray doing it. Two passages in the Bible perhaps most often sinned against in this manner are Genesis 1:1-2, where an enormous gap is suggested by some as occurring between the verses; and Daniel 9:26-27, where the last of a series of seven sevens is often cut off and separated from the rest by a period now more than 2000 years long. There is absolutely nothing in the phraseology, meaning of the words in the original tongue, or context in either passage indicating that this should be done, nor does the Lord so indicate anywhere as He does in the case cited from Isaiah. The breaks are introduced largely to buttress and justify preconceived hypotheses of creation or millennial theory, hypotheses that find their origin elsewhere.

There may well be justification for making such divisions with more or less clearly defined breaks between the 24th chapter of Matthew and some portions of Revelation, but the necessity arises rarely and should be treated very carefully.

5. Hold firm convictions about the major and well-defined prophecies when these are adequately established in your mind, but do not be intolerant of other views with regard to some of the more perplexing passages. The other interpreters may have a more penetrating mind than you; you may be wrong, especially when beginning the study of the subject. The writer was brought up under a rigid Futurist leadership and accepted wholly the positions of that group, defending them vigorously. I recall

several great Christian leaders that I considered heretics and modernists, and called them so, because they did not hold to the Dispensational-Futurist position. In my first experiences attending the Bible class of the Providence, R.I., Advent Christian Church I found there those who disagreed kindly but effectively with my rigid preconception. I was confused. Some of these men were obviously most devout believers in the Bible and deep students of the prophetic books, yet they held views other than those I had equated with proper Orthodoxy. They also brought to my attention large areas of Scripture that I in my circular thinking had completely ignored. On one occasion, having run across a booklet expressing a variant view, I rushed up to the pastor of the Church, whom I knew did not agree with the view either, saying with some force, "What do you think of this man?" The pastor made no reply for a moment but looked at me mildly and then said, "Well, I guess he's like most of us, a lot of truth and a little error." This was a new outlook for me, but a true one. Anyone who feels that he is going to construct a complete system of prophetic interpretation that will be free from error and not susceptible to intelligent criticism and disagreement on the part of others as devout and studious as he himself needs to consider the simple truth conveyed in the statement of this learned pastor.

6. Do not be too positive or dogmatic; you antagonize those who disagree with you and you may have to backtrack later. Some of the nineteenth century Historicists made the most definite predictions about the Turks and the Mohammedans that never came to pass. The Dispensational Futurists are continually fixing on some current world figure and demonstrating him to be the Man of Sin. Kaiser Wilhelm Mussolini, Hitler and Stalin have all been positively so identified yet they are all safely dead. The volumes written proclaiming them to be the Antichrist and identifying them by the mystic number 666 are so much wasted paper. Furthermore by being over positive one may set up a theory that later he may find himself forced to defend as dogma rather than seeking the truth. Very symbolic prophecy is too indefinite to

enable one to be over positive about detail. As new light appears and historical fulfillment progresses a certain flexibility is to be desired. When I was a young graduate student I spent some time discussing these matters with Rev. Harley Hewitt, then head of the Advent Mission Society. Mr. Hewitt was a much older man, rich in experience and a student of prophecy for many years. I recall speaking rather intolerantly of certain writers who did not seem to have any positive stand about the millennium and referring to them as "fence-sitters." I recall this elder brother giving me a rather quizzical look up and down and saying, "Son, when the mud is ten feet deep on each side, the middle of the fence is a mighty fine place to be; you can climb down on whichever side dries out first." "When in doubt, attack," was all right for Napoleon but produces mistakes, absurdities and future retrenchings for the student of prophecy. It may take you several years to determine precisely, which is the "right" side of some perplexing issues.

7. Be prepared to leave some questions unanswered. The student of prophecy (particularly if he is a young person just beginning the study), cannot reasonably expect to solve permanently and completely all the problems that have been perplexing the minds of able students for centuries. Many younger persons feel insecure unless they have rational and fairly complete answers to all moot questions in any area of knowledge they are exploring. This is a very natural feeling and the writer recalls it well as an aspect of his own early theological studies when in college and graduate school.

The great danger of such an attitude is twofold. First, it is an evident fact that complete and definitive answers to all complex problems do not exist in any field of knowledge known to man; indeed, it is common to find a consensus only on a relatively few basic propositions and a wide diversity of interpretations with respect to many lesser items in most fields of study. There are more questions than answers in human learning and as the body of known data increases the volume of questions rises in geometrical proportion. As a result, some who feel very strongly the need of certainty become discouraged and give the whole matter up. Second, there is a common tendency to accept, after superficial examination, some one interpretation so definitely and positively that it becomes dogma that we feel pressed to defend even to the point of irrationality in order to preserve the pattern in which we feel secure.

The very nature of the prophecies as unfolding in interaction with history makes absolute resolution of all problems impossible. Some predicted events such as the birth of Christ, Calvary, the resurrection, the descent of the Spirit and numerous forecasts concerning Israel, Babylon and other ancient nations can be identified positively in historic time. Some prophecies may be applied with more caution and less certainty to existing times. With regard to other prophecies, as mentioned in earlier chapters of this study, the Church is completely divided; equally brilliant and holy men hold quite contrary opinions very firmly. Prophecies regarding the millennium and the Antichrist are of this nature. In this latter situation the wise student will grasp firmly the great basic prophecies that are clearly fulfilled and are directly related to the roots of his salvation, and prepare in his mind a large and broad shelf upon which he will put many concepts with regard to which there seems to be reasonable question or doubt. From time to time he will take down and dust them off and reconsider them in the light of new data or further discussion. With respect to some he may eventually come to satisfying conclusions that will settle the problem in his mind; some he may never wholly resolve.

8. Be prepared to consider new data or opinion. If future historic development or discovery should prove your opinion to be untenable, or to need modification do not be like the ostrich and hide from the facts behind the shelter of blind dogma, nor like many who ignore such data altogether, but like the intelligent scientist be prepared to reconsider your position so as to incorporate the newly discovered data.

9. Read books on prophecy critically and understandingly. Remember that the writers of these works very likely have some personal prejudice or peculiarity of interpretation for which allowance must be made in evaluating their writings. Few interpreters today do much more than digest and rearrange the commentaries of previous writers. If you have your annotated "Schofield Bible," a volume of Cummings, Mauro or Guinness at hand, and a good understanding of the programs of the principal schools of prophetic thought, you will usually be able to forecast the stand a new writer is going to take on most points after reading the first chapter of his work. There are some happy exceptions.

10. Be cautious of new and startling interpretations or those who claim some special revelation of God. Remember that there are more "freak" theories in the field of prophetic research than in most other aspects of Scripture study. There is probably some truth in most of them; many may be right; most of them no doubt contain a great deal of error. Prophecy has been studied by some of the finest minds in the world for hundreds of years. Novel interpretations that "lift the veil, dispel the clouds, loose the seals, make perplexing points convincingly plain by unanswerable arguments," or positively identify some contemporary individual as Antichrist are generally unsound and do not last long. Absolute identification of the date of the second coming of Christ by prophetic exegesis or Pyramid has proved to be unsound and special visions claimed by such persons as Mrs. Ellen G. White and Joseph Smith should require some validation to be accepted.

11. Do not permit yourself to be hurried to premature conclusion. Regardless of the pressure of friends, circumstances or that of fashion-following by the group to which you belong, take time in sorting out and settling your views. These intricate problems merit much thought. Read widely and critically, think and pray much, and give ideas time to settle and relate themselves in your mind.

12. Finally, in summary, I can do no better than quote the wisdom of a devout and scholarly Christian preacher who wrote and studied in the field of prophecy over many years in the nineteenth century.

"We must not seek to be explicit in that which God's Holy Spirit has been pleased to leave dimly revealed. Rash hands must not tear, but sacred hands must reverently draw aside the apocalyptic veil; we may not rush in where angels fear to tread; we must not dogmatize where the Spirit has not spoken decidedly; we must be content to be ignorant in many places, thankful to be instructed in others, and patient students throughout the whole.

We must not do as Edward Irving did – pronounce our views of unfulfilled prophecy to be among the very essentials of salvation; we must not give the least countenance to any idea that the great truths of evangelical religion are to be placed in the same category with any theory of interpretation of prophecy. The first seven seals may or may not refer to the Roman Empire, but there is no doubt that 'the blood of Jesus Christ cleanses from all sin': the first may be true; the last must be true. I will allow you to reject my expositions of the Apocalypse, as far as its symbols are involved; but I cannot for a moment consent that there should be any question whether my Savior be God, or whether his righteousness be my only covering, His sacrifice my only trust, His crown my happy and imperishable hope. All that I can say on unfulfilled prophecy may be wrong – what I preach of the gospel I know to be true: 'I know whom I have believed, and am persuaded that He is able to keep that which I have committed unto Him against that day'" (John Cumming, in the Preface to *Apocalyptic Sketches*).

*Edited by Clinton E. Taber, 2011

RECOMMENDED READING *

Alves, David. *We're the 'sons of God'* . . .*So What?* New York/ Bloominton; i Universe. 2009.

Barton, Freeman. *Heaven Hell and Hades: A Historical and Theological Survey of Personal Eschatology.* Lenox: Henceforth, 1990. Print.

Barton, Freeman, et al., comps. *God's Prophetic Calendar.* Ed., Millie H. Griswold. Charlotte: Advent Christian General Conference, 1983. Print.

- - -, comps. *Our Destiny We Know: Essays in Honor of Edwin K. Gedney.* Ed., Freeman Barton. Charlotte: Venture Books, 1996. Print.

Braun, Neil H,; Edwin K Gedney; and Austin R Warriner. *We Believe: A Biblical Anthropology.* 2nd ed., 1978. Osaka, Japan: The Japan Advent Christian Mission, 1980. Print.

Burch, Helaine. *Asleep in Christ.* New Berlin: Bible Search Publications, 1999. Print.

Carpenter, H. F. *Our Loss in Adam Our Gain in Christ.* Boston: Advent Christian Publication Society, 1867. Print.

Collins, Oral Edmond. *The Final Prophecy of Jesus: An Introduction, Analysis, and Commentary of the Book of Revelation.* Eugene: Wipf and Stock, 2007. Print.

Constable, Henry. *Hades; or the Intermediate State of Man.* Reprint of the London Edition ed. Boston: Advent Christian Publication Society, n.d. Print.

Crouse, John H.; J. William Denton; and Orrin Roe Jenks. *The Hebrew Prophets -- Studies in Old Testament Prophecy.* Boston: Advent Christian Publication Society, 1950. Print.

Crouse, Moses C. *Modern Discussions of Man's Immortality.* Concord: Advent Christian Publications, Inc., 1960. Print.

Dean, David A. *Framing the Prophetic Puzzle; A Guide for Interpreting Prophecy.* Lenox: Himes, 1987. Print.
- - -. *Resurrection Hope.* 2nd ed. Charlotte: Advent Christian General Conference of America, 1977. Print. Original Title – *Resurrection: His and Ours*

Froom, LeRoy Edwin. *The Prophetic Faith of Our Fathers, The Historical Development of Prophetic Interpretation.* 1-4 vols. Washington, D.C.: Review and Herald, 1950. Print.

Fudge, Edward William. *The Fire That Consumes: The Biblical Case for Conditional Immortality.* Carlisle: The Paternoster Press, 1994. Print.

Gedney, Edwin K. *A Primer of Prophecy, Part I: A Key to Understanding of Prophetic Prediction.* Concord: Advent Christian, 1964. Print.
- - -. *A Primer of Prophecy, Part II: A Survey of Biblical Prophecy.* Concord: Advent Christian, 1964. Print.

Grant, Miles. *The Kingdom of God; or, The Final Home of the Saints to be on the New Earth*. Boston: The Advent Christian Publication Society, n.d. Print.

Hastings, H. L. *After the Verdict*. Lenox: Himes, 1982. Print.

Hewitt, Clarence H. *A Class Book in Eschatology*. Boston: Advent Christian Publication Society, 1942. Print.
- - -. *Faith for Today*. Boston: Warren Press, 1941. Print.

Hewitt, Clyde E. *Devotion and Development*. Charlotte: Venture Books, 1990. Print.
- - -. *Midnight and Morning: An account of the Adventist Awakening and the founding of the Advent Christian Denomination 1831-1860*. Charlotte: Venture Books, 1983. Print.
- - -. *Responsibility and Response*. Charlotte: Venture Books, 1986. Print.

Ladd, George E. *Crucial Questions About the Kingdom of God*. Grand Rapids: Wm. B. Eerdmans Publishing, 1952. Print.

Lewis, Eric. *Christ, the First Fruits*. Boston: Warren Press, 1949. Print.
- - -. *Life and Immortality*. Boston: Warren Press, 1949. Print.

Nichols, James A., Jr. *Christian Doctrines, A Presentation of Biblical Theology*. Nutley: Craig Press, 1970. Print.

Niebuhr, Reinhold. *The Nature and Destiny of Man: A Christian Interpretation*. 1941. New York: Charles Scribner's Sons, 1953. Print. Gifford Lectures: Complete in One Volume

Northup, Arthur B. *The Scenario of the Savior as Sovereign: The Book of Revelation as a Christian World View and Philosophy of History*. Charlotte: Venture Books, 1991. Print.

Parnia, Sam. *What Happens When We Die: A Groundbreaking Study into the Nature of Life and Death.* Carlsbad: Hay House, 2006. Print.

Payne, J. Barton, ed. *Encyclopedia of Biblical Prophecy: The Complete Guide to Scriptural Predictions and Their Fulfillment.* Grand Rapids: Baker, 1973. Print.

Pentecost, J Dwight. *Thy Kingdom Come: Tracing God's Kingdom Program and Covenant Promises Throughout History.* Grand Rapids: Kregel, 1995. Print.

Prestige, Warren. *Life, Death and Destiny.* Auckland, New Zealand: Resurrection Publishing, 1998. Print.

Sauer, Erich. *The King of the Earth: The Nobility of Man According to the Bible and Science.* Carisle, UK: The Paternoster, 1962. Print.

Sheldon, William. *Man's Future State: or, Where Do Dead Folks Go?:* n.p., n.d. Print.

Stockman, E A. *Our Hope or Why Are We Adventists.* 10th ed. 1880. Boston: Advent Christian Publication Society, 1915. Print.

Stott, John. *The Gospel & the End of Time: The Message of 1 & 2 Thessalonians.* Downers Grove: Inver Varsity, 1991. Print.

Taylor, Daniel T. *The Great Consummation and the Signs that Herald Its Approach.* Boston: Advent Christian Publication Society, 1891. Print.
- - -. *The Reign of Christ on Earth: or The Voice of the Church in All Ages Concerning the Coming and Kingdom of the Redeemer.* Boston: H. L. Hastings, 1883. Print.

Thompson, H. E. *Adventism Triumphant.* Boston: Advent Christian Publication Society, 1924. Print.

Tillich, Paul. *The New Being*. New York: Charles Scribner's Sons, 1955. Print.

Warren, Thomas S, II. *Dead Men Talking: What Dying Teaches Us About Living*. Lincoln: IUniverse, 2005. Print.

Wright, N T. *New Heavens, New Earth: The Biblical Picture of Christian Hope*. Cambridge: Grove Books Limited, 1999. Print.

- - -. *The Resurrection of the Son of God*. Vol. 3. Minneapolis: Fortress Press, 2003. Print. Christian Origins and the Question of God.

- - -. *Surprised By Hope: Rethinking, Heaven, the Resurrection, and the Mission of the Church*. New York: Harper One, 2008. Print.

Young, G. L. *Fundamental Christology: A Discussion of Foundation Doctrines Concerning the Christ*. Boston: Advent Christian Publication Society, 1906. Print.

- - -. *The Return of the Redeemer and the Objects of His Return*. Boston: Advent Christian Publication Society, 1899. Print.

* Additional resources available on request.
To reference out of print material, please contact:
The Adventist Collection, Gordon Conwell Theological Seminary.

CPSIA information can be obtained at www.ICGtesting.com
261341BV00001B/2/P